-4

Gew

14/7.

ERIC PARTRIDGE

In His Own Words

ERIC PARTRIDGE

In His Own Words

WITH TRIBUTES BY
ANTHONY BURGESS, RALPH ELLIOTT,
WINSTON GRAHAM AND
RANDOLPH QUIRK

Edited by David Crystal

ANDRE DEUTSCH

FIRST PUBLISHED 1980 BY
ANDRÉ DEUTSCH LIMITED
105 GREAT RUSSELL STREET LONDON WCI

PRINTED IN GREAT BRITAIN BY
EBENEZER BAYLIS AND SON LTD,
THE TRINITY PRESS, WORCESTER, AND LONDON

British Library Cataloguing in Publication Data
Partridge, Eric
    Eric Partridge in his own words.
    1. English language – Addresses, essays, lectures
    I. Crystal, David
    420'.8 PE1072

ISBN 0 233 97300 1

These pieces were originally published as follows:
'The Etymology of Medicine' in Everyman,
February 1931; 'Familiar Terms of Address'
(shortened version) in Action, 1931; 'Genesis of a
Lexicographer' (shortened version) in Tomorrow,
March 1951; 'The Language of the Underworld'
in The Quarterly Review, April 1948; 'Quacks
and Quackery' in Everyman, February 1931;
'Slang and Standard English' in The Persian
Quarterly, 1944.

Contents

═══

Acknowledgements		7
Foreword by David Crystal		9
Serving a Life Sentence by Ralph Elliott		13
An Adjunct to Ourself by Randolph Quirk		19
Partridge in a Word Tree by Anthony Burgess		26
Some Club Reminiscences by Winston Graham		31

Part I Word-Books

1	Adventure in Words from *Adventuring Among Words*	37
2	How it All Began from *The Gentle Art of Lexicography*	41
3	Genesis of a Lexicographer from *From Sanskrit to Brazil*	51
4	The Problem of Alphabetical Order from *The Gentle Art of Lexicography*	64
5	Some Aspects of Etymology from *A Charm of Words*	81

Part II Word-Levels

6	Slang from *Slang Today and Yesterday*	103
7	Slang and Standard English from *Here, There and Everywhere*	114
8	The Language of the Underworld from *Here, There and Everywhere*	120
9	Clichés from *A Charm of Words*	131
10	Euphemism and Euphemisms from *Words, Words, Words!*	141
11	What's in a Catch Phrase? from *Greetings Card, Christmas 1971*	150
12	Business English and its Confederates from *A Charm of Words*	154
13	The Shaggy Dog: A True Story from *A Charm of Words*	162

Part III Words

14 The Real McCoy and the Real Mackay from *From Sanskrit to Brazil*   169
15 The Etymology of Medicine from *A Charm of Words*   177
16 Quacks and Quackery from *Literary Sessions*   182
17 Whence *Hogmanay?* from *A Charm of Words*   186
18 Familiar Terms of Address from *Words, Words, Words!* 191
19 Naming Influences and Fashions from *Name This Child* 196
20 Vignettes from *From Sanskrit to Brazil*   200

Part IV Dictionaries

Abbreviations   207
21 from *Usage and Abusage*   210
22 from *Name into Word*   212
23 from *A Dictionary of the Underworld*   214
24 From *A Dictionary of Clichés*   216
25 from *Origins*   218
26 from *Shakespeare's Bawdy*   220
27 from *A Dictionary of Forces' Slang, 1939–45*   222
28 from *A Dictionary of Slang and Unconventional English* 224
29 from *A Dictionary of Catch Phrases*   226
30 from *Name This Child*   228

Envoi A Short Story from *The First Three Years*   233
A Partridge Bibliography   239
Name and Subject Index   247
Word Index   250

Acknowledgements

WE GRATEFULLY ACKNOWLEDGE the kind permission of all those concerned to reprint material from the following books: *A Charm of Words*: estate of Eric Partridge, *A Dictionary of Catch Phrases*: Routledge & Kegan Paul/Stein and Day, *A Dictionary of Clichés*: Routledge & Kegan Paul, *A Dictionary of Forces' Slang*: estate of Eric Partridge, *A Dictionary of Slang and Unconventional English*: Routledge & Kegan Paul/Macmillan, New York, *A Dictionary of the Underworld*: Routledge & Kegan Paul/Macmillan, New York, *The First Three Years*: estate of Eric Partridge, *From Sanskrit to Brazil*: Hamish Hamilton, *Here, There and Everywhere*: Hamish Hamilton, *Name into Word*: Secker & Warburg, *Name This Child*: Hamish Hamilton, *Literary Sessions*: estate of Eric Partridge, *Origins*: Routledge & Kegan Paul/Macmillan, New York, *Shakespeare's Bawdy*: Routledge & Kegan Paul/Dutton & Co. Inc., *Slang Today and Yesterday*: Routledge & Kegan Paul, *Usage and Abusage*: Hamish Hamilton, *Words, Words, Words!*: estate of Eric Partridge. 'Serving a Life Sentence' by Ralph Elliott has been reprinted from *Meanjin*, 4, 1979, (Melbourne, Australia) with the kind permission of the editor.

Foreword

BY *David Crystal*

═══

ERIC HONEYWOOD PARTRIDGE was born on 6 February 1894 on a farm in Waimata Valley, near Gisborne, North Island, New Zealand. In 1907, he moved with his family to Brisbane, where he went to grammar school. He left school at the age of sixteen, and spent some years as a trainee teacher at schools in Queensland and New South Wales. A scholarship to the University of Queensland enabled him to read first Classics, and later French and English. The First World War interrupted his studies: he joined the Australian infantry in April 1915, and served in Egypt, Gallipoli and on the Western Front – experiences which are recorded in his contribution to *Three Personal Records of the War*. He returned to university between 1919 and 1921, and received a B.A. In 1921 he was made a Queensland Travelling Fellow, and went to Oxford, where he worked simultaneously for an M.A. on eighteenth-century English romantic poetry, and a B.Litt. in comparative literature, both of which were in due course published. A short period of teaching at a grammar school in Lancashire followed, and then appointments at the Universities of Manchester (1925–6) and London (1926–7) He was married in 1925, and had a daughter.

1927 proved a turning-point. He gave up his academic career, partly because of his difficulties with public speaking, on account of a vocal cord weakness, and partly because of his preference to become, as he liked to put it, a 'man of letters'. His love of writing had appeared early. By the time he was thirteen, he had attempted a novel and several short stories. Verse translations from French poetry were privately circulated in 1914. Then there was *The Bakara Bulletin*, other wartime writings, and several literary studies in the mid-1920s. In 1927 he founded the Scholartis Press (see Envoi) as a private venture, and directed it until 1931, when the pressures caused by the economic recession of the time caused bankruptcy. During this period, he edited several of the elegant volumes himself, perhaps the most well-known of his own contributions being *Songs and Slang of the British Soldier* and *Francis Grose's Dictionary*. Under the pseudonym of Corrie Denison, he wrote three novels.

1932 was another turning-point, with his free-lance writing activities beginning in earnest. His first major work on slang appeared in 1933, followed in 1937 by the first of his big dictionaries. The period saw several essays on literary, linguistic and other themes, in addition to the regular revisions of his early work. During the Second World War, he joined the Army Education Corps, and later transferred to the correspondence department of the RAF. 1945 saw him back at his desk in the British Museum library, and the commencement of a further productive period of essays and lexicographical projects. His *Dictionary of the Underworld* was completed in 1949; *Origins* in 1958. Several other essay projects followed, but the bulk of his time was taken up with the meticulous revision of all his dictionaries, and his editorial work for the Language Library series. His last major project, *A Dictionary of Catch Phrases*, appeared in 1977. He died on 1 June 1979.

The essential biographical facts are easy to state, and reference to the bibliography at the end of this book will quickly fill out the above sketch. But such a synopsis does scant justice to its subject matter; there is little hint here of the personality which appears so readily from the pages of Eric Partridge's own writing. Indeed, it would be difficult to have a better account of his early life than those he wrote himself (see Chapters 2 and 3). For my part, I have no alternative but to rely on these accounts, supplemented by the enthusiastic and full reminiscences of his many friends, and by the barrage of correspondence which I received from him when I joined him as co-editor (the 'working editor', as he liked to put it) of the Language Library in 1977. I never had the fortune to meet him myself. Accordingly, it is not my place to present a personal appreciation of the man in these pages: this must be left to those who knew him well.

But it is an impressive publishing life, under any criterion. I know, for I have just read all of it, in preparation for this volume, and it has taken a long time. Like most people, I had come across several of his essays, and dipped into his dictionaries, but I was quite unprepared for the enormous range and variety of his output. This made itself apparent the hard way, when I left the house of one of Eric Partridge's oldest friends, Mr Alan Steele, staggering under the weight of the many books, clippings and cards that he had been kind enough to lend me from his collection. It was a prodigious output – always informative, lucid, entertaining, and only occasionally repetitive. For Partridge, language was a key to our understanding of civilization – its present social structure and its history. English was the language and culture at issue; but the discussion and illustration goes well beyond this. The scope of his work was at once macrolinguistic, in its focus on universal themes, and microlinguistic, in its concentration on language detail.

What should a luckless editor do, under such circumstances? I have, firstly, tried to give this volume some coherence, by restricting it to Eric Partridge's study of language; I have not included his fiction, his writing on literary and other topics (such as may be found in *Journey to the Edge of Morning*), or his editorial work. I could not however resist putting in an account of the Scholartis Press (Envoi), for it meant so much to him. Apart from this, I have stuck carefully to his two main themes: lexicology – the study of the history and the modern use of words, and their patterns of relationship; and lexicography – the art and science of dictionary-writing. In Part I (Word-Books) I have included pieces dealing with lexicographical principles and practice; in Part II (Word-Levels) I have focused upon the varying uses of words at different stylistic levels; Part III (Words) illustrates the detailed study of individual lexical items; and Part IV (Dictionaries) is self-explanatory – the end product of it all. I have tried to illustrate the breadth and the depth of his knowledge, his ability simultaneously to inform and entertain, the freshness and appeal which he brought to the study of language and its history – and all the time I have been aware that I am presenting only the tip of the iceberg.

But 'luckless' is not really the word. Editing this volume has been an immensely enjoyable task, and I hope the many friends and students of Partridge will think it a worthy tribute. My one regret, felt all the more now that the book is complete, is that I came into personal contact with the man so late. I wish I'd met him.

David Crystal
University of Reading
31 December 1979

Serving a Life Sentence

BY *Ralph Elliott*

—

WHEN ERIC PARTRIDGE DIED he was working on a revised edition of his *Dictionary of Catch Phrases*, first published two years earlier when he was eighty-three years old. It was the final labour of 'an addict', as he once described himself, 'who is cheerfully and incorrigibly serving a life sentence'. It was also the final contribution to English lexicography by an assiduous toiler who, by temperament, education and scholarship, was exceptionally well fitted to follow in the footsteps of Nathaniel Bailey, Samuel Johnson and Francis Grose.

Partridge was indeed a cheerful and incorrigible toiler. For many years his gaunt figure was regularly to be seen in the Reading Room of the British Museum or at morning coffee at Oddi's café across the road. It was not until November 1976 that he finally had to leave London for health reasons, and move into a friend's house in Devon. Although he continued to work, the pace inevitably slowed down, as he wrote to me a few weeks before his death, 'for some time I must do scarcely any work. Have been working too hard for too long.' By this time he had written over forty books, some of them running into several revised editions, and many of them still in print.

Eric's energy never ceased to amaze me. It is well illustrated by his total involvement in his productive, albeit short-lived, publishing enterprise between 1927 and 1931. 'For the first year,' Partridge wrote, 'I did absolutely all the work by myself, even to delivering parcels.' Nineteen books were published in this first year, twenty-four in the second, nineteen more in the third, several of them edited, introduced, or even written by Partridge himself. There cannot be many people who can claim to have written, published and delivered their own books.

Along with *Songs and Slang of the British Soldier (1914–1918)*, which he published in 1930, it was probably his edition (also published under the Scholartis imprint, in 1931) of Francis Grose's *A Classical Dictionary of the Vulgar Tongue* (first published in 1785) which confirmed Partridge's growing interest in less conventional forms of English. In a manner reminiscent of Chaucer's apology for his churls' vulgarisms, Partridge disclaims offensive expressions and sentiments as not his own 'but as the sentiments of the persons by whom such terms were first invented, or those by whom they are used'. It served as an appropriate disclaimer for much of Partridge's subsequent work, for books of slang and cant and catch phrases and literary bawdy are easily mistaken for pornography by the squeamish and the uninformed, and the suspicion may not be entirely unfounded that the lack of public or academic recognition accorded to Partridge in Britain may be due to the belief that he revelled in obscenities.

The first of his three big dictionaries, *A Dictionary of Slang and Unconventional English*, was published in 1937; the second, *A Dictionary of the Underworld*, in 1949; and the third, *Origins: A Short Etymological Dictionary of Modern English*, in 1958. All three were repeatedly revised and enlarged, all three are still in print, and all three are major contributions to English lexicography.

The first two are both historical dictionaries in the manner made familiar by *The Oxford English Dictionary*. Wherever possible, early occurrences are dated and sources given. Clearly, this is much more difficult and as a rule less precise for slang and other forms of 'low' English than for 'polite' or received standard English hallowed by literary usage. As in his much later *Dictionary of Catch Phrases*, Partridge is often compelled to approximate or to hazard a guess; but neither the approximations nor the guesses are arbitrary. He possessed both a thorough knowledge of English linguistic history and a detailed acquaintance with his sources – British, American and Australian especially – to lend substance to his datings.

But these dictionaries are historical also in another sense. Slang is the most evanescent of linguistic phenomena, and what is here enshrined for present and future edification or amusement is for the most part no longer alive in English speech. All the great dictionaries of English slang and cant from Thomas Harman's *A Caveat for Common Cursetors* of 1567 to Partridge's are linguistic museums. That is not to belittle their achievement, but it does define their usefulness.

Origins is quite different. It was Nathaniel Bailey's peculiar contribution to English lexicography to add etymologies to the words listed in *An Universal Etymological English Dictionary* of 1721, but it was not until the last quarter of the nineteenth century that W. W. Skeat produced the first specialist English etymological dictionary, to be followed by Ernest Weekley's and then Partridge's. Eight years after the latter came C. T. Onions' *Oxford Dictionary of English Etymology*, so that we now have two excellent reference books to satisfy our etymological curiosity. The difference between the two is instructive. Onions has given us a straightforward dictionary in the best Oxford tradition, dependable, cautious, a reference rather than a bedside book. Partridge's lexicon, on the other hand, is 'both abundantly informative and delightfully readable', as the *Times Literary Supplement* said of the first edition. Its particular merit is to assemble families of related words in one entry, thus displaying connections often totally unexpected. Thus, looking up 'watch' for example, guides you to 'vigor' where a veritable feast of vegetables and vigilantes and waitresses and numerous other cognates awaits you.

A further merit of *Origins* are its 150 pages of prefixes, suffixes and elements, the latter mainly scientific and technological like 'acro-', '-morph', '-phobe', etc. The aim here is to help the reader to 'ascertain, at least approximately, the meaning of a vast number of erudite terms', a welcome aid, indeed, in an age of ever-increasing verbal complexity. The success of this work may be gauged by the fact that by the time Onions' *Dictionary* appeared, *Origins* was in its fourth edition. It was success well merited.

The process of constant revision and enlargement which *Origins* underwent, was applied to the other dictionaries as well as to Eric Partridge's smaller works. Among the latter were a few acknowledged pot-boilers, like *From Sanskrit to Brazil* (1952), *The 'Shaggy*

Dog' Story (1953), and *Comic Alphabets* (1961), the latter illustrated in his own inimitable fashion by that master, Michael Foreman, who, more recently, has contributed so successfully to Alan Garner's *Stone Book* Quartet and four *Fairytales of Gold*. But there were works of greater substance too, dating from this most productive period of Partridge's life, and one of them in particular, *Usage and Abusage: A Guide to Good English* (1947) was destined to immortality when, as a Penguin Reference Book (1963), it took its place alongside Fowler and Gowers in countless homes and offices throughout the English-speaking world. It was this book which Partridge dedicated to C. T. Onions for his 'lucid lexicography, severely impeccable etymologies, and humanely corrective English syntax'.

Usage and Abusage is, yet again, 'both abundantly informative and delightfully readable'; it has its impish moments, but it is at heart what the sub-title claims: A Guide to Good English. People who insist on 'commencing' instead of 'beginning', on 'eventuating' instead of 'happening', or using 'disinterested' for 'uninterested', and on committing innumerable other offences against 'Good English', need the gentle yet insistent therapy of this excellent book.

The same year, 1947, saw the publication of *Shakespeare's Bawdy*, in which Partridge's long-standing interest in English literature is profitably nurtured by his unrivalled knowledge of sixteenth- and seventeenth-century slang and innuendo. It is, as he describes it, 'A literary and psychological essay and a comprehensive glossary', which opened the window upon a long-avoided aspect of Shakespeare criticism. Although the introductory essay is by no means negligible, the meat of the book is in the glossary which begins with 'Abhorson' in *Measure for Measure* and ends with an innuendo on 'youth' in the same play. By 1977 the book was in its fourth edition and available in British and American paperbacks. Its status as a pioneering study remains unchallenged.

Partridge's own favourite, *English: A Course for Human Beings*, followed in 1949. Its writing, he admits, brought him much pleasure. Drawing upon his experiences as a teacher both in

Australia and in England, Partridge devised a course in three parts, each designed to be a year's study, intended primarily for schools. It is a lively, well-devised book which still reads remarkably well, although attitudes to, and methods of, the teaching of English have changed considerably during the last thirty years. Like Lindley Murray's *English Grammar* (1795), Partridge's book is a classic of its kind.

It is also, with its 560 pages, a very big classic. Indeed, the sheer volume of Partridge's literary output, much of it demanding the most exacting scholarship, is astonishing: even more so, when one remembers some of his other time-consuming activities. Thus, he acted for many years as an examiner in English to three examining boards; and in 1952 he started the Language Library, a respected and successful series published by André Deutsch, of which he was sole editor for some years until joined by Professor Simeon Potter. This venture continues to thrive, now with over fifty titles to its credit, under the editorship of Professor David Crystal. It is a worthy tribute to its founder.

Partridge, moreover, throughout his long life was a tireless correspondent. He answered letters punctually and was always ready to discuss matters of linguistic interest or to answer queries. He kept friends, librarians, institutions informed of work published or in progress, sent lists of errata or addenda, and sought advice from numerous correspondents in many countries. He was an informative and witty conversationalist over coffee at Oddi's or luncheon at the Savile Club.

Among his best friends were his publishers. In honour of Eric Partridge's seventieth birthday (commemorated in Australia by a tribute in *Meanjin Quarterly*), ten British and American publishers combined to issue a leaflet with a biographical sketch and a bibliography of his major books. Characteristically, the last section dealt with future works. A similar leaflet, headed 'Not yet old enough to know better', as well as a large advertisement in *The Times Literary Supplement*, marked his seventy-fifth birthday. These were unusual tributes.

Only two academic honours, both Australian, were awarded

to Eric Partridge: an honorary doctorate of letters from the University of Queensland and an Honorary Fellowship of the Australian Academy of the Humanities. An anonymous reviewer of the seventh edition of *A Dictionary of Slang* in the *TLS* of 16 October 1970, commenting on the lack of official recognition of Partridge's work, noted that 'Princeton University has made a doctor out of Bob Dylan ... And yet this book is one of the glories of the British Commonwealth . . . and that this most human lexicographer – now in his seventies – should not receive some public recognition, however grudging, must seem to many a public disgrace.' Moves to remedy this omission were set afoot when Eric reached his eighty-fifth birthday. They came too late.

But public, as against official, recognition of Partridge's work was never wanting. He made a contribution to the historical study as well as to the practical use of the English language so substantial and so individual in its scholarship, breadth, imagination and wit that his name is now a household word in every country where English is spoken and studied. Unlike Oliver, he did not ask for more. His was a life sentence well and faithfully served.

An Adjunct to Ourself

BY *Randolph Quirk*

==

A NATURAL ENOUGH TITLE for an essay on Eric Partridge, when this is precisely what many of us felt we had lost on his death. In almost any aspect of humane letters – literature, languages, book-craft, and of course word-study – he not only had a staggeringly wide knowledge: he had a limitless capacity for sharing it. No query went unanswered. Almost by return of post, always in his own elegant hand, and usually on a tightly packed self-sealing letter-card, came the information we sought, together with references to where more could be obtained. For the hundreds of correspondents who had the good fortune to enjoy his friendship, decade after decade, he became indeed an indispensable adjunct to themselves in their research and writing.

But to Eric himself my title would of course have called up primarily its source in *Love's Labour's Lost* (and the title of the play itself would be a fitting epitaph):

> Learning is but an adjunct of ourself
> And where we are our learning likewise is.

And this would naturally have turned his thoughts to the British Museum – I doubt whether he ever came to speak of the 'British Library'. If, as was claimed by Tze-sze, the grandson of Confucius, merely to be fond of learning is to be near to knowledge, few men ever edged themselves nearer. He was, indeed, fond enough of learning to make it his daily practice not merely to get 'near' but to put himself right in the centre of one of the world's chief repositories of learning. 'Oh no, madam,' a not altogether pleased American scholar was told. 'You can't occupy K1: Mr Partridge will be coming in a few minutes and that is *his* seat.' And so it was – year in, year out. He made the BM his second home, with a ticket first issued in November 1923 and regularly renewed (with only a short war-time break while he was serving in the RAF) for well over half a century. No scholar made more exiguous demands on the staff but none was better known to them, and each Christmas he acknowledged his modest debt with a cheque, tentatively suggesting 'chocolates for the girls and some Embassy Panatellas for the men . . . to the limit of what the traffic will bear.'*

And for Partridge what the traffic could bear was never very much. Though the scores of friends he generously hosted at the Savile were given no reason to suspect it, he remained a man of acutely slender means. ('Business, you know, may bring money, but friendship hardly ever does,' Jane Austen tells us in *Emma*, and Partridge's instincts were unshakeably set on friendship.) In a period when almost all others engaged in writing on language had the financial security of an academic post behind them, with any royalties merely easing the mortgage a bit, Partridge lived for the major part of his fourscore years and five on royalties alone. The brief exceptions are revealing: a couple of years in the twenties as a university teacher and four running his own small publishing business until the 1931 slump put him out of business. They are revealing because they highlight the extent to which Partridge's strengths were limited: he was at his best with a pen in his hand, with none of the responsibilities of administering a business or of teaching students. In truth, although he was a delightful conversationalist, he froze into calamitously dull immobility of mind when he went before a microphone (he broadcast occasionally) or a lectern (he was invited to do so less and less frequently).

Unfortunately, this did not merely constitute an incidental limitation: it actually contributed to a far more serious and more central one. His dependence on royalties diverted his attentions all too often from the historical study of slang (his forte, as well as his prime interest from about 1930). If he had been able to get

---

* I am indebted for this charming detail to Mr J. A. Marks of the British Library.

into the school market with one widely used text-book, he would have had a financial cushion on which his serious interests could have reclined. But this he never achieved, and he came to depend on the layman's interest in the byways of language (widespread enough, but not fortune-making) and the layman's concern for 'good usage' (already pretty well catered for by Fowler, not to mention other 'readers over your shoulder' like A. P. Herbert). This meant not just a diversion of his interest but a dilution of them. Let me give one example, about which I have something of a bad conscience because I chided Partridge over it in my naïvety, before I had come to realize the economic pressures on him.

After his fairly successful attempt to up-stage Fowler with *Usage and Abusage* (New York 1942, London 1947), he wrote *Chamber of Horrors* for the André Deutsch Language Library series of which he was founder and general editor. But he published it under the name 'Vigilans'. In the Preface, 'Vigilans' warmly thanks Partridge: to him 'I owe a special debt. He has encouraged and helped me in the search for jargon . . . and written an Introduction.' And in the said Introduction, nine pages long and of course signed by Partridge, he in turn (page 14) commends the work of 'Vigilans'.

This seemed more than a literary jest, as he represented it to Ivor Brown (the dedicatee: 'Gracious Guardian of English') as well as to me and other friends. Coming so soon after *Usage and Abusage* (and containing in large measure material already in that book), it would have looked a bit repetitious to have the *Chamber of Horrors* in his own name – in his own series. But the 'Vigilans' device not only relieved its author of this embarrassment but enabled him to quote himself glowingly on page after page, with the name of Partridge linked with Fowler, Gowers, Alan Herbert and Ifor Evans, whose handbooks were held up along with Partridge's as the authorities on good usage – as well as being rifled for supportive quotations. Thus on *priority* (page 102), 'Vigilans' writes: 'All loyal to the cause of good English would do well to heed the verdict expressed in Eric Partridge's *Usage and*

Abusage.' On page 124 we find no fewer than three such puffs; for example, 'I recommend all diligent inquirers to go to both "Fowler" and "Partridge"'.

If financial pressures led him to dilution and self-advertisement, it diverted him also to write – engagingly enough – ephemera like *Comic Alphabets* and *The 'Shaggy Dog' Story*, as well as layman's guides to such diverse matters as onomastics and punctuation (*You have a Point There* – Partridge had a flair for titles). And his nose for what should sell produced *Shakespeare's Bawdy* – which, if he could have taken more time and space, his nose for bawdy could have made so very much better.

Whether everything he wrote could have been much better is hard to say. It is perhaps significant that even his most serious work was more highly praised by the literary than the philological establishment. His etymologies (*Origins*, 1958) were based on literary scholarship and intuitive judgement more than on philological theory. In fact, he seemed to distrust theory and certainly ignored most theoretical adventures from Bloomfield and the Prague School onwards. It was characteristic that he should have spent his last years on a dictionary of catch phrases without in the least being troubled by the vagueness of the term itself: 'Friends – and others – have often asked me, "What the devil *is* a catch phrase?" I don't know' (Introduction). Yet in his knowledge he was profound and in his reading omnivorous (as the present memorial volume illustrates clearly enough). It was on these grounds – together with his endlessly patient kindness – that he was so invaluable 'an adjunct to ourself'. He helped others of like mind. The encouragement he gave to scores of young writers in – or at the fringe of – language studies put many of them on the first rungs of the career ladder, as well as introducing them to an exciting circle of friends such as Christopher Fry, Gilbert Harding and Robert Morley.

It is difficult and perhaps too soon to make a proper assessment of the impact that this prolific scholar has had: still more difficult to assess the impact he will have in the future. Few libraries are without at least some of his books, yet he is little read – and is least read (and perhaps always has been) by those most concerned with the direction of language studies. Nonetheless, and gloomy as are the implications of this, there seem to be three areas in which one can speak of positive influence.

First, there is his standing among those whose job involves writing: I don't mean poets, novelists, dramatists (though I don't exclude them either) so much as civil servants, solicitors, administrators, secretaries. For such people (who are arguably the most vulnerable to critics of their usage and style), 'Partridge' became something of a household word in the same category as 'Fowler', though never with the same aura of authority or anything like the same ubiquity. His staying-power as such a household word is doubtful, but I am confident that his many writings on usage will continue (along with comparable contributions by Fowler, A. P. Herbert, Ivor Brown, Ernest Gowers and Bruce Fraser) to have a pervasive if perhaps anonymous influence in alerting the writing public to the need for clarity and the avoidance of pomposity.

Secondly, there is the stimulus he gave to writings upon language, especially on English, and especially for students and the lay public. This stimulus he exercised above all through the books he edited for André Deutsch, and while some of the volumes have been of so low a standard as to risk damaging the series as a whole, there is little question that the Language Library has had (and under its new direction will increasingly have) a beneficial effect in extending a knowledge of language studies. Indeed, it is chiefly by this means that Partridge has been able to have some influence within universities and other institutions of higher education.

But in my view it is in the third area that he will have a really lasting impact: his lexicographic work, and especially that on slang (even his etymological dictionary, *Origins*, is at its best with slang and tabu).

Given the quite severe limitations self-imposed by Murray and his colleagues, the great *OED* left the field of argot, slang, colloquialism wide open – and much in need of care and attention.

Partridge gave it both. Though he regrettably lacked the means to emulate Murray in subjecting primary sources to detailed study, he did a very useful job in collating the evidence presented in numerous collections of slang words, liberally adding material from his own eclectic reading and – for the present century – from his own memory. The results (*A Dictionary of Slang and Unconventional English*, 1937, with its pre- and post-war supplements) lack the magisterial scholarship, meticulous authentication, and consistency of presentation that give us confidence in the *OED*, but Partridge's work is the best we are likely to have for a long time. And as a one-man product, it is deeply impressive. The three or four column-inches on *pross* and its derivatives are a good illustration (see page 224 below).

One of the strong points of the *Dictionary* is the attention paid to phrasal colloquialisms such as 'right as ninepence', and in a sense Partridge's last major work, *A Dictionary of Catch Phrases* (1977), can be seen as a final supplement (after forty years) to the *Dictionary of Slang*. To the *Catch Phrases* in turn there was to be a supplement, and in one of his last letters to me (8 March 1979), Partridge resolutely maintained his intention of continuing with this (he had already got to 'T'), though now weak and confined to a Devon nursing home. While resenting his grievously reduced capacity and the indignities imposed by his ageing body, he could find the irony to blame only himself for his condition ('far too much hard work, over far too long a period') and even to take grim pleasure in permuting a catch phrase he might well have put in his collection: 'one need not grin; it is enough to be obliged to bear it'. *The Dictionary of Catch Phrases* is marred by some dilution and prolixity: for example, in comparing two obviously similar phrases (page 197), he says that the first 'is a naval lower-deck variant' of the second, 'than which it is felt to be slightly less coarse, slightly less offensive, and slightly more polite'. And there is the rather too frequent practice of tantalizingly omitting textual support. Thus *don't want to know* is asserted to originate in British jails of the present century – perhaps correctly, but evidence would have been welcome from the one man who was likely to have some. The dictionary is none the less invaluable, if only (again) because we cannot realistically expect to have anything better in the foreseeable future.

At the same time, it is invaluable also in providing a late demonstration of Partridge's wide-ranging interests and the sheer delight he took in the byways of language. There is an article, for example, on 'Oh, Mother, is it worth it?'. Oh, Eric, it was.

Partridge in a Word Tree

BY *Anthony Burgess*

I FIRST BECAME ACQUAINTED with Eric Partridge in the
1960s, when he was already old but still very vigorous. I had
been commissioned by Penguin Books to produce a dictionary
of contemporary slang, but I did not want to do it. My agent had,
however, accepted the advance, which I later had to return,
though not she her ten per cent. I toiled at the letter B, always the
biggest section of an English dictionary, and saw the problems.
'Contemporary' means from now on till the end of time. I
envisaged a life spent in updating the dictionary. When I had
finished B 'bovver boots' came in and had to be admitted. Meeting Eric Partridge by chance at his club, when I was lunching
with somebody else, I had the chance to discuss the whole lexicographical agony with him.

First, though, knowing of my project, he cordially invited me
to cannibalize him to the limit: dictionary-making was a matter
of eating others and always had been. Then he admitted that his
craft was one of perpetual revision, that no dictionary was a
finished book but merely a photograph of the language at a
point in time, always ready to be replaced with a new picture.
His life was mostly given up to dealing with correspondents,
most of whom were helpful. I became one of those correspondents myself when I decided that I was not a dictionary man,
one of the thousands who sent him new words, idioms and
etymologies. One of the pleasures of new editions of his slang
dictionary was in meeting expressions of warmth, gratitude,
friendship within the text itself.

Eric was a human lexicographer, like Samuel Johnson. He was
a philologist rather than a linguist. He knew what Chomsky was
doing and what had happened to phonology in Prague, but he
eschewed the strict scientific approach. Linguistics is scared of

semantics and prefers to concentrate on structures, leaving the study of the meaning of words to anthropologists – or, perhaps with misgivings, to Johnsonian word-lovers like Eric Partridge. Eric's etymologies were often, as he admitted, shaky, but he preferred a shaky etymology to none at all. I remember discussing with him the origin of the word *camp*. As it happened, I had written an article in the *Spectator* using the word, and a retired general had asked precisely what it meant and where it came from. I wrote a letter of some length in explication but got no thanks. My view was that *camp* had nothing to do with *kempt*. I thought of camp concert parties with men dressed up as girls and making exaggerated feminine gestures; I thought of those camps set up in nineteenth-century America for the constructions of the railroads, when a temporary homosexual culture developed with secondary features of effeminate display. The latest general dictionary (Collins, 1979) defines *camp* and its derivatives admirably but says 'etymology unknown'. I maintain, as Eric always did, that it is better to guess than to be silent. This is amateurish, but it is human.

No academic linguist could be expected to be interested in frivolities like the 'comic alphabets' on which Eric wrote a whole book. I had, like him, heard Clapham and Dwyer on the radio in the 1930s reciting the whole liturgy: 'A for orses, B for mutton, C forth Highlanders, D for payment,' and so on, penultimating with the brilliant 'Y for secretary' (I forget Z). What fascinated Eric in the direction of his book was the anonymous human brilliance of this fantasy, and it was the creativity of humble users of language which, of course, inspired him to that lifelong devotion to slang and catch phrases which produced the great dictionaries. The catch phrase book, which, alas, he did not live to be able to complete revising and enriching, got a great number of his admirers digging in their memories. I wanted him to put in (from ITMA) 'NWAWWASBE' – never wash a window with a soft boiled egg – and great gestures of phatic communion like 'Roll on death and let's have a go at the angels' and 'Put another pea in the pot and hang the expense' and 'Never mind, lads, it'll soon be Christmas'. Many people did not appreciate these catch phrases. I wrote a novel in which a character says, 'Ah well, as one door shuts another door closes' and this was silently corrected to a statement that made sense. Naturally, I unsilently uncorrected it.

Eric had learnt these ludic tropes and others like them in the army. It was in the army that I learned to appreciate the great humorous stoicism of ordinary men and the way in which they expressed it in language. He, like myself, was fascinated by the slow folk development from trope to trope in the direction of greater sardonic truth. In 1939 soldiers were saying: 'The army can do anything to you including fuck you.' This, in 1941, had become 'The army can fuck you but it can't make you have a kid.' At the end of the war the army could give you a kid but it couldn't make you love it. I don't know what the latest embellishment is.

A New Zealander, an Australasian, hence a great mistruster of what Joyce called 'those big words that make us all unhappy', Eric was brought up in a kind of dispossessed demotic tradition which prized the speech of the people as the repository of a dour philosophy of life. The downtrodden, who are the great creators of slang, hurl pithiness and colour at poverty and oppression. Language is not, like everything else, in the hands of the haughty and educated: it is the people's property, and sometimes all they have.

I would have wished that Eric, who spoke the finest classless English of his generation, could have paid some attention to the pronunciation of demotic speech, though of course he had enough to do in other linguistic fields. I have always had my tinpot theories about, for instance, the relation of Cockney pronunciation to the whole corpus of English phonology, but I have never dared – as he might have done – to present possibly false but probably acceptable speculations. Why, for instance, are *v* and *w* interchangeable in the speech of Sam Weller? I like to believe that traditional London speech had a bilabial fricative, as in the Spanish *vaso*, which served for both the voiced labio-dental and the voiced labial semivowel. Dickens, hearing the sound, knew it was not quite right but could not tell how it really differed from standard phonemic use: hence he effected a literal transposition. Sam Weller's rendering of *widow* was neither *vidder* nor *widder* but /βidə/. As Eric made the study of meanings and (in his *Origins*) etymology a great philological joy, so he might have ventured imaginative flights about the Great Vowel Shift and related, with humanity and humour, the pronunciation of Shakespeare's English to that of modern Dublin and Boston. After all, it was language as a living experience that concerned him.

For Dublin's Swift, or rather his modern readers, he performed a great service. The *Polite Conversations* were perfectly annotated, and those dialogues in which nothing is really said were shown to be a kind of ultimate repository of socio-linguistic truth, demonstrating that conversation is never about anything but it is perhaps the only thing that matters. For Shakespeare he performed a service which more orthodox scholars winced at. In *Shakespeare's Bawdy*, it was alleged, he dug out more dirt from Shakespeare than was really there. The 'Will' sonnet, for instance, was shown to be a virtuoso concert about the male and female pudenda. I do not think Eric went very far wrong, and if he did it was on the right side. (In his imagined presence one need never be ashamed of bulls.) Slang was, as he showed, mainly subversive. Literature was closer to slang than to governmental directives, and that had to be subversive too. The people's way of being subversive had always lain in the, figurative, lowering of trousers and the raising of skirts. 'Apples be ripe and nuts be brown. Petticoats up and breeches down.' Slang and literature alike tend to greater obscenity than decent people like to imagine. Eric celebrated indecency.

Because he dealt in a field traditionally trivial, as well as subversive, Eric never received the public honours that were his due. He served the Queen (and Kings before her) as well by glorying in the posterior of her, and their, English as staider men did by debasing it (I am thinking of politicians and newspaper proprietors, not jockeys). He never visited America to tell Americans about the riches of their own language. Reading room, study, club sufficed him, and the pleasure of having friends who, like him, loved English. I once toasted him with 'May you live for ever and I live to bury you.' Sadly, the second clause has just about been fulfilled. So, not sadly at all and not fancifully either, is, or will be, or is being, the first.

Some Club Reminiscences

BY *Winston Graham*

———

ERIC PARTRIDGE and I were elected to the Savile Club in the same year, 1950. There we met, casually, and exchanged names and views once or twice. I knew him of course as a distinguished etymologist, but I didn't then know that he had included a passage from one of my novels in his book, *British and American Usage*, which was to be published the following year. Then one day he invited me to his birthday party, which he was giving for a few friends at the Club, and our acquaintance ripened into the warm friendship that persisted until the day he died.

He was a quietly spoken, easy, friendly person, *extremely* modest in manner, so that his later Christmas cards telling the world of his numerous publications seemed to belie the man one knew. I think if asked about these he would have drawn a distinction between self-advertisement and legitimate pride of achievement – of which he had reason to have plenty.

Although he had friends of all kinds, he was most at home among bookmen, and really only happy when talking about words and phrases and synonyms and syllogisms and all the varied and variable features that go to make up a living language.

As a club we are fond of words, their derivation, their use and misuse, the way they change in mid-life and take on new or contrary subtleties of meaning; so the cry was always being heard: 'We must ask Eric!' For many years he used to lunch and dine at the Savile on Thursdays, but as he grew older it became lunch only; otherwise, he said, he was not fresh enough for the invariable cross-London journey to the British Museum Reading Room early next morning, a part of his regime that must never be interfered with. But almost always, while he was sitting talking before lunch, or at the table in the dining room, some member would come up to him and say: 'Oh, Eric, I wanted to ask you; we had

[31]

an argument last night about the use of the word Blank.' Or: 'Tell me, Eric, I came across it the other day: is the word Blank a recent importation from the Greek and if so when was it first used in English?' And always he knew. It was as if all the books he had written were filed away page by page in his head, like a miniature British Museum Reading Room, and he only had to take down the correct volume.

He was a very generous man. My grandfather used to say: 'My happiness lies not in the greatness of my possessions but in the fewness of my wants.' Of few people was this truer than of Eric Partridge. If a little money came to him unexpectedly he would find some reason to give it away. It probably never entered his head, until I suggested it to him, that he might use this money taking a taxi to and from the British Museum to avoid the fatigue of the journey; and when I did he just smiled and shrugged it off. His birthday parties at the Savile were annual events and became quite famous. They were quiet, discreet parties, usually for a dozen or so. Nothing showy or designed to impress, but thoroughly agreeable evenings of food, wine and conversation. They were the only parties I have ever been to at which the host *gave* presents to the guests instead of receiving them. Most often the presents were books of his own, which he would distribute at the end of dinner; but twice he bought and gave away books that I had written.

At these parties I first met Alan Steele, Peter Cochrane, Christopher Fry, Randolph Quirk, Oliver Stoner, some of whom have since become friends of my own. So it came as a special pleasure to be able to organize (with Maurice Goldman's willing help) Eric's eightieth birthday luncheon. At Eric's request, he being then very frail, the numbers were restricted to twenty. So many Savilians wished to be present that I received a lot of black looks from those who could not join in.

A memory of Eric would not be complete without mentioning his enthusiasm for, and expert knowledge of, cricket and tennis. His absences from the British Museum Reading Room while Wimbledon was on were no doubt made more excusable to himself during the years when he was contributing a page to *Time and Tide* on the tennis fortnight; but his visits to Lord's and the Oval were one of the few self-indulgences he permitted himself. A member of both the Middlesex and Surrey County cricket clubs, he was most often to be found at the Oval watching Surrey with a keen and appreciative eye. On one occasion in the late fifties he correctly forecast all the winners at Wimbledon.

After his retirement to Devon the Club no longer saw him, and neither did I. But we continued to correspond, and the last letter I had from him was two weeks before he died, from the hospital, from which he wrote to assure me that he hadn't had a stroke, that it was unfortunate his illness had interfered with his revision of *A Dictionary of Catch Phrases*, but that he hoped to resume work on it that week. His last sentence was: 'Thank you for all your news about the Savile. Do keep me in touch.'

Eric Partridge has left a lasting monument to himself in all the books he has written; but for a little while yet a further monument will remain in the warm and affectionate regard of his friends.

PART I

Word-Books

1

Adventure in Words

I N   S H O R T, every adventure of the mind is an adventure vehicled by words. Every adventure of the mind is an adventure *with* words; every such adventure is an adventure *among* words; and occasionally an adventure is an adventure *of* words. It is no exaggeration to say that, in every word of every language – every single word or phrase or every language, however primitive or rudimentary or fragmentarily recorded, and whether living or dead – we discover an enlightening, sometimes a rather frightening, vignette of history; with such a term as *water* we find that we require a volume rather than a vignette. Sometimes the history concerned may seem to affect only an individual. But, as John Donne remarked in 1624, 'No man is an island, entire of itself; every man is a piece of the continent, a part of the main; . . . any man's death diminishes me, because I am involved in mankind; and therefore never send to know for whom the bell tolls; it tolls for thee.' History is not merely individual, it is collective or social; not only national, but international; not simply terrestrial, but universal. History being recorded in words and achieved partly, sometimes predominantly, by words, it follows that he who despises or belittles or does no worse than underestimate the value and power, the ineluctable necessity of words, despises all history and therefore despises mankind (himself perhaps excluded). He who ignores the enduring power and the history of words ignores that sole part of himself which can, after his death, influence the world outside himself, the sole part that merits a posterity. Comparatively few men and women were affected by Christ himself, by his spoken word and his still more moving example: myriads were influenced by the Apostles repeating those words and extolling that example: countless millions have responded, either to the later preachers, drawing their inspiration from manuscripts and printed books, or to their own reading of the recorded words (The New Testament) or of works based thereon.

Phrased thus, the importance of words seems almost painfully evident – trite – platitudinous. Yet how many people *know* this importance, instead of merely *knowing about* it and recognizing it when it is stated? How many go further and *believe* this inescapable truism? And how many go further still and *believe in* it? If they did, they would realize that no word is 'a mere word', no word is an island, entire of itself. Every word presupposes a context – a situation – the persons forming or participating in or, at least, witnessing that situation. Every word implies either an emotion or a thought or an act, or any two or all three of those things. Rarely do we know exactly where and when and why and how an act originated. With words we fare better. Admittedly we can rarely pinpoint a word in its every aspect, but usually we can trace it satisfactorily or, at least, fairly adequately.

We can trace a word much more easily if we know some history; the more history we know, the more words we can trace and, what is nearly as important, the more we can trace about any given word. (For example, *mayonnaise*, elliptical for *sauce mayonnaise*, recorded in 1807 and probably representing *sauce mahonnaise*, commemorating not Field-Marshal Mac*Mahon*, who wasn't born until 1808, but the brilliant capture, in 1756, of Port *Mahon*, the capital of Minorca, by the Duc de Richelieu, Maréchal de France. The lapse of some fifty years between that event and 1807, the date of the earliest printed record, presents a difficulty more apparent than real, for the term could well have existed for many years without being recorded; moreover, research may yet discover a much earlier date.) By using history, we go direct – a very different matter from trying to trace a word by deduction from deductions, which is what we do when we attempt to trace a word by the so-called laws of sound-change and sound-correspondence, laws that derive from and depend on and generalize the evidence afforded by a collection or a group of relevant or supposedly relevant words, many of which may originally, and for a long period, not have been pronounced as the philologists assert.

We do not at all precisely know how Classical, let alone pre-Classical Greek was pronounced – a tremendous battle has been fought, nor is it yet decided, concerning Greek *oi*; we do not even know precisely how Medieval Latin was pronounced, let alone Late Latin, Classical Latin, Old Latin; about such earlier languages as Hittite and Sumerian we guess wildly. On such assumptions and presumptions are many of the 'laws' of the Indo-European languages built. As I've already declared, phonetics may or may not supply us with a useful servant, but it certainly supplies a fickle, ignorant and dangerous master. Phonetics should be utilized and – with many reservations – respected. Even I often use phonetics and the philological 'laws', but I don't make a song and dance about it; nor do I trust these treacherous and ever-shifting sands. The layman may not believe me when I mention that, at this very moment (and for several years preceding it), there are two bitter, internecine wars being waged concerning the validity or the falsity of two fundamental 'laws' or principles of applied phonetics or 'practical' philology: reputations are being slain, friendships severed, enmities engendered: by the members of each party or 'school of thought' (? rather, 'prejudiced sect') the theories of their opponents, whether those opponents be the revolutionaries or the traditionalists, are declared to be either absurd or ignorant or futile or irrelevant or obsolete or newfangled, and the tenants to be either fools or rogues or preferably both. What amuses an outsider like myself is the bland assumption that the one party or the other must be right: it never seems to cross their minds that both of them could be wrong.

Rather than entrust myself to the quicksands of fanatical phonetics or to the raging seas of parochial philology, I prefer, when I confront a difficulty insoluble by ordinary means, to enlist the aid of history or, if I'm desperate, to resort to imagination; often I combine these two means, either by an imaginative use of history or by a pragmatic use of imagination. 'What *sort* of persons or *which* tribe or people or nation – living *where*, doing *what*, feeling or thinking or acting *how*, and at *which period* in their civilization or at *which stage* of their growth – *would* or, at worst, *could* have evolved and developed, or borrowed and, having borrowed, transmuted either the form or the sense or, usually, both the form and the sense of the word that is causing all this trouble?' These are merely a few of perhaps many questions I ask myself before I do anything so drastic as to begin the search. One doesn't just dart all over the place and hope for the best and muddle through; one doesn't grab at the first straw or, worse, essay brick-making without straws; one doesn't try to show how clever one is or what a fine intellect one has. What one does attempt is something very different. To explain the difference would necessitate a fair-sized book.

2

How it All Began

———

AS ONE MIGHT EXPECT, Dr Johnson has permitted himself three or four remarks upon lexicography or the art of writing dictionaries. As one might expect, they tend to be both wry and dry. Like most great – as opposed to merely famous – men, he was modest and humble.

'Dictionaries,' he once said, 'are like watches: the worst is better than none, and the best cannot be expected to go quite true'. He defined *lexicographer* as 'a writer of dictionaries' and characteristically added the words, 'a harmless drudge'. Within his great work, he exemplified *dull* with the sentence, 'To make dictionaries is dull work'. Even a cursory glance at a few pages of *A Dictionary of the English Language* (1755) shows us that he did not find the work dull; that he did not regard himself as a drudge; that it is unlikely he thought of himself as harmless. But lexicographical hacks are drudges: and the result of their work is dull and lifeless: and they themselves are, one supposes, harmless fellows, who would be so much better employed in compiling pedestrian encyclopaedias – as doubtless many of them are. For me, lexicography is not dull, but exciting; otherwise I should not be writing this little book at all. Nor have I ever been a drudge.

Clearly, when I use the word *dictionary*, I primarily mean a word-book, not a reference work that, for reasons of convenience, is arranged in alphabetical order, as in (say) *A Dictionary of Architecture* – as opposed to *A Dictionary of Architectural Terms*. The dividing-line is sometimes hard to draw; but let us not diverge upon that fascinating theme!

Near the end of a not too dull life, Albert Jay Nock proclaimed: 'As sheer casual reading-matter, I still find the English dictionary the most interesting book in the language' (*Memoirs of a Super-*

fluous Man, 1943): and that's as it should be, for what more fundamental than, what so indispensable as, a dictionary? Nock's proclamation reminds me of the trivial story of that old lady who, on borrowing a dictionary from her municipal library, returned it with the comment, 'A very unusual book indeed – but the stories are extremely short, aren't they?' A remark, one feels, rather more applicable to the *Who's Who* of any country whatsoever.

For most of us, a dictionary is hardly a book to read; a good dictionary, however, is a book to browse in. Some dictionaries are so well written that one just goes on and on.

To write such a dictionary has always been my ambition.

I began early in life: and it is the course of my life which, allied to a natural propensity to original sin, has made a lexicographer out of me. Perhaps I should have become one even if I had lived always in one country and always done the same work; but probably the migrations and the changes have pin-pointed the predilection and transformed the advisable into the profitable, and necessity into a virtue – if 'virtue' be the right word. As I look back, I seem to discern a pattern or, if you prefer, a series of happenings, some pushing vulgarly, others slyly nudging, me into a career that, since 1930, has been predominantly lexicographical. Here I must enter a caveat. Sometimes I grow a little tired of being called 'the dictionary man' or 'the word man' or even, as Edmund Wilson, far too generously and, for once in a well-integrated life, inaccurately, called me, 'the word king'.

My first book was a slim, privately printed volume of not at all good verse translations from French poetry, 'way back in 1914. Ten years later, the next two represented my M.A. and B.Litt. theses. In 1925–29, I published a collection of literary essays, some editings of English literature, pseudonymously a volume of short stories. Since 1930, I have – in addition to lexicographical labours of love – issued eight collections of essays, one literary, one autobiographical, the others mainly linguistic; pseudonymously a novel; *Slang Today and Yesterday: A History and a Study*; small books on 'shaggy dogs' and 'comic alphabets'; *English: A Course for Human Beings*; *You Have a Point There* (a guide to punctuation and its allies); *What's the Meaning?* (an introduction to etymology). Admittedly, most of those books deal with one aspect or another of language; but they are not dictionaries – and neither, except in alphabetical arrangement, are *Usage and Abusage* and its offshoot, *The Concise Usage and Abusage*.

Nor is that caveat a mere interpolation; much less is it a self-indulgent effluence of egocentricity. It bears very closely on much of what is to follow. Much of what follows would be inexplicable or, at the least, perplexing without the caveat. After all, I'm a writer and therefore unlikely to fall over my own feet as I this simple tale unfold.

Born, 1894, in New Zealand, I passed the first ten or so years in a country district (its first white child) situated fifteen miles from a small town. Hilly sheep country it was, with a few cattle and only occasional crops, small, domestic. There I naturally gained a pretty intimate knowledge of country life and rural fauna and flora: not the worst basis on which to build a solid foundation for an urban and sedentary life devoted mainly to learning.

Learning very early became a passion; it has remained a passion. 'How so, among the hayseeds?' Easily enough. My father was not uneducated. Apart from being quite well-read, he had received a grounding in Greek and Latin and French and he was a far from average mathematician. He introduced me to books as soon as I could read and before I could read well; he encouraged me to read; he showed me (aged seven) how to use a dictionary – I forget which, but probably an Annandale recension of an Ogilvie.

Inadvertently and perhaps a year later, he inculcated an invaluable lexicographical principle; the pundits are not necessarily right even when they're utterly self-confident. I can remember, vividly remember, how, one summer day, he came in to lunch still fuming from an argument he had had with a visiting farmer, who, as one flew by, said 'That's a large bumble bee'. My father maintained that he had never heard it called anything but a humble bee and that '*humble* bee' was correct, '*bumble* bee' incorrect. The visitor asked why it should be described as *humble*; he was told, 'Because it's a large, good-natured bee that doesn't sting'; to which he replied that, on the contrary, it was named '*bumble* bee' for two reasons; it bumbled and blundered about the place and made a booming sound – on a small scale. My father stuck to his opinion. I felt suitably impressed, although not quite as he supposed. Later I somewhat guiltily looked up *humble bee* in the dictionary; it wasn't there. So, disloyally, I tried *bumble bee*, and there it was. At least I had enough sense to refrain from telling my formidable father this; and for years, whenever I saw or heard of a *humble-bumble* bee, I vaguely wondered which of the disputants had been wrong. When, aged fourteen, I could at last consult an authoritative dictionary, I learned – to my delight and ribald amusement – that both of them had been right about the term. *Humble bee* is apparently the earlier: the OED records it for 1450 and derives it from the now long-obsolete *humble*, to hum or buzz, as a bee does. *Bumble bee* is recorded for 1530, but it probably existed from fifty or more years earlier, and it derives from *bumble*, to boom or to buzz. Etymologically, our visitor was almost right; my father, entirely wrong. As a result – well, I've already dotted the *i*'s; you may cross the *t*'s.

Yet, before I was quite fourteen, I received a still more valuable lesson. In October, 1907, we migrated from New Zealand to Australia, my father having wearied of the life of 'retired gentleman'; that life had lasted for three years, much to the surprise of my mother and her family, for he was a very active, somewhat restless, decidedly energetic person.

Well, there was I, with a tolerable vocabulary possessing a ruddy New Zealand complexion; cast upon a world so different as to startle anyone except a mature philosopher – and I was neither mature nor philosophical. Although only twelve hundred miles apart, New Zealand and Australia are 'poles apart' in physical composition and nature; in fauna and flora; in climate; ethnically, in respect of their native peoples; and in the very character of the white populations, with their fundamentally different history of settlement and early growth and with the tremendous influence of environments differing so sharply. Not least of the differences was that in speech; a difference of accent and tempo, of intonation and enunciation. The difference in vocabulary was perhaps even greater: new names to learn for the beasts and the reptiles, the birds and the fishes; for the trees and shrubs and grasses; for the soils and the winds; for customs and occupations, and, in short, a new way of life. One of the first things I noticed was that what had, in New Zealand, been called a public school was, in Queensland, a State school or, as I learned very much later, a primary school, not necessarily elementary; to add to the confusion, I had somewhere read that, in Britain, a public school or, rather, a Public School, was a very superior sort of secondary school – a glorified grammar school. I realized, perhaps for the first time vividly, that, in these questions of nomenclature, it was no good guessing: one had to *know*.

I bought a little note-book and industriously entered all those strange names and words and phrases which came my way or which I learned by eager inquiry. 'If you wish to know, ask!' Probably I made a damned nuisance of myself; certainly my youth protected me from the rude answers some of my informants must have felt very much tempted to make. Most people respond very kindly to a starry-eyed innocence and an ingenuous enthusiasm. Luckily, my father had an equally inquiring mind; luckily he perceived that my motive was less daft than it seemed. That spirit of inquiry has served me well throughout my life. By the time I was sixteen or thereabouts, I possessed a technique rather more subtle, much more indirect: but as it's one that might not work with most, nor even with many, I shall not divulge it: thus I shall spare the naïve investigator a busted nose or an indelicate recommendation. (Until the Second World War, most of us regarded ourselves either as inquirers or, if we were scientists or thesis-writers, as researchers; nowadays, the 'inquirer' has become an 'investigator' or a 'field-worker'. The language of simple, honest inquiry has become pompous and pretentious; and so have many of the inquirers.)

Language, however, has an aspect that, in the main, is insusceptible of inquiry, except from oneself and one's reading and one's constant observation of speech, especially of intelligent and preferably educated speech: the *way* in which words are used, by means of syntax, phrasing, idiom, and so forth, to express need or action, thought or meditation, dream or aspiration. Here, the differences between one country and another, one district and another, one occupation and another, one social class and another, and, in one person, between childhood and youth, youth and maturity, are less readily grasped and analysed and systematized – if, indeed, they can be systematized at all. Linked with these features of language are those of differences of meaning; it is exceedingly difficult to prevent the connotations and implications of words, as opposed to their denotations (themselves difficult enough, heaven knows!), from slipping through the semantic net, no matter how finely and cunningly it is meshed. Australian syntax and semantics, phrasing and idiom, I soon perceived, differed appreciably from those of New Zealand. Thus it was that, early in – and throughout – my teens, I became aware of and, at first, perplexed by one of the most delicate characteristics of language: usage; hence, by comparison, abusage too. From usage, one may pass to the perilous and exciting game of attempting to determine sociological and racial characteristics by a searching examination and comparison of accidence and syntax, words and phrases and idioms. If one does, one has to guard against nationalist prejudice and preoccupation. Several otherwise excellent dictionaries have been vitiated by national prejudice, as for instance Noah Webster's by his intensely anti-British bias or Friedrich Kluge's by an almost pathological phobia against everything non-Germanic in general and against everything Semitic in particular. Not, of course, by Kluge (1856–1926) himself, but by Nazi-minded German philologists during the approximate period 1933–1945. The vast majority of words escaped contamination; but all those which could be made, or bent, to subserve the Teutonic dream of world-domination and the constant Teutonic ambition to glorify everything even remotely German and to claim, as

German, words or devices or inventions or ideas, not to forget persons, and such human manifestations as they suspected might help to shore up a gigantic fabric of make-believe: all these rather numerous words fell under their malefic sway. All good Germans – for whom scholarship transcended frontiers – squirmed in spiritual discomfort, and a few of them contrived to get out of the country. (But I did not interest myself in nationalist philology until during the First World War.)

That war ensured a further somewhat drastic development of my linguistic interests. Early in 1915, I enlisted in the Australian Imperial Force and, in May, departed for further training in Egypt. I began my obscure military career as a private in an infantry battalion, with only one blemish. After the Second Australian Division's 'first Pozières', I was the only 'Anzac' left in my section; in a frail moment, I was persuaded to lead the section, a week later, into 'the second Pozières' (4 August, 1916). Much good it did either the section or myself. Crossing No Man's Land, I 'stopped one'. On returning to the battalion some months later, I kept quiet about my promotion to the dizzy rank of lance-corporal and, although several times urged to take a commission, I successfully resisted the influences endangering my independence. Nor was I being entirely unselfish: I'd have made a very poor officer, for I hate to boss people about.

Nor is that a digression. As a private, I learned much more about Australian speech, about Australian English, than I could possibly have done as an officer. I was meeting all the roughs and the toughs, as well as many decent fellows coming from trades and professions of which I knew nothing – or so little as to be worse than nothing. Although I had earned my living since I was sixteen, I had, as teacher and then as undergraduate, met only a few different types of mankind: now I was meeting all conceivable types, from the wealthy pastoralist to the petty crook; from the cane-cutter to the 'wharfie'; from the rural storekeeper to the urban shopkeeper; from the book-keeper to the bookmaker; from the journalist to the 'sundowner' and the 'swaggie'; from the Civil Servant to the commercial traveller and the 'con man' proper; from the shearer to the sailor; from the railway official to the tram-driver. Not only meeting but living with them, in conditions where men regard modesty and reticence as unwanted luggage. Having a quick ear, a comparative mind, a retentive memory, and no hesitation in asking for full and precise information whenever I was in doubt and could ask without giving offence, I naturally acquired a considerable store of technical and semi-technical standard Australian English, as well as a not inconsiderable stock of slangy and colloquial and other unconventional words and phrases and senses and idioms. At the time, I was not intending to specialize in – better, to concentrate upon – English: I had left Queensland as a Classic ('Theocritus' Cholmeley had been one of my University teachers); so far as I thought about the matter – survival being or, at the least, seeming rather more important, I assumed that if ever I had the luck to return, with faculties unimpaired, to Australia, I should continue to be a Classic – no bad training for anyone so rash as to study language in general, the English language in particular. To some extent or, rather, to the requisite extent I have remained one, partly urged by inclination and partly driven by conscience. How anyone can pretend to be an adequate philologist or, at any rate, a good etymologist, without possessing a 'pretty useful' knowledge of Greek and Latin, has always defeated me. Oh! I admit that my Latin has become rather, and my Greek very, rusty, but for many years they were something more than a smattering and I can still 'find my way around' in them with a reasonable approximation to comfort and security.

On the other hand, I cannot truthfully say that, during the First World War, I learned very much about the speech-habits of the English and the Welsh, the Scots and the Irish. I played inattentively on the vast periphery of knowledge; I came to know something about, but hardly knew, the extensive, bewilderingly variegated, field into some of whose corners I was later to roam and pray.

But the influence of those war years is a subject upon which I could expatiate until I lost every friend and estranged every acquaintance. I hated that war. Yet it benefited me more than I can tell.

Then in 1921 I came to England and went to Oxford. This meant that I was obliged to habituate myself to yet another way of life – almost another civilization – and to augment and, in some respects, change or modify a vocabulary, a usage, a pronunciation; it was pronunciation which took me the longest. I have not acquired, nor have I wished to acquire, that variety of Standard English pronunciation which is known as Southern, or Public School, English. Mine is one of the Modified Standards. My aim has always been to speak a clear and lucid, rather than a dulcet, English and to write a lucid and expressive, rather than an elegant, English; and to be occasionally subtle, never precious.

As when I had left New Zealand for Australia, so now the task of learning new names in fauna and flora, in urban and in rural life – new social and professional and commercial customs – strange usages and idioms – confronted me, in circumstances enforcing or, at best, rendering advisable a still more thorough and much more speedy adjustment. Such an adjustment, largely conscious, and such an adaptation, partly unconscious, had three results worth mentioning in this brief account of a progress in the study of language and in the practice of lexicography: they considerably enlarged a vocabulary that was, perhaps, already more various than that of most of my coevals; they increased a natural predilection towards the study of language especially of the English language wherever and however spoken; and they sharpened an innate curiosity about the origins and nature of this or that word, that or this phrase or idiom.

Not that I took my B.Litt. in language. I took it in a literary subject intimately connected with language. (As if one could divorce literature and language!) 'The Influence of English Literature upon the French Romantics.' When, early in 1919, I had returned to Australia, I changed from an honours course in Classics to one in French and English. Perhaps my interests had, during the war years, moved slightly away from Greek and Latin and towards English, with a strong secondary affection for French and other modern languages. An intimate study of French, a language that had fascinated me ever since I was introduced to it as a young boy, certainly refined my study of English; linguistically, I've never been quite the same person since; but then, only an insensitive could have been. Through my work for this degree, I met three very fine scholars: A. J. Carlyle, my supervisor, and my two examiners, Gustave Rudler and David Nichol Smith. Indirectly, I came also to know George Gordon and H. C. K. Wyld, who held the senior chairs in English Literature and English Language respectively. To enumerate the benefits accruing from acquaintance with two, friendship with three, of those five men would take far too long. It would be difficult, if not impossible, to evaluate the total collective benefit, whether in scholarship or in the imponderables.

3

Genesis of a Lexicographer

━━━

IN HIS FAMOUS *Dictionary*, Dr Samuel Johnson defined a *lexico-grapher* in two ways. Literally as 'a writer of dictionaries'; not, you will notice, as 'a compiler . . .', for he was thinking of scholars, not of hacks. And idiosyncratically as 'a harmless drudge, that busies himself with tracing the original, and detailing the signi-fication of words'.

One and three-quarter centuries later, Osbert Burdett, who met his death in 1936 by falling down an escalator but who had made his mark as a literary critic and historian, of rare distinction and who was an authority upon mushrooms, published a volume of short stories, *The Very End*, in which he caustically yet not unsympathetically remarked, 'A maker of dictionaries is an active laborious creature, the navvy of scholarship, carrying his head backward and forward from one learned library to another.' Burdett himself was a very good scholar.

Well, every lexicographer would agree that, to be one at all, he must be 'active' and 'laborious' (that is, very hard-working), but few would admit that he need, unless he's a hack, be 'a drudge'; fewer still, that he is 'harmless', for the most damning thing you can say of anybody is that 'He's so well-meaning'.

Lexicographers differ among themselves as much in method as they do in style; as much mentally as they do morally; and as much in ultimate motive as they do in immediate aim. I cannot speak for other lexicographers; nor, even if I could, should I. They go their ways, I mine. Here, I shall confine myself to my own aims, motives, methods, experiences: and to do that I must, since this is not an academic disquisition, be frankly egotistic, although not, I hope, disgustingly egocentric.

Why did I become one of what some compassionate soul has called 'these poor, misguided creatures'? I could hurriedly answer:

predilection. That answer is correct, it is also far too easy. A murderer might say the same thing. It would be more accurate to reply: training in (and by) life; training in literature.

If I believed in the Argument from Design, I should say that life has made me a lexicographer, or, more fully, that the very course, even the most unpredictable vicissitudes, of my life have 'conspired' to direct, rather than to force me into this adventurous path and, perhaps even more decidedly, to keep me there.

Born in a remote rural community in New Zealand, I had, until I was ten or eleven, to find most of my own amusements. Luckily my father, a well-educated person, had a good, though small, library. He encouraged me to read. If I remember rightly, I needed very little encouragement. The first three books I read, and frequently re-read, were Thomas Hughes's *Tom Brown's Schooldays*, Defoe's *Robinson Crusoe* and Dean Farrar's *Eric, or Little by Little*, all set in circumstances and amid scenes quite alien from my own. The slightly archaic language of *Robinson Crusoe*, like the old-fashioned language of the other two books, sent me thus early (at the age, I suppose of seven and eight) to a dictionary, with the result that, at even that immature age, I became accustomed to using these invaluable aids to knowledge and sources of sober, never-disillusionizing entertainment. Truth, although it may not be stranger, is both more durable and more satisfyingly exciting than fiction.

That dictionary and that reading stimulated an imaginative and, I fear, sensitive and perceptive child of eight into the writing of three or four extremely short stories. Then I never wrote another until I reached the advanced age of twelve, when I began – at thirteen, I completed – a novel of English Public School life, a pleasurable task from which I was not in the least deterred by the fact that I knew precious little about England and precisely nothing about Public Schools. The odd thing is that I did not return to fiction until 1915, when, at the age of twenty-one, I amused myself, by the light of a candle in a dug-out on Gallipoli, and wrote a suitably gloomy short story of love unrequited; nor again until 1928, when, with the pseudonym 'Corrie Denison', I published *Glimpses*, a volume of short stories, which, to my amazement, *The New York Times* reviewed favourably. To the novel, I did not return until 1932, when I wrote and succeeded in getting published a pseudonymous, not at all good fantasy, entitled *The Scene is Changed*. To my very considerable relief, both of these books have been out of print these many years. Since then, the only fiction to which I have committed myself has consisted, on the one hand, of a short, intimate (probably much too intimate) love-story, written in 1944-45, rejected by one shrewd publisher and since submitted to no publisher whether shrewd or credulous, and, on the other hand, a short story I self-indulgently yet not altogether uncritically allowed myself to incorporate in a work that appeared in 1949.

To the not improbably irate suggestion that this talk of fiction may appear irrelevant and, in a lexicographer, unseemly, I can only reply that I'm so unrepentant that, the opportunity occurring, I shall, not improbably (and not entirely by way of parergon), write other novels and other short stories; more, that I am so irretrievably lost to grace and decency that I believe the mental and moral exercise proved by the writing of fiction to be not only salutary to all authors whatsoever but also beneficial to their art – yes, even to the art and craft of a lexicographer. The ability to write about words is a speciality, but so is the ability to write about life; the man able to write about both is thereby enabled to write all the better about words in particular and language in general and to bring to a dictionary that breath of life which all too often is excluded from dictionaries.

To return to the chronological order, especially important in any account of the genesis of a writer, my family emigrated from New Zealand to Australia late in 1907, when I was some four months short of fourteen. The change from rural and, later, urban New Zealand to urban and rural Australia proved to be something of a shock, for not only are the countries sharply contrasted in climate and physical features, but also the people of Australia are startlingly different from those of New Zealand. The impact of those differences was so great that, young though I was and therefore wholly inadequate, I wrote in my otherwise deficient diary a long series of notes upon the contrast in characteristics; and among those contrasts I included those of language, Australians having speech-habits almost as sharply alien from those of New Zealanders as Americans have from Britons in general and Englishmen in particular. But I also realized and duly noted the fact that, despite all those differences in pronunciation and enunciation, in word and phrase and catch phrase, New Zealand English and Australian English had far more in common than in dissonance – as, indeed, have American and British English.

From late 1907 until early 1915 and from early 1919 until mid-1921 I lived in Queensland. For the whole of the interval between 1915 and 1919, I was serving with the Australian Imperial Forces. I came, therefore, to absorb Australian English and, much more important, unforgettingly to acquire the knowledge, invaluable to a student of speech and literature, that even one language can and does change from clime to clime, from colony to colony, from city to country, from one generation to another, even from one social group to the next, and from childhood to youth to early manhood to middle-age to old-age: that language has its collective as well as its individual aspects, its deviations as well as its usage and usages: that it springs not from books but from life, not from pundits but from the people: that it progresses or, at the worst, moves, not along narrowly, but only along broadly established lines of development: that it is almost as much subject to the vicissitudes of fate as are the lives of the most impressionable of men and women.

The war of 1914–1918; the war of 1939–1945: four years' service in the first, as a private in an infantry battalion – Gallipoli and the Western Front; and again four in the second, private and officer in the Army, aircraftman in the RAF, but, owing to age and indifferent health, all the time on the Home Front, although at first with duty quite exciting enough in London during 'the Blitz'. Those eight years out of my life were years very significantly in it: more, they probably were by far the most important, not only to me as a person but to me as a potential, then as a realized, writer – whether novelist or essayist, and whether philologist or etymologist or lexicographer. They brought me into the most human and intimate, the most searching and illuminating contact with men in both deed and word; that word, at its most deedful and urgent and fateful. In the Combatant Services, I could and – in the main, subconsciously – did watch men's characters develop, and their thinking, hence their speech, with them. Life there acted as both a catalyst and a precipitate, which is more than war can do of itself: most of us, resilient and unthinking, rebound and recover from the mere mechanical impact of war, partly because that impact, however frightening, is so very obvious; from communal life, lived in such circumstances, we never rebound, never 'recover', partly because we seldom think about it, that life being, as it were, the air we breathe, the ambience of our existences. Some, of course, pay a price so heavy that the benefits do not accrue. But they are not many. In its general aspects a curse and a disaster, war should, for all such reflective individuals as suffer no irremediable damage, turn out to be, in its total effect, a blessing. It did for me; perhaps I was lucky. Certainly I account myself fortunate to have met with those experiences which did come my way. Certainly I've paid a price: but the price was comparatively low.

Neither in 1914–1918 nor in 1939–1945 did I plan to 'cash in on' a world-wide misfortune. But I did have to 'get it out of my system'. This I succeeded in doing by writing either about or near them. The earlier conflict produced, long after, *Three Personal Records*, 1929 in England, 1930 in America – published, that is, during the worst of the depression, yet long out of print; *Songs and Slang of the British Soldier*, now hard to find; and *A Martial Medley*, an anthology of original articles and stories, now more than merely hard to find. All were collaborative works. So is *A Dictionary of Forces' Slang, 1939–1945*, happily in print. Two of those books are dictionaries; the other two, mainly autobiographical.

On returning from World War I, I completed my long-interrupted course at the University of Queensland, and in 1921 I went, on a travelling fellowship, to the University of Oxford, where I took a B.Litt, with a comparative study in French and English literature. Some research had to be done in Paris, where, on and off, I spent much time until about 1934. At Oxford, I met, and enjoyed the counsel of, three outstanding men: Dr A. J. Carlyle, the Puck of scholarship; Professor George Gordon, later President of Magdalen College; and Professor H. C. K. Wyld, author of several very well-known books upon English language. All of them are dead. To my two years at Oxford I owe an unrepayable debt.

During the two years beginning in September, 1925, I was a lecturer in English literature at the Universities of Manchester and London. At this point, therefore, I may fittingly interpolate a brief mention of the second of the two trainings that have contributed to the genesis of a lexicographer: life and literature. One cannot honestly pretend to a knowledge of any civilized language unless one has an adequate knowledge of the literature. Whatever my failings, I can at least say that I have continuously read works of literature ever since I unintentionally started off with *Robinson Crusoe*. My first two published books were *Eighteenth-Century English Romantic Poetry* and *The French Romantics' Knowledge of English Literature*, both issued in Paris in 1924. From then until 1932 inclusive, my publications consisted mainly of studies in English literature. Since 1931, however, I have worked mostly at one or other phase of English language, the exception being *A Journey to the Edge of Morning*, a volume of essays published (although not in America) in 1946. This almost life-long association with literature has helped to preserve me from the morass of ingrown philology; that is, from such philological writing or compilation as seems to imply a belief that words and language itself have an existence apart from the countless millions of men and women who originated and developed the words and languages.

But to revert, once more, to chronology. In 1927 I founded and until late in 1931 controlled a small publishing firm known as The Scholartis Press. In 1929 it issued *Three Personal Records of the War*, by R. H. Mottram, John Easton and myself. As a result of reading that book, John Brophy suggested that he and I should collaborate in *Songs and Slang*, which appeared in June, 1930. While we were working upon it, we both had occasion to consult Captain Francis Grose's *A Classical Dictionary of the Vulgar Tongue* (1785). Mr Brophy urged me to publish an edition of 'Grose', with a biographical essay and a copious commentary. I did. The book, issued in 1931, has for several years been out of print and is now obtainable only at a price I myself am assuredly not prepared to pay. Those two works attracted the attention of a far-seeing publisher, who invited me to write a study of slang and, that completed, a dictionary of slang.

Three Personal Records started a train that has run for some years. But I had been profoundly interested in language ever since 1907; the war brought above the surface a seed that had germinated long before. To *Eighteenth-Century Romantic Poetry* I added an appendix dealing with the neologisms occurring in the verses of the poets concerned. Philologically I owe most to the works of Henry Bradley, Logan Pearsall Smith, H. C. K. Wyld and Ernest Weekley; I owe much also to the guidance of J. J. Stable, my old Professor of English at the University of Queensland.

Of my development in lexicography, however, there remains something to say – something to add to those early indications. My first really big piece of work was *A Dictionary of Slang and Unconventional English*, published in February, 1937, second edition in 1938, and the third, very much enlarged, late in 1949.* The second is *A Dictionary of the Underworld, British and American*, commenced in October, 1936 and completed in 1949. And they *were* big, for both of them cover a period of more than four centuries. Other works have appeared since I 'turned author' in December, 1931, the most successful being, I suppose, *Usage and Abusage*, appearing (October, 1942) in America nearly four and a half years before it did in England; *The World of Words*, an

---

* Since then, the fourth edition has appeared; it is virtually the same as the third. [The much-enlarged fifth edition appeared in 1961. Ed.]

exercise in popularization; *A Dictionary of Clichés*, conceived in jest, borne mirthfully, and born in September, 1940, at the height of 'The London Blitz'; and *Name into Word*, which also was great fun to write. And there were three collections of philological essays – a form to which I am distressingly addicted. The first has long been out of print; the other two are *Words at War: Words at Peace*, 1948, and *Here, There and Everywhere*, first and second editions in 1950.

The most cursory consideration of the books mentioned above may serve to show that I like to deal as much with language in general as with particular aspects. That affection underlies the book on which I have recently been working and which will (we hope) appear* during the Festival of Britain: *A History of British and American English since 1900*, where I handle both the general and the British themes and John W. Clark, Associate Professor of English in the University of Minnesota, the American. But what fascinates me the most is etymology. Since mid-1948 I have, with the exception just mentioned, been engaged upon an enterprise that will, I fear, keep me out of mischief until 1957 or perhaps 1958 or even 1959. An etymological dictionary of English, British and American, upon entirely new lines.†

For this work, I shall require not only all the courage and resources that can be afforded by a powerful predilection, by knowledge, and by industry, patience and perseverance, but also an enduring, open-minded enthusiasm – ingenuity – and imagination rather than mere fancy. One cannot exemplify most of those requisites, but one can perhaps indicate what is meant, in lexicography, by ingenuity and imagination.

Established for some 150 years as the commonest of the British slang terms for 'sixpence' is *tanner*, dismissed by all the most authoritative dictionaries as of 'uncertain, or obscure, origin'. Origins in Latin and Romany can be ignored. Perhaps I may be allowed to quote from 'Neither Cricket nor Philology . . .', an

---

* It did.

† *Origins: A Short Etymological Dictionary of Modern English* (1958). [See the extract on pp. 218–19. Ed.]

essay included in a self-anthology, *A Covey of Partridge*, published in 1937 but long out of print. 'The origin I submit is more fantastic; but many slang words are of an origin that at first seems fantastic. As early as the late seventeenth century, there was a slang word for sixpence [– it survived until about 1820]: and that was *simon* or *Simon*. I don't pretend to know the origin of *Simon*, though it is probably a fanciful name, precisely as *bob* (a shilling) may be *Bob* and *susie* (sixpence) may be *Susie*; but *tanner* may well have been suggested by that Biblical passage which later accounted for "the old joke" . . . about St Peter's banking transaction, when he 'lodged with one Simon a tanner' " (*Household Words*, June 20, 1885)'. The exact passages in *Acts*, *x*, 6 and 32, are respectively: 'He [Peter] lodgeth with one Simon a tanner' and 'He [Peter] lodgeth in the house of Simon a tanner': in both of which, modern punctuation would put a comma after 'Simon'; the more relevant passage is 'He lodgeth with one Simon a tanner'. But to continue with the quotation from *A Covey*: 'Incredible? Well, I won't argue about it further than to equate the semantics; thus:

"one Simon a tanner"

1 Simon = a tanner

a sixpence = a Tanner

hence,   a Tanner = sixpence.'

Having been at first derided for excessive ingenuity, that proposed etymology has gained ground. So has the following, which exemplifies imagination – or so I like to think. The *tarot* pack of cards has caused much trouble. *The Oxford English Dictionary* adduces such European forms as Italian *tarocchi* and Old French *tarau* or *tarault*, Modern *tarot*, the form adopted by English, but states that the word is 'of unknown origin'; so do 'Webster' and 'Weekley'. To quote again from 'Neither Cricket nor Philology . . .' (where 'not cricket' alludes to the English statutory condemnation of anything dishonest): – 'These cards have, for centuries, been used in fortune-telling; originally and still mainly by the Gypsies. . . . Of the 78 cards of a Tarot pack, 52 are those of an ordinary pack; only 26 are essential Tarot. These 26 represent powers that are friendly, but also, and more, powers that are inimical to man. By a wholly unphilological reasoning I said to myself: "Fortune-telling cards; Gypsies; coming from India, but – witness their old name, *Egyptians* – almost certainly connected with Egypt at one time; so have a look at Wallis Budge". That great Egyptologist's *Egyptian Dictionary* . . . contains . . . *taru* . . . "fiends, demons, devils, enemies". (He also has "*Tar* . . . a fiend . . .", as well as a host of other terms cognate with *Taru*.) There is not, I think, much need to gild Egyptian gold', especially as Old French *tarau* corresponds so closely to *taru*, which, let me repeat, is a plural.

'Yes! But how, in general, does a lexicographer go about his work?' I cannot answer for others, although I do most heartily disagree with the late Professor W. W. Skeat's reputed, although probably apocryphal, dictum that if he failed to solve an etymology in twenty minutes, he left it alone or, in other words, discarded it – with the label 'Origin obscure'.

Since generalizations can become very tedious, I shall briefly tell how I went about two of my dictionaries.

For *A Dictionary of Slang and Unconventional English*, as for *A Dictionary of the Underworld*, I spent three well-occupied weeks in planning the book: the period to be covered; the scope – involving the solution of some very knotty problems of delimitation and classification; the alphabetical system to be followed, there being, contrary to general belief, two systems, each with much to recommend it – the absolute, as in 'Webster', and the something-before-nothing, as in these two dictionaries of mine,* the order of procedure within every single entry – whether, for instance, etymology should come first or last, and to what extent, if any, quotations should be used; and many others, several of them too erudite for mention here. For the earlier work, I decided to deal with the slang, colloquialisms, catch phrases, and so forth, of the entire British Commonwealth of Nations; for the latter, with the under-

---

* [See further, Ch. 3 below. Ed.]

world speech of the United States as well. For both, I read widely, moved in many circles, and listened hard; necessarily, I listened very discreetly, wherever I might be prosecuting my researches.

That precaution held doubly good for *Underworld*. (For America, by the way, I had the assistance of some very able and suitable persons, both during and after my search in literally every American book and periodical available in Britain. All collation, all etymological work fell to me, although occasionally I had to apply to an American for the solution of an etymology.) Only a little of the underworld material that came to me direct was in written form, professional criminals being, with the exception of confidence tricksters ('con men'), notoriously inept with the pen, even 'penmen' or 'scratchers' being useless – outside of forgery. Luckily, famous criminals have employed 'ghosts', and they and other criminals have frequently been tapped by journalists and authors; prison chaplains and governors, or wardens, are, to coin a phrase, mines of information; police officers, especially detectives, pick up many words and phrases; tramps and hoboes, whether ex-professional or amateur, tend much more than criminals to write of their experiences; special investigators into prostitution and the drug-traffic – that is, those of them who take their work seriously and are engaged therein for long periods – learn much of the cant (the philologists' term for 'language of the underworld') used by the purveyors and their customers; police-court proceedings are occasionally helpful. That is an incomplete though not a grossly inadequate list of the more accessible sources available to a researcher into cant.

But he who deals, or professes to deal, directly with the underworld has to be very careful. Criminals are naturally suspicious of a stranger: and usually they either withhold information or supply 'phoney' material. But unconsciously they let things out, for the very simple reason that, unless (as is rare) they are well-educated and unless (as is equally rare) they are speech-conscious, they are often unaware that a term or a phrase does, in fact, belong to cant. When a criminal has been using an underworld expression for five or ten years, he forgets when and, above all where he acquired it. More than one British, and more than one American, journalist and social worker and philologist have had their legs pulled. Rarely will a 'working' criminal impart the required information; when he does, it is because he trusts the inquirer not to divulge names or other police-useful details; that confidence has to be earned. Ex-criminals, however, are less reticent. As for the dating and the etymology of material supplied by criminals (and hoboes), whether active or retired, one cannot, as a rule, trust their statements or opinions. One settles the question either by collation, by external evidence, by internal evidence, or, in the last, desperate resort by the intelligent, carefully controlled exercise of that flair without which the delver into the byways of language would do better to refrain from delving at all.

Concerning the aims and methods I pursue in the etymological work in which I am now engaged, I can hardly be expected to speak. But in the introduction to *Name into Word*, I furnish certain clues as to how I went to work on this particular 'sectional' dictionary; in another, *Clichés*, the task was apparently simpler, yet really harder – observation and note-taking over a long period.

The economic problems confronting a professional lexicographer (a lexicographer primarily an author, not a university professor) are much the same as those confronting any other writer, the worst being the precariousness of his livelihood. But whereas a reputable English novelist has his books manufactured in America, and a reputable American one his in Britain, and thus earns royalties in both countries, a lexicographer has usually to be content, in one of the two countries, with a percentage on the sale of sheets, i.e. with one-quarter to one-third of what the royalties would bring to him. Moreover, like certain other British writers, I had the stocks of several books destroyed during 'the London Blitz'.

And domestic problems? The gravest is the need for quiet in which to concentrate upon work far more exacting than that done by a nominally creative writer. (Lexicography itself can be creative. But that's another story.) Most of the research into written sources, I do in the world's greatest library, that of the British Museum; and my 'field work' – well, naturally that isn't done at home.

Yet, despite all the difficulties, lexicography (except the inferior variety 'cooked up' by hacks) is always fascinating. And often it's fun. Indeed, any fairly well-known writer of readable books on language finds it so. One learns how to 'take it'; from adverse criticism, whether by reviewers or by academics and whether one is at first irritated or amused, one learns, or should learn, more than from favourable comment. The puzzles that arise may, in the attempt to solve them, lead one to discoveries either valuable or entertaining – or both. Etymology, particularly, can be genuinely exciting: a good etymologist, who combines academic learning with human interests, and activity with alertness, might be described as a detective among words, one clue suggesting another, and the second a third, and so on until the quarry is run to earth in Bantu or Basque, in Armorican or Algonquin, in Hittite or Hebrew, in Chinese or Chinook.

Moreover, one's interest is sharpened by correspondents, known or unknown, literate or illiterate, erudite or ignorant, admiring or abusive. Most of them do truly wish to know; many wish to inform; a few – very few – wish to tell one where one 'gets off'. Now and then, one encounters a most fruitful and learned, courteous and helpful correspondent, and then, as like as not, one gains an amicable assistant. One may even make a friend. The most valued of my collaborators (I've had a hand in several works that benefited by being collaborative) has become a collaborator precisely because he had first been an extremely welcome correspondent, whose worth I immediately perceived. I should have had to be quite unusually stupid, not to perceive it.

Although I have linguistic interests other than lexicography and eytmology, and shall, I hope, be able to indulge myself in expressing them, yet, being a passably honest man, I am bound to admit the justice of the charge, 'Once a lexicographer, always a lexicographer'. There are worse fates.

4

The Problem of Alphabetical Order

ON READING the proofs of *Slang Today and Yesterday*, Colonel Egerton must have conferred with the directors of Messrs George Routledge & Sons and applied his eloquence and charm with good effect, for in May or early June, 1933, I was invited by that excellent firm to write – not merely to compile – *A Dictionary of Slang and Unconventional English*. The two years stipulated by the contract had, by mutual consent, to be extended to three: and how I worked during those three years on the dictionary and during the next seven months on the proofs (slips or galleys, then pages)! I swore that I'd never again 'slave' like that; and yet, some years later, I 'slaved' even harder at *Origins*. That's what happens when one is engaged upon a large and fascinating piece of work. (Fascinating to the 'slave', I mean.) Unless one is a hack, adapting someone else's dictionary, lexicography is hard work; the conscientious lexicographer, if he has a passion for his subject, adds to the strain by doing more than, strictly, he needs to do, not so much because he wishes to perpetrate a supererogation as because he must. We hear of the compulsions of the creative writer – the poet and the dramatist, the novelist or the short-story practitioner. Those are genuine compulsions; the results, genuinely creative. Yet the true scholar also has his compulsions: and his results may, in a different mode, be almost as creative as those of the other wielders of words. But enough of that – for the present, anyway.

As soon as I began to ponder the method, the technique, of writing *A Dictionary of Slang and Unconventional English* (or *DSUE*, as it is often called nowadays), I found that I had to solve problems of demarcation and classification and arrangement: what was, and what was not, eligible to figure in these august pages; to increase the value of the book, a classification into slang proper, colloquialism, catch phrases (frequently difficult to distinguish from proverbial sayings) – and, at the very bottom of the social scale, vulgarisms on the one hand and, on the other, cant or the language of the underworld; and the arrangement, both that of senses within any given entry and that which is known as alphabetical order.

Alphabetical order? 'But surely,' the philistine exclaims, 'there is only one alphabetical order? Why mention the subject at all? We don't need to learn the A B C; we know it.' Many scholars not concerned with language, and even many non-lexicographical philologists, if they have not thought of the matter (after all, why should they?), are either totally unaware or, at best, very hazily aware, of the fact that there are two main alphabetical systems, with a third – combining the other two – employed by those humanitarians who do not wish either to carry logic to an absurdity or, like a house-proud woman, to pursue an ideal of perfection to the point where everyone else is discomforted and discomfited. Lexicography is not an abstraction, devised and practised for the delight of lexicographers. 'The operation was brilliantly successful.' – 'And how is the patient?' – 'Oh, unfortunately he died, poor fellow.' That sort of thing simply won't do in lexicography. Even the 'perfect' alphabetical order has, on occasion, to be 'bent' a little to suit the customer's convenience.

The words that go to form the vocabulary of a language are much less tractable and malleable than most people seem to realize; even the words forming a specialist or sectional dictionary, as, for instance, of slang, can show themselves infuriatingly intractable. The two principal reasons for such unexpected recalcitrance are these: words aren't the only units of a language, for there are also phrasal verbs, phrasal prepositions, phrasal adverbs and adjectives, in addition to the phrases formed by metaphors and similes and idioms; and especially there are compound adjectives and nouns (and even verbs) as well as simples. All compounds have, at least potentially, three stages. At first they consist of two (or more) separate words, still regarded as two or more entities; thus, *lower class*, a noun used as an adjective. Then they are linked by means of a hyphen; *lower-class*, adjective. Finally they become one word, written 'solid'; *lowerclass*, adjective. (The preference of most Britons and many Americans for *lower-class* to *lowerclass* springs partly from habit and partly from aesthetic considerations and partly for reasons of convenience. Let us not quibble about aspects irrelevant here.)

The compromise method being, for a moment or two, deferred until we can clearly see which two systems the compromise is between, we have to consider the 'absolute', as it is usually known, or 'logical'; and the 'something before nothing' – the predominant name – or 'sensible'. Both 'logical', so much less logical than it may seem, and 'sensible', yet not always nor necessarily the best, are question-begging terms; yet, in so delicate a decision, so subtle an arrangement, it is difficult to avoid the begging of questions. For some dictionaries, the 'absolute' is probably the best; for others, the 'something-before-nothing'; for yet others, few but very important, some compromise is advisable, although it may not be indispensable.

The third method – 'the compromise' – arose because we human beings are not yet gods and are hindered and held back by imperfect memories and imperfect intellects. This method, in one or other of the varieties determined by circumstance, has therefore much to commend it.

The second method – 'something before nothing' – is perhaps the most satisfying, if considered at the psychological and aesthetic levels and judged by psychological and aesthetic criteria; yet because of compounds, it too has occasionally to be humanized by recourse to compromise.

The first method – 'the absolute' – cannot be faulted on grounds of either logic or methodology or economy. It never necessitates a repetition. Yet, because of its very perfection, it is the best only for a non-exclusive, hence a huge, dictionary; it makes no allowance for human imperfections and frailties.

The preceding trio of paragraphs may, to the carping and the querulous, look dangerously like a dramatic trick or a narrative 'gimmick': a contrivance of suspense. Those paragraphs are, in the fact, something very much less artful, for they aim only at an atmospheric adumbration; they amount to a genial hint that, thus forewarned, the layman is forearmed against the tedium that can so easily result from a consideration of what, to him, appears theoretical and is, in reality and practice, a set of devices designed to introduce clarity into obscurity, a light into darkness, a bulwark against chaos and despair. If anyone should think, 'This is rhetorical exaggeration,' he thereby condemns himself as both ignorant and stupid, and also as hopelessly imperceptive and insensitive. Lexicography is an art vastly more complex and difficult and arduous than the lay consulters of dictionaries can possibly imagine. Lexicographers, you may be sure, wish it were otherwise.

The 'absolute' order, provided that it be prosecuted 'to the letter' and then mitigated by additions or insertions wherever the consulter's convenience is involved, is theoretically the best order of all; yet such modification would, of course, remove it from the first to the third, or 'compromise', group. The genuine or 'one-hundred-per-cent' absolute order has never been followed, even in that great work which professes to have adopted the system. *Webster's New International Dictionary* has gone the closest to observing 'the absolute alphabetical order'. (The ensuing 'specimen section' has been based upon – indeed taken from – that scrupulous recension which appeared in 1934 as the Second Edition.) Not only has it apparently done so; it has also really done so in the main.

Before I take a difficult example and analyse it, let me give an easy one, first in absolute order, then in 'something before nothing'. (As it's an easy example, there is no need for compromise; and, to be a valid, not a contrived, example, it must come from a small dictionary.)

SET, v., to place, to put, etc. Its various senses. Followed, within the same entry, by *set*, adjective, and *set*, noun, with their various senses. Then, still within the entry: the compound nouns, as *set-back*; a compound adjective; the derivatives *setter*, with its off-shoots, and *setting*; then, in one alphabetical list, both the phrasal verbs, beginning with *set about*, and the true phrases, *set at naught – set eyes on – set one's teeth – set speech* – etc.

That main entry, which, even in this excellent general-purpose smallish dictionary (*Chambers's Twentieth Century Dictionary*), is dauntingly large, is followed by SETA, SETON, SETTEE (two distinct words), SETTER and SETTING referred to SET, the technical verb SETTER, SETTLE, noun and verb (-MENT, -R, etc.) – SETWALL (or SETUALE) – SEVEN . . .

But, you'll notice, there are no separate entries, even of cross-reference, either for such a compound as *set-back*, now often written *setback*, or for phrases of any kind. Then why are SETTER and SETTING cross-referenced? Clearly, they represent a compromise – a concession to those consulters who may not immediately connect them with SET.

And if this happens in a smallish dictionary, what's going to happen in a large, especially in a vast, one? The 'defect' – if that be the right word – should not be blamed on the particular dictionary: as I've said, it's a very good piece of work. I could take any other small or smallish dictionary and display similar 'defects': 'defects' caused by the very nature of the English language – by the very nature of any analytical language. (A Greek or a Latin dictionary is much easier to handle.)

That *Chambers's Twentieth Century* specimen is fundamentally and predominantly an example of 'something before nothing': all SET senses and compounds and phrases are disposed of before SETA, SETON, etc., are treated.

The 'absolute' arrangement of those words and phrases would run something like this; only 'something like this', for I do not include every single compound and phrase.

SET, v., n., adj. – or separated into SET, adj. – SET, n. – SET, v. (or some other order)

SETA	SET ASIDE
SET ABOUT	SET AT NAUGHT
SET AGAINST	SET BACK and SETBACK
SET APART	SET BY (to put aside)

SET DOWN	SETTER
SET EYES ON	SET TERMS
SET FIRE TO	SETTING
SET FORTH	SETTLE (1), noun
SET IN	SETTLE (2), verb; SETTLEMENT,
SET OFF	SETTLER, etc.
SET ON (to incite)	SET UP, v., and SET-UP (or SET
SETON (thread)	UP), n.
SET PIECE	SET UPON (to attack)
SET SPEECH	SETWALL
SETTEE (1)	SEVEN
SETTEE (2)	

That, an example of the 'absolute alphabetical order', has much to commend it: the consulter will be able to find immediately any word, whether simple or compound or direct derivative, and any phrase whatsoever. Yet, if he did not know that this order governed the arrangement or did not fully realize its implications, he might be brought up short and feel perplexed and perhaps resentful. An 'absolute' lexicographer might well hesitate; and, hesitating, be not lost but sane; he would probably arrange the phrasal verbs and the phrases in one alphabetical order immediately after the verb – and *not* repeat them; such a compound noun as SET-UP (or SETUP) would cause him a headache, nor would it be the only one. The 'absolute' order has ceased to be absolute: a concession has been made to good sense and to semantic congruity and unity. Yet if the lexicographer carries semantic congruity – senses following senses in what seems a natural order – much further, he will be sacrificing convenience.

'That's all very well,' an irritated reader may understandably exclaim, 'but what would *you* do about it? Can you suggest a method that will preserve both the consulter's convenience and a degree of congruity and commonsense?' That's a good question.

First of all, I should hope to make it clear that every consulter of any dictionary of the words and phrases forming the vocabulary of an analytical language (English, French, German, Spanish,

[69]

Italian, etc.) must bear in mind the irrefutable and inescapable fact that, in this matter of alphabetic order, perfection is impossible. Secondly, I should compromise; yet, for the compromise to be appreciated or even understood, the consulter should be induced to read the preliminary 'Note on Arrangement' – if there is one. If the dictionary is either small or specialist, there may be no need for a 'Note'.

The compromise would take the form of 'something before nothing', with an occasional repetition made for the sake of convenience: a modified 'something before nothing'. Theorizing is here of little use. This is how, if I were confronted with the task of editing the *Chambers's* material, I should do it; but, both that lexicographer and I preferring a 'something before nothing' to an 'absolute' arrangement, we should differ only in details.

> SET (1), adjective
>   *set back,* recessed
> SET (2), noun
>   *set-back* or *setback,* a reverse
>   *set-down,* a rebuff
>   *set-off,* a claim offsetting another claim
>   *set-out,* a display
>   *set-to,* a bout of fisticuffs, a momentary quarrel
>   *set-up* or *setup,* an arrangement
> SET (3), verb

All the phrasal verbs and the full phrases arranged in one alphabetical order and, as for the noun, indented and italicized, thus:

> *set about*
> *set against*
> *set apart*
> *set aside*
> *set at naught*
> *set back,* to check, etc.
> . . . .
> *set eyes on*
> . . . . . .

> *set little,* or *much, store by*
> . . . .
> *set one's heart on*
> *set one's teeth*
> . . . .
> *set piece*
> . . . .
> *set terms*
> *set to* (to begin a meal, etc.)
> . . . .
> *set up* ('That'll set you up')
> *set upon*

SETA
SET BACK or SETBACK. See SET (2)
SET-DOWN. See SET (2)
SET-OFF. See SET (2)
  (But, if economy were necessary:
    SET-BACK, SET-DOWN, SET-OFF. See SET (2))
SETON
SET-OUT. See SET (2)
SETTEE (1), the seat
SETTEE (2), the sailing-ship
SETTER (1), noun
SETTER (2), verb
SETTING, noun
SETTLE (1), noun (a long bench with a high back)
SETTLE (2), verb, with its derivatives,
  SETTLEMENT, SETTLER, SETTLING-DAY, etc.
SET-TO. See SET (2)
SET-UP. See SET (2)

The critical consulter will inevitably and most properly ask, 'But if the compound nouns receive the honour of a cross-reference, why not the phrasal verbs and the full phrases?' My answer would be, 'Because they immediately precede the new series (beginning with *seta*) and because they are so very numerous that repetition would amount to one of the "larger lunacies" and because, unlike the compound nouns, they are not written "solid" as one word, the general rule for nouns in American English (witness *setback, setdown, setoff, setout, setup*, etc.) and a practice increasingly common elsewhere in English.' If the critical fellow then objected, 'That isn't very logical, is it?' – I should reply, 'If the arrangement of any large dictionary were entirely logical, as opposed to part-logical, part-sensible, and to part-absolute, part-convenient, you would probably lose your way in it'. Compromise is not merely advisable, often it is necessary and – except to fanatics – unavoidable.

In the *Chambers's* entry, I suppressed one item. The phrase *dead set*, as in 'to make a *dead set* against someone', occurs, within the main SET entry, at the beginning of the list of phrases and is disposed of in the instruction, 'see DEAD-SET'. This is the more usual of the two main techniques, the other being to list the phrase as SET, DEAD, and to place SET, DEAD, immediately after the last of the simple SET entries. The latter is the practice I adopted in *A Dictionary of Slang*, where '*have* (a person) *set*' appears as 'SET, *have* (a person)' and comes next after SET, DEAD. All such phrases naturally – in the 'something before nothing' system – precede all such phrases as *set about, set at naught, . . . set upon*.

Perhaps that comparatively simple cluster of SET entries and the reasonably compact indication of the three best ways of dealing with the cluster as a whole, hence with its distinct parts, will have adequately conveyed to the layman the (I hope) salutary fact that non-imitative lexicography requires unceasing care, unflagging awareness, unwearying alertness – and a very clear head. Like other men, lexicographers are, despite a deplorably widespread belief to the contrary, only human; they occasionally nod drowsily and 'drop a (verbal) brick'; and, like the legendary pianist in a Wild West saloon, they should not be shot, but merely forgiven.

After that relatively simple exemplification of alphabetical order, a rather more advanced exposition will be nonchalantly taken in their stride by all intelligent readers: and anyone who reads this little book stands self-condemned as intelligent and properly inquisitive. But I'll try to render the exposition acceptable by continuing with SET. This time, I shall analyse the entries in *Webster's New International* (in its ever to be cherished recension of 1934) and *The Shorter Oxford Dictionary* (edition of 1956) and *A Dictionary of Slang* (1961 edition): for treatments respectively 'absolute' or, rather, predominantly so – 'something before nothing' – 'compromise'. This time, however, I shall make the treatment as mercifully brief as possible; I certainly don't want my patient readers to die from sheer boredom.

Webster's deals with our SET thus: verb, adjective, noun. The verb, defined in its multiple senses, is followed by all the phrases, the phrasal verbs (*set about, set by*, etc.) merged with the true phrases in one continuous 'absolute' alphabetical order, the final *set up one's pipes* coming next after *set upon*. The adjective – strictly, the past-participial adjective – is shrewdly defined; its use in combination (*close-set, thickset*) receives an immediately following separate entry. The noun is then defined in detail.

All that is sufficiently obvious. But what happens next? The ensuing SET entries are these:

SET, a standard of value	SETHEAD
SET, a dialectal variant of 'to *sit*'	SETH GREEN
SETA and its derivatives	SETHIAN – SETHIC – SETHITE
SETBACK	SET HOOK
SET BAR	SETI-
SETBOLT	SETIBO
SET BOOK	SETIFERA
SET CHISEL	SET-IN
SETDOWN (British *set-down*)	SETLINE
SETEBOS	SET NUT
SET-FAIR	SET OF ASSOCIATED
SET GAUGE	ELEMENTS
SET GUN	SET OF DAY
SETH	SET OF EXCHANGE
SETH	SETOFF (British *set-off*)
SET HAMMER	SET OF THREADS
SET-HANDS and a derivative	SETON, n. (1)

[73]

SETON, V.
SETON, n. (2)
SETOPHAGA
SETOSE – SETOUS
SETOUT (British *set-out*)
SETOVER (British *set-over*)
SET PIECE
SET PIN
SET POINT
SET POT
SETSCREW (British *set screw*
  or *set-screw*)
SETSMAN
SET SQUARE
SET-STITCHED
SETT – three distinct nouns
SETTECENTO
SETTEE – two distinct nouns
SETTEE BED
SET TEMPER
SETTER – two distinct nouns
SETTER, verb
SETTER-FORTH
SETTERGRASS
SETTER-IN
SETTER-ON
SETTER-OUT
SETTER-TO
SETTER-UP
SETTERWORT
SETTIMA, SETTIMO
SETTING
SETTING BLOCK or BOARD
  and some eighteen other
  setting combinations
SETTLE, noun (the long,
  wooden, high-backed seat)

SETTLE, verb and ten derivative
  phases, e.g. SETTLE
  ACCOUNTS
SETTLE, n. (2) – a physical
  settling
SETTLEABLE
SETTLE BED
SETTLE-BENCH
SETTLE-BRAIN
SETTLED, adjective, and six
  dependent combinations
SETTLEMENT and four
  combinations
SETTLER
SETTLER'S-CLOCK
SETTLER'S MATCHES
SETTLER'S TWINE
SETTLING, participal adjective
  and verbal noun; with four
  dependants
SETTLOR
SET-TO
SETTSMAN
SET TUB
SETULA and SETULE
SETULIFORM
SETULOSE and SETULOUS
SETUP (British *set-up*), n.
SET UP, adj.
SETWALL (which has nothing
  to do with SET)
SETWISE
SETWORK
SEUGH
SEVEN
etc.

The list, one notices, is itself in 'absolute' order – except that it omits both the phrasal verbs and the true phrases based upon the verb *set*, all of which have appeared immediately after SET (verb) and have thus followed, not the 'absolute' but the 'something before nothing' principle. Had the 'absolute' principle been rigidly adhered to, every word, whether simple or compound, and every phrase of any sort would have been displayed in one continuous and exceptionless order: thus would a kind of doctrinaire logic and systematic purity have been preserved – to the detriment of good sense and semantic congruity.

How, then, does the treatment in *The Shorter Oxford English Dictionary* differ from that in *Webster's*? Compressed and rationalized as far as it is possible to go without obscuring the argument ('I labour to be brief and I become obscure'), the SET material in the *SOED* is exhibited in this engagingly intelligent manner:*

> SET, noun (1), corresponding to the verb
> SET, n. (2), group of persons, collection of
> things
> SET, verb, scrupulously and subtly defined
> under ten heads; at the end of each head,
> the relevant phrases or proverbs. After
> the tenth sense: 'combinations' (phrasal
> verbs) with prepositions (*set about*, etc.)
> and – a very long list – with adverbs (*set
> afloat*, etc.)
> SET, participial adjective, with the relevant
> 'combinations' (*set dance*, etc.)

SET-, the combining-form of the v. *set*	SET-OFF
	SETON
SETA, followed by SETACEOUS	SETOSE
SET-BACK	SET-OUT
SET-DOWN	SETT
SETI-, combining-form of SETA	SETTEE (1) and SETTEE (2)
	SETTER and, within the entry,
SETNESS	its combinations

* I have changed all unnecessary initial capitals to small letters.

SETTERWORT	SETTLER
SETTING, noun and its 'combinations'	SETTLING, noun, and a derivative
SETTING DOG	SETTLOR
SETTLE, noun	SET-TO
SETTLE, verb, defined under six heads, with relevant phrases under each head	SETULE
	SETWALL
	SÈVE
SETTLED, participial adjective	SEVEN
SETTLEMENT	etc.

There you have a truly excellent example of 'something before nothing': everything is placed where the sense demands that it should be, and nothing is repeated; the principal meanings are followed immediately by the shades of meaning and by the phrases connected with those meanings and nuances: or, at least, all this has been so brilliantly achieved, that one guiltily wonders 'Why were the compound nouns *set-back, set-down, set-off, set-out* and *set-to* singled out for the special treatment of a separate entry?' Also, perhaps, 'Why have these nouns been separated from the corresponding phrasal verbs?' The answer, as I see it, is that they are sufficiently important to merit a separate entry. Moreover, you will probably have noticed that *Webster's* does exactly the same thing, as you will certainly have noticed that neither dictionary repeats the phrasal verbs and that you must go looking for them at the verb SET.

Two facts emerge. Firstly, no alphabetical order is perfect. Even if every simple and compound word, every possible combination, every phrase of every sort, every proverb and proverbial saying, were placed in the literally 'absolute' order, there would still be problems arising from the 'Which is the key-word in "to *set at naught*" – *set* or *naught*?' class of question; the solution being the simple one of cross-reference. Secondly, the consulter of any large dictionary should study that preliminary section (if any) which tells him how to use the dictionary. The *OED* provides no such section, nor does the *SOED*; Webster does, under the title 'Explanatory Notes'.

So do I in *A Dictionary of Slang and Unconventional English*, where, the material being vastly smaller in quantity, all I need to provide is a brief, perhaps a too brief, 'Note on Arrangement'. Yet various worthy persons have written to tell me that they could not find this word or that phrase. What they couldn't find was usually there, and in its right place; the complainers had omitted to read the 'Note'; but then, you can't help some people!

Perhaps the list of SET entries in *DSUE* will dispel a few remaining doubts. It cannot, of course, dispel all doubts, for reasons already laboured quite sufficiently in this tedious yet – by the honest lexicographer – unavoidable chapter. (The list is that of Volume I, the first edition revised. To incorporate the SET entries of the Supplement would merely confuse the issue yet further.)

SET, noun	SET UP, verb
SET, verb	SET-UP, adjective
SET, adjective	SET UP FOR, BE
SET, DEAD	SETACEOUS
SET, HAVE (a person)	SETS-OFF, -OUT, -TO
SET ABOUT	SETTA
SET BACK	SETTER
SET-DOWN	SETTER, CLOCK-
SET IN A CRACK	SETTING DOG
SET JEWELS	SETTLE
SET-ME-UP	SETTLE (a person's) HASH
SET-OUT	SETTLEMENT-IN-TAIL
SET THE HARE'S HEAD . . .	SETTLER
SET THE SWEDE DOWN	SETTLER'S BIBLE, THE
SET-UP, noun	SEVEN, ALL IN THE

The increasingly common practice among lexicographers engaged in any major work is to supply a set of hints on How to Use This Dictionary. They cannot, however, supply to would-be users either the intelligence to think of looking for such hints or the patience to read them very carefully. In small, still more in very small, dictionaries, such a key is hardly necessary: yet the

proper and especially the effectual use of any dictionary whatsoever calls for the exercise of a modicum of average intelligence
and of commonsense. And no matter how small the dictionary
may be, there is always a list of abbreviations. Not to go to the
slight trouble of assimilating that list is to ask for much greater
trouble.

In the selfish ardours of intellectual abstraction, I have said nothing
about an aspect of much greater interest to the general reader,
however intelligent and tolerant he may be.

I could not begin to estimate how many times I have been
asked, 'How on earth did you go about gathering the material
for *A Dictionary of Slang*?' The better-informed have usually
added a number of sensible remarks which might be compounded
and summarized in some such way as this: 'After all, the problem
is quite different from that which faced the editors of the *OED*
or *Webster's*. They examined thousands of books and periodicals
and presumably they depended to some extent upon oral tradition. Also, they had scores – probably hundreds – of helpers; one
rather supposes that such helpers are still available to them. But
you are, for the present century, dealing with a vast body of
material of which rather a lot, surely, isn't available in the usual
way.'

First of all, I'd like to make it clear that, after material has been
collected, it needs to be sifted; then collated; finally, edited – a
term that veils an entire complex of operations. Secondly, any
such undertaking as the *OED* or *Webster's* must be carried out by
a large team. Thirdly, that the 'lone wolf' is less lonely than, to
the uninformed, he may seem. Fourthly, this particular 'lone
wolf' has enjoyed advantages denied to the majority of such
creatures: advantages afforded partly by environment and circumstance, partly by predilection and addiction.

'That's all very well. That's "fine, wide and handsome". But
could we,' asks an irritated consulter of dictionaries, 'could we,
please, "cut the cackle and come to the 'osses"? Could we "get
down to cases"? We wish to know how you went about gather-

ing and checking the material for *DSUE*, not how other lexicographers might have done it nor even how they think *you* should
have done it. You wrote it, not they – nor do we think it at all
likely that any one of them *could* have written it.'

Ah, well! On your own heads . . .

I did not come to the task a virgin. Already, you will remember, I had been concerned with *Songs and Slang of the British
Soldier*; I had published a number of articles on slang and colloquialism; I had edited Grose's *Vulgar Tongue*; I had just finished
studying the entire field of slang and its related subjects in order
to write *Slang Today and Yesterday*. So much for a tolerable preliminary knowledge of the subject and so much for some slight
experience of technique. No less important, however, was the
fact that the publication of those three books and of those articles
had brought me many acquaintances, several of whom became
good friends and a few of whom became faithful correspondents
over periods varying from a couple of years (people die or are
either submerged or immersed) to thirty or more. Then there
were others: people I met, people who met me: and these others
communicated by word of mouth.

'Oh! One presumes that any and every writer, especially upon
such a subject as English, receives such communications and perhaps goes so far as to maintain such contacts. But what *sort* of
person got into touch with you? And for what *reason* – or
reasons?'

All sorts of persons communicated with me: 'dons' and dust-
men; school teachers and schoolboys, but not, if I remember
correctly, schoolgirls; butchers and bakers – but no candlestick
makers; sailors and soldiers and airmen; games-players and
gamesters; Civil Servants and domestic servants; railwaymen
and busmen and tram-drivers; huntsmen and motorists; actors
and authors, doctors and divines; journalists and publicity men
(and women); social workers and prison warders; beggars and
tramps; petty crooks and one or two (I suspected) major criminals; sheep farmers and sheep shearers; cattlemen and commercial
travellers; shopmen and clubmen. You name them; I got them.

Whereas some could hardly write, others wrote almost too well, or was it rather too much? Often those who wrote most, told me least. A very few 'tried it on', either by making up words and phrases or by pretending they meant something quite different: they forgot that I have myself 'been around' and that I could, and would, check their fantasies. I often wish that I had kept all those letters. Clearly, I couldn't. There were far, far too many of them. I own a small house, not a warehouse.

The reasons these good people had for helping me can, in the last resort, be reduced to three. The majority wished to help, and that's all there was to it, for most people are helpful; a few hoped to see their names in print; a very few, I believe, wished to prove how much they knew about the subject – in brief, to 'show off'. Among scholars and among all kinds of writers, some – indeed, the greater part – were attracted by the project itself and, like the general majority, wished to contribute, with no thought of gain and, apart from an occasional publicity-hunter, with no desire to be named. I did not name all my correspondents; some of them expressly asked not to be named. But, whenever I could, I named all those who had contributed considerably or otherwise notably.

Although I shouldn't need to say this, I instituted a vast number of oral and scriptural inquiries and received almost no rude answers. I read a vast number of books and periodicals, including many sources that had apparently eluded all my predecessors. I had, moreover, the great good fortune to be allowed, by my publishers, to use, as freely as I desired, a work that was entirely their property: Farmer & Henley's *Slang and Its Analogues* (seven volumes, 1890–1904) – the relevant entries of which, in fact, I adopted as an expansible framework. I owe a great deal to that work and I have never tried to minimize the debt; nor do I wish to do so. On the other hand, even for the period up to (say) 1890, I have dealt far more richly and, above all, far more pertinently with the subject.

5

Some Aspects of Etymology*

Etymology, Greek *etumologia*, literally means 'an account of the true' – that is, of the true, especially the original, form and meaning of a word: *etum-*, stem of *etumos*, true+the connective *-o-+-logia*, from *logos*, word, account, discourse, and even thought and, as in *logic*, reasoning; an account of the *etymons* or true origins of words, whether individually or collectively: hence the art and science of ascertaining the original forms and meanings of one word or of many. That etymology is a science, no one will deny; that it is also an art, far too many deny.

By the way, it is convenient to restrict the term *etymon* to the original word in its entirety and to apply *root, radical* or *base* to the unchangeable core of the etymon concerned. But three cautions must be stated; the first is that *etymons* and *roots* exist at various historical or linguistic levels; the second, that the root is often identical with the etymon: the third, that many words, especially nouns and verbs, have two stems – certain Greek and Latin verbs have three or even four stems – and I'm not talking about those anomalous verbs which have had their conjugation built up from different roots, as, for instance, the (je) *vais*, (j') *allais*, (j') *irai* of the French verb for 'to go', and the three unrelated roots that form the conjugation of the English *be, is, was*. Perhaps an example or two will help. The etymon of *cow* is Old English *cū*, which is both etymon and root. But the Indo-European root of *cow* must have had some such form as **gwō-* or **gwū-* or **gwōu-* becoming *gwou*, for we must account for the cognate Sanskrit *go* and Scandinavian *ko*. English *crime* goes back to Latin *crimen*, with root *crim-* [creem]; but the oblique stem of

---

* Designed for the general *intelligent* public and for those students who have not yet qualified as philologists; not for scholars.

[81]

crimen is *crimin-*, seen in our *criminal*. Then take the Latin verb 'to see': Medieval *vidēre*, Classical *uidēre*, root *uīd-* [weed], ML *vīd-* [veed], seen in our pro*vide*. But the present participle *uīdens*, *vīdens*, has oblique stem *uīdent-*, *vident-* as in our pro*vident*. And the past participle *uīsus*, *vīsus*, has stem *uīs-*, *vīs-*, as in our *vision* and *proviso*.

In those examples I have scamped, not distorted, the evidence. One could discourse for an hour, two hours, a day, on the ramifications of English *cow* or those of Latin *uidēre*. But I'm no sadist.

As you know, *etymology* might be defined as the history of change – the changes in a word or in a group of words or, again, in a vast corpus of words. If languages did not change, there could be no *native* etymology, which would then be reduced to a consideration of the cognates in other languages and of the probable Indo-European root. But, everywhere and in many diverse ways, all languages change – or have changed. And, by the way, it is foolish to speak of *dead* languages. Ancient Greek lives on in Modern Greek; Classical Latin in Italian; both Classical and Vulgar Latin in French; Hebrew, though far less vitally, in Yiddish; Sanskrit in Hindi and in Hindustani; Ancient Egyptian in Coptic, itself akin to Ethiopian. Hittite and Tokharian do not lack modern kindred. Even Basque has a dimly discernible ancestor.

To return to our mutations. The changes are of two kinds: in form and in meaning. Besides, every language borrows – or at least tends to borrow – words from abroad and then either to discard native words that are synonymous or to narrow their meanings. As Professor John W. Clark, of the University of Minnesota, has remarked in his article 'Etymology' in the 1954 recension of *The Encyclopedia Americana*, 'the English-speaking person can hardly read Chaucer or even Shakespeare and can certainly not read *Beowulf* without perceiving that some changes have occurred; and even the relatively incurious and unread can hardly help observing, and wondering at least a little about, such facts as the occasional formal resemblances between words of different meanings (e.g., *cow*, noun, and *cow*, verb) and between words of similar meanings in different languages (e.g., English *beef*, French *boeuf*), and, conversely, the formal differences between words of related meanings (e.g., *cow* and *beef*) and between different meanings of the same word – meanings sometimes co-existent (e.g., *interest*, "fascination" and "income") and sometimes not (e.g., *usury* – now "illegal interest", but formerly "any interest").'

Since languages change, they tend, within any one language-family, to change in much the same way; and all languages whatsoever, irrespective of family relationship, tend to change in certains ways – for instance, they must keep pace with the civilizations they serve, and they borrow from other languages. One's solution of the problems caused by, and involved in, all change, whether operative in any language as a whole or only in its etymology, depends for its success upon the amount and worth of the information gained from research in fields where 'the following kinds of data are available', as John W. Clark,* from whom I forthwith quote, has postulated:

'(1) Considerable masses of at least roughly datable documents yielding a fairly continuous record of the language throughout its history; (2) relevant records of languages from which any considerable number of words have been borrowed; (3) relevant records of the other languages of the same linguistic family. These several kinds of data,' he adds, 'are available in sufficient quantities for only relatively few languages, pre-eminent among which are the languages of the Indo-European family.'

Since the rest of this paper concerns that linguistic family, perhaps I might, even though the generalities of the subject are familiar to you, do worse than risk one or two more generalities.

Indo-European is a far better name than either *Aryan*, which is vague and misleading, or *Indo-Germanic*, which is still more misleading and inadequate. The Indo-European languages have descended, and in descending have increasingly diverged, from a single language or, some of them, from one or two extremely important dialects of that language, which we call either Primitive

---

* Loc. cit.

Indo-European or simply Indo-European and which was probably spoken at least as early as 4000 B.C. You will, in passing,
notice that we have pushed ever farther back the 'chronological
frontiers' of all languages and indeed of all language: for instance,
where formerly we used to assign the ulterior limit of Sanskrit to
about 1500 B.C., we now assign it to about 2000 B.C. Perhaps I
might also recall that the chief branches of the Indo-European
family are these: Indic, notably Sanskrit and modern Hindi;
Iranian, especially Persian and Afghan; Greek; Latin and its
Romance descendants, Italian, Spanish, Portuguese, French,
Rumanian; Tokharian – the two dialects or, maybe, parallels;
Celtic – the long extinct Gaulish, the recently extinct Cornish,
Breton, Welsh, Irish, (Scots) Gaelic, Manx; Slavic, especially
Russian; Baltic, e.g. Lithuanian; Armenian; Albanian; and Ger-
manic – the extinct Gothic, German, Dutch, Old Frisian, English,
the Scandinavian languages.

More than the Chinese, and more than the Semitic and the
Hamitic, the Indo-European languages are, as a group, notable –
all, in some respects, and some, in all respects, unique – in the
following ways: their historical importance; the wealth of their
literatures; the sweeping and remarkably diverse changes they
have experienced. Moreover, their inter-relations have been
studied more intensely than those of any other linguistic family.

The cultural or civilizational importance of the Indo-European
languages combines with the generally high level of intelligence
among the speakers of these languages to account for the com-
plexities of Indo-European etymology, but also to supply an
astounding quantity and diversity of evidence. If the complexity
has caused numerous problems, it has also – and inevitably – presented us with numerous clues. Professor Clark has noted the
astonishing fact that 'the English verb *was* and the *-er-* in *Canter-
bury* go back to the same Indo-European base'. But hardly less
astonishing is the fact that English *am, is, are* belong to the same
Indo-European stem as Latin *sum,* Greek *eimi,* I am – to Greek
esti, Latin *est,* German *ist,* he is, wherein the *-t* indicates the Third
Person Singular – to Old English *sind,* Gothic *sind,* Latin *sunt,*

Sanskrit *santi* [sahn'tee], they are; to the *-sent* in *absent* and *present*, and the *ent-* in *entity*; more distantly yet no less certainly, to the *et-* in *etymology* (a story I tell elsewhere) and also to *sooth*, true, real, from a hypothetical Primitive Germanic root *santh-*, with which, rather obviously, compare the just mentioned Sanskrit *santi*, they are, and the Sanskrit combining-form *sant-*, existing, real. All those various and apparently very diverse forms derive ultimately from a Sanskrit root **es-*, to be. In fairness I should like to add several tiny clues that etymologists do not always mention: to Attic Greek *eimi*, and Thessalian Greek *emmi*, I am, there exists an arresting cognate in Old English – *ĕom*, I am; the *-nd-* and *-nt-* forms are not necessarily due to nasalization, as such, and they constitute a predominant feature in the formation of present participles.

But etymology has not always been so intelligent; or rather etymologists only in the latter part of the eighteenth century began to acquire the knowledge requisite for an intelligently comparative study of the Indo-European languages, much of the credit being due to an Englishman, Sir William Jones (1746–94). Britons, it might be remembered, have done more and better work in philology in general and etymology in particular than most foreigners and too many Britons will admit; and in this excellence I associate Americans. Before Jones and, except among a few scholars, for thirty or so years after his death, etymology merited the definition, attributed to Voltaire: 'A science in which the consonants are of very little importance, and the vowels of none at all.' Even Noah Webster, who should have known better, had several exceedingly odd ideas; yet, in the 1820s, Jacob Grimm and Rasmus Rask were formulating 'laws' of the utmost importance, 'laws' notably supplemented in the 1870s by Karl Verner. With the more recent 'giants of philology' (as I once saw a newspaper describe them) it would be invidious – and probably dangerous – to deal.

What philologists in general and etymologists in particular have come to realize is that, despite the rather numerous *apparent* exceptions and anomalies, philology and, although perhaps slightly less, etymology rank as sciences precisely because (again to quote John W. Clark) 'they proceed on the assumptions, justified by the results, on which all science proceeds – to wit, that nothing happens without cause and that the same cause under the same conditions will always bring about the same results'. The doctrinal position is now such that nine out of ten philologists hold that if a proposed etymology of any Indo-European word fails to conform to the 'laws' of *sound*-correspondence, that particular etymology is almost certainly wrong. And at least one philologist further holds that meaning is entirely and always subordinate to sound; by which, I presume, he intends to say, 'meaning is always subordinate to that inseparable duad, sound-and-form'.

The word he selects is *dream*. John W. Clark's semantic explanation of this word is based upon the very reasonable assumption that the sense of the Primitive Indo-European etymon from which descend both the Old English *drēam*, primarily 'joy', secondarily 'music', and the Old Norse *draumr*, almost solely 'dream', was 'sound' or 'noise'. 'The main Old English meaning, "joy", presumably results from [some such development as] "sound, sound of merriment, festival music, festival activity, pleasure, joy"; the Old Norse meaning, from some such development as "sound, noise, rumor, lying rumor, lie, deception, deceptive vision, vision, dream".' He concludes thus: 'The Modern English *form* is apparently Old English in origin; the *meaning*, Old Norse. This is very far from improbable considering (1) the close genetic relation between English and Norse, (2) their mutual intelligibility *ca*. 900 A.D., when most of the Norse settlements in England occurred, and (3) the virtual blending of the language of Scandinavian settlers in England with the language of their English neighbors.'

But to revert to *sound*-correspondences. The 'laws' governing them should not be prosecuted beyond the limits of good, as opposed to mere common, sense. We do not, for instance, know precisely how Primitive Indo-European was pronounced, nor precisely how Sanskrit or even Greek was pronounced. Take

Greek! There has been a controversy raging about the pronunciation of χ *(khai)*: is its phonetic value merely that of a strongly
aspirated *k* (the old, long-held, not yet disproved opinion) or does
χ represent a barely audible division *k-h*? Then there are οἱ, *hoi*,
the masculine plural of the definite article, and οἵ, *hoi*, the masculine plural of the relative pronoun 'who, which'. That is the old
pronunciation: the modern school holds that, to take a phrase we
all of us know, *hoi polloi*, the many, should be pronounced *hwah
polwah*, although some of the moderns hold that *hoi* becomes
hwah only in the relative pronoun, their reason – an excellent
reason – being that obviously *hwa* stands very much closer to our
who, Early Middle English *hwo*, Old English *hwā* [hwah] than *hoi*
does, and also to the Latin relative. Latin, by the way, has its
problems too.

Here we may interpose a few words on Semantics or the so-
called 'science' of meaning: the science that treats of the nature,
the inter-relationships and especially the developments and
changes in the meanings of words and phrases and also (though
I've heard no one remark the fact) in the turns of phrase and
clause and sentence. By itself, *Semantics* (a word plural in form
but singular in construction) is not enough, but as Professor
Weekley has often shown, it is a valuable ally, in that it sometimes
provides a clue, notably as to the direction – e.g., the language –
in which to search for the origin of a troublesome word. Sense-
identities occur rarely, but sense-contiguities and sense-parallels
occur frequently.

To be dogmatic for a moment, one may postulate the following
axioms:

(1) If between a Modern English word and (say) a Hittite word,
there exist correspondences in sound, form, meaning, those words
are akin, as e.g. *water* and Hittite *watar* [wahtar]. Despite the
arresting correspondence, only a linguistic lunatic would derive
water from *watar*; the correspondence merely illustrates the fact
that Hittite is in some way related to the Indo-European languages.

(2) If, however, we set the English adjective *lucent* beside Latin
lucent- [loo-kent], the oblique stem of *lucens* [loo-kens], the

present participle of *lucēre* [loo-kay'-ree], to be light, to shine, we know that, there, we have the origin. (By the way, compare Latin *lux*, light, with Hittite *lukzi*, lights up.)

(3) The *lucent* example shows that, providing both the form and the meaning of a word agree, the sound need not exactly agree. For English there is a compulsive reason for this: the letters representing the long vowels denote certain phonetic values that are the same in all languages – except English. Britons and Americans just have to be different! Their independence is, in most ways, an admirable characteristic: but in a comparative study of language it is rather a nuisance. This linguistic characteristic forms one of the major difficulties blocking the way to a reformed spelling.

(4) If two words agree in form and sound, yet differ somewhat in sense, that sense-discrepancy has to be explained; it cannot be allowed to outweigh the form- and sound-correspondences, provided there be sufficient evidence to link the modern word with the proposed original. Take the modern slangy adjective *rum*, meaning 'odd, strange, (in short) queer', and the sixteenth-to-seventeenth-century adjective *rum* meaning 'fine, excellent'. The modern meaning is very different from the old. But the semantic change can be quite easily explained: the old adjective *rum* was a term used by the London underworld, and its opposite was *queer*. Now, the underworld senses of *rum* were 'fine, excellent, costly; briefly, superior or even the best'; of *queer*, 'of bad quality, cheap, cheap and nasty; briefly, inferior or even downright bad'. But what seemed good to the underworld might seem very bad, because extremely disadvantageous, to the honest citizen. The two adjectives, therefore, are etymologically identical. (But this *rum* is merely a homonym of *rum* the potent spirit.)

Thus we arrive at homonyms, and by the term I understand words that are spelt and pronounced alike but have different meanings and are of different origin, not such homophones as *b-o-a-r* and *b-o-r-e*. A good example is afforded by that *policy*, akin to *police* and *politics*, which comes from Greek *polis*, a city, and that other, the insurance *policy*, which comes from Italian *polizza*, which, by aphesis, comes from Medieval Latin *apodixa*, itself from Greek *apodeixis*, proof. There, no doubt exists; but certain supposed homonyms probably derive from a common origin; one must be on guard against excessive differentiation. More than once it will be found that the fact of common origin has been overlooked simply because of that *I-him* relationship, more ambitiously described as the subjective-objective relationship, which occurs in so many words and even in syntax. *His* success perhaps means my failure, *his* victory my disaster, *his* good my ill, as we saw in the rogue's sixteenth-to-seventeenth-century and the honest man's nineteenth-to-twentieth-century interpretation of the adjective *rum*. I put forward this suggestion in the hope that, one day, someone will make a thorough study of homonyms.

Most of those aspects of etymology have been fully treated elsewhere; several of them, indeed, by many scholars. I should like to pass to a few aspects deserving, I believe, far more attention – and much greater care – than they have received. I can deal with them only very briefly, hence very inadequately. Please regard them as, in the better sense of that word, provocations.

The first aspect is the historical. In general, too little recourse has been had to, and too little verification has been made by, history. On the negative side, however, history has not been neglected, especially where anachronism is suspected; nor has scholarship failed when it needs to determine the order and the nature of successive borrowings of the same word, as, for instance – it is John Clark's instance – *dish, desk, dais, disk, discus.* (Here I wish to make it clear that several of the short-comings of etymology result, not from deficiencies in the etymologists themselves, but from lack of time: for that etymologist who 'loves' his work, and nobody should be one unless he does, life is far too short.)

No; I wish here to urge upon you the value – often, indeed, the necessity – of going to history for clues as well as corroborations. With history I link the physical framework of history: geography: and, above all, historical geography, which is of primary importance to the etymologist. Of history itself, the most helpful kind is that which concerns itself with civilization or, rather, civilizations or, as is now the fashion to say, with cultures. In this sense, *culture* has recently been defined as 'the concepts, habits, skills [what we used to call 'crafts'], arts, instruments, institutions, etc. [including, presumably, customs] of a given people at a given time'. (*Webster's New World Dictionary of the American Language*, College Edition, 1952.) If any of you thinks this definition the apotheosis of the letter as distinct from the spirit of civilization, I shall not invite him, much less *her*, to 'coffee for one'; apart from the mention of 'concepts', it ignores religion and philosophy: it refers to the arts, yet omits literature; it implies mind, yet almost entirely excludes spirit, without which mankind would be doomed.

But we were speaking of the value of history and geography. To take a shamelessly egotistic example, I could not have solved the problem inherent in the etymology of *tarot* (the *tarot* cards used in fortune-telling) without some knowledge of the history of the Gypsies. I sha'n't bore you with it, for I have briefly told the story in *From Sanskrit to Brazil*, a title that caused a very good scholar to imply, although he didn't in so many words say, that he thought it damn' silly [see pp. 59–60 above. Ed.].

History, I need hardly emphasize, is implicit in all philology; nor have philologists underestimated its general importance. Just now and again I find myself wishing that its importance in the lexicography of languages not their own were less sporadically recognized, and utilized, by them. At the moment I'm thinking of Greek and Latin, about which I should like to make two or three extremely brief and doubtless unsatisfactory remarks.

In dealing with Greek, one should transliterate correctly and, in several instances, complementarily. That seems obvious; yet how very seldom is it done! In one or two dictionaries you will not even find the Greek characters transliterated; in most, you have the transliteration but not the Greek, and in one respect the transliteration is misleading, that of *ch* instead of *kh* for χ, and in another, affecting that group of four combinations which we might call 'the nasalizing-*gamma* quartette', not only misleading but wrong. The table is easy:

γγ, gamma gamma = *ng*;
γκ, gamma kappa = *nk*;
γξ, gamma xi = *nx*;
and γχ, gamma khai = *nkh*.

To transliterate gamma gamma as *gg*, gamma kappa as *gk*, gamma xi as *gx* and gamma khai as *gch* is, for the non-Grecian, even more misleading than to put the Greek characters without transliteration. Examples that are relevant to *English* may help us: Greek κλάγγη [klang-ē], a confused or inarticulate cry, especially if shrill, apparently spelt k-l-a-g-g-ē, should be transliterated '*klang-ē*' or '*k-l-a-g-g-ē*', pronounced *klang-ē*', for only thus can the non-Grecian see its kinship to English *clang*. The Simple Future κλάγξω [klanx-ō], I shall shriek, exemplifies γξ, gamma xi, although a better example is afforded by λύγξ, *lunx*, our *lynx*; the combination γκ, gamma kappa, appears, for instance, in λυγκός, *lunkos*, the genitive of *lunx*; and γχ, gamma khai, in λόγχη, *lonkhē*, lance or javelin, literally 'the long thing', the Greek word being thus seen to be kin to English *long*.

For Latin, I shall confine myself to a couple of scriptural-phonetic points: these concern the letters we call *i* and *j*, and those we call *u* and *v*. On *i* and *j* I quote probably the best all-round British Classical scholar of this century: the lamented Alexander Souter, who, in *A Glossary of Later Latin*, says, 'The letter *J*, which is really an elongated *I*, is first used in cursive writing to indicate an initial *I*, but in the semi-vocalic sense is not used until about A.D. 800 and then only in South Italy and Spain.' Never, in referring to Latin before that date, spell with a *j* a word beginning with *i*; and remember that even after that date it is pronounced approximately *y*, not as our English *j*; remember also that only English pronounces *j* as we pronounce it. If you see *i-a-c-ē-r-e*, to lie down, written with a *j*, it is still pronounced *ya-kay'-re*.

As for the letters *u* and *v*, there are several points to notice.

Small *v*, as it is printed, is a reduction to lower-case of upper-case or capital *V*, as it is printed; in Classical and even in Late Latin (roughly A.D. 180–600) capital *V* was the way capital *U* was written, as you have doubtless seen in inscriptions; the displacement, in Latin, of *u* by *v* does not precede the darkest Middle Ages – that it took place *then*, we can deduce from Old French. The importance of writing and pronouncing Classical and Late Latin words beginning with *u* as *u*, pronounced *oo*, is greater in etymology than some people seem to realize. Take Latin *uinum* [wee'-num], meaning primarily 'wine', secondarily 'vine': that, the correct, pronunciation links the word not only with our *wine* but also with Greek *oinos*, which, if pronounced *wah'-nos*, does away with the need to postulate that the word was originally written with a digamma – a letter that, discarded before Classical Greek existed, has the form of a sans-serif capital *F* but is pronounced like our *w*. But the Medieval Latin pronunciation *vinum* [vee'-noom] accounts for French *vin*; *vin*, of course, does not form the origin of our *vine*, which comes from Old French *vine*, whence Modern French *vigne*; OF *vine* derives from Medieval Latin *vinea* [vee-nay'-ǎ], the vine, from Latin *uīnea*, oo-ee-nay'-a, that is wee-nay'-a, properly the feminine of the adjective *uīneus*, wee-nay'-ooss; with *uīnea* [wee-nay'-ǎ] compare the synonymous Greek *oiné* [wah'-nay]. By the way, the word variously represented in Indo-European by *oinos* [wah'-nos], *uinum* [wee'-noom], *vin, vine, vēne* [way'-ne] (the Albanian form) and *gini* [ghee'-nee] (the Armenian), occurs also in Semitic languages, for example Hebrew *jajin* [yah'-yeen], and in the Hamitic. But I sha'n't weary you with my theory on the subject of such 'Mediterranean words', as Boisacq calls them; nor shall I expatiate upon my opinion that, in English etymology, Greek is rather more important than Latin – and that Latin is indispensable.

Latin has, in one sense, more ramifications than Greek: whereas the modern descendant of Greek is Modern Greek, the modern descendant of Latin is the entire group of Romance languages – Italian; Spanish; Catalan and Provençal; Portuguese; French; and Rumanian.

The Romance languages present a very tricky problem in chronology. If, however, you keep in mind the 'colonies' or settlements founded or made by Roman soldiers, camp-followers and more reputable traders, you will not go far wrong, especially if you remember that trade sometimes preceded conquest or military occupation. Here you have language in a phase where Historical Geography will help you considerably. Every Romance language has existed in the three phases – Old (or Ancient), Medieval, Modern – with the proviso that Old Italian is better known as Late, and Early Medieval, Latin. Unfortunately, the records of the earliest phase of two or three Romance languages are meagre.

Complicating the problem of Romance chronology is that of Celtic chronology. Of the thorny subject of Celtic elements in Old Germanic, I shall say nothing, for the most compulsive of all reasons: I know nothing about it. I know almost as little about the Celtic elements in Romance – apart, at least, from the Celtic influence on Latin, especially on Silver Latin (*ca.* A.D. 14–180) and Late Latin. The question of the Latin element in Celtic as a whole needs to be restated: that of the Celtic element in Latin, from early Republican days until the end of (say) the fifteenth century, demands a comprehensive study and perhaps a glossary. But then, we further need at least two comparative dictionaries of Celtic: one from the earliest days until (say) 1500, the other for modern times.

The trouble is that, of all the fields of Indo-European philology, the most neglected is that of Celtic – the most neglected, that is, in proportion to the wealth and importance of Celtic in general and in particular. The number of British chairs in Celtic – although this stricture applies more to the Dominions than to these islands – would disgrace the seating accommodation in the foyer of a third-rate hotel.

Celtic falls into three periods: Old, Middle, Modern. Irish and Welsh possess a very fair amount of lexical evidence for all three: Gaulish, for only one – the Old; Cornish, to which Breton is so closely related, died, as an *active* language, *ca.* 1800. Irish and

Gaelic (or, if you wish, Scottish Gaelic) are very closely linked; the most independent and the least studied of modern Celtic languages is Manx, spoken by a proud people in an island long existing in isolation – a language *not*, as several dictionaries state, 'almost extinct'. One of its most interesting features, and philologically perhaps its most important, is this: if you take the usually presumed Old Celtic root as the norm, you find that whereas Gaelic and Irish in one or other of its phases, and Welsh in one or other of *its* phases, possess or possessed a word varying in an easily recognizable form; that whereas the Cornish and Breton words, though usually not quite so obviously akin, bear resemblances at least cousinly – when they bear any at all; that whereas Gaulish words may, superficially, look somewhat outlandish; the Manx word, more often than not, exhibits differences explainable only in the light of vowel-changes and consonantal alterations or, at least, shifts; yet the Manx word often illuminates the apparently Cimmerian gulf between the Common Celtic root and the (say) Latin root or, better, the Common Indo-European root. Nor, in these random remarks, am I forgetting that whereas Breton, Cornish, Welsh belong to the south-western or Brythonic (or Brittonic) branch, Irish, Gaelic, Manx belong to the Goidelic branch; or that Gaulish stands rather apart, perhaps for geographical reasons (the language having been spoken very far afield, even in parts of Asia Minor), certainly for its structure, probably for its chronology, Gaulish having either fallen into disuse or perhaps disintegrated – that is dispersed – somewhere about A.D. 500. The chief point I wish to make is that most philologists, even some of the Celtic philologists, very rarely, when they are comparing one Celtic language with another, still more when they are comparing a (say) Romance language with Celtic, deign to adduce a Manx word. I feel very strongly on this subject of Manx; perhaps because of my abysmal ignorance.

One thing, however, I do know or, at any rate, *seem* to know. In the Celtic languages, one cannot escape the impression that here is a speech, here a vocabulary, very intimately related to mountains, high hills, the uplands: and that impression has not

arisen as 'wisdom after the event', based upon the attractive interpretation of the word *Celt* as 'man of the mountains'. That is a
tempting theory, because, like so many other ancient racial desig-
nations, the term existed as a plural before there was a singular:
so perhaps the Celts were, after all, originally 'the people of the
mountains', in opposition, it is possible, to 'the men of the plains',
especially of the great Tigris–Euphrates basin, so often called 'the
cradle of civilization'.

After all that haziness, I somewhat belatedly hasten to make a
few casual remarks upon two pairs of 'mystery words' – that is,
words of unknown origin – and finally to issue a grave warning.

The mysterious pairs are *lad* and *lass*, and *boy* and *girl*. I cannot
solve them for you, but I may be able to set you on a couple of
likely paths.

Boy and *girl* seem to be as far apart as, except for the suffix of
the second pair, *brother* and *sister*. *Lad* and *lass*, on the contrary,
probably have a common origin, much as those two disguised
compounds *lord* and *lady* have a common origin. The usual guess
that lass derives from an Old Norse word meaning 'weak' or
'idle' strikes me as feeble and the usual assumption that *lass* is
independent of *lad* fails to convince me. On the other hand I like
the suggestion that *lad*, Middle English *ladde*, derives from late
Old English *-ladda*, occurring only as a second element in place-
name and by-name compounds, an element akin to the Old
English element *-led*, sprout, as in the name *Sumerled* [soo'-mer-
led], literally 'summer sprout', and to the Gothic element *-lauths*,
sprout, as in *juggalauths* [yoong'-gă-lauths], young man, literally
'young sprout or growth'. This etymology postulates for *lad*
the entirely suitable basic sense 'young sprout or growth' – compare the phrases *young sprig* and *a sprig of the nobility* and, more
vaguely and remotely, *young things*. If you accept that etymology
for *lad* and further accept the probability that *lass* derives from
lad, you are forced to accept some such derivation as *lad* – *lad-ess* –
la'ess – *lass*. Although I lack the evidence to corroborate that
derivation, I think that it may well exist: after all, our linguistic
records are, at many points, far from complete.

Boy and *girl*, however, are obviously independent, the one of the other. *Boy*, Middle English *boie*, is probably akin to East Frisian *boi*, a young gentleman, perhaps also to German *Bube* [boo'-bū], a knave, and Old Norse *bufi* [boo'-fee], a rogue – compare semantically, although in reverse, English *knave* from Old English *cnafe* [knah'-fa], akin to German *Knabe* [knah'-be], a boy. Those few details have been well known since late in the nineteenth century, but the lexicographers should, I think, have made it clear, even though it is obvious, that the comparison of English *boy* with German *bube*, Middle High German *buobe* [boo'-o-be], Old Norse *bufi*, is probably valid only for the first element *bu-* [boo]. That element *bu-* is important, for it at least suggests an Indo-European stem and a Latin cognate, perhaps a Greek cognate – and certainly a semantic parallel in *lad*. The Indo-European stem, I'd say is *pu-* [poo-], occurring perhaps in Sanskrit and in Latin and, with vowel-change, in Greek; with Germanic alteration *bu-*. The basic sense of Indo-European **pu-* would be 'to grow' or 'growth', specialized as 'young growth'. But can we substantiate that airy proposal? Sanskrit has *pumán* [poo'-mahn], a man: by a man we tend to understand a man in full growth, yet before he begins to lose his strength and energy. Latin has two significant words, in which the idea of growth is manifest: *pubes* [poo'-base], one who is physically adult, at least essentially; and *puer* [poo'-er], a boy, 'a *growing* male', literally a *grow*-er', the *-er* being agential. (*Puella* [poo'-ella] derives from *puer* and consists of stem *pu-+-ella*, feminine diminutive suffix, *puella* being 'the little female *grow*-er'; *puellus* doesn't help, for it has been refashioned upon *puella*.) What, then, is the Greek word? *Pais* [pice], a boy, *pu-* having, by 'popular' vocalism, become *pa-*[pah]; *-is* being a masculine suffix; the original form may have been *pa-wis** – *pá-+*digamma+*-is*. If we accept the Indo-European and Latin kinship, we necessarily abandon the 'boy'-'rogue' semantic parallel, which clearly is neither essential nor even relevant.

---

* I owe *pais* to Ernout & Meillet.

Thus we reach that difficult word *girl*. The Middle English forms *girle* (gheer'-le], *gerle* [gher'-le], *gurle* [ghoor'-le], meaning a young person of either sex, but especially towards the end of the period, mostly a girl, apparently derive from Old English *-gyrl* [gheer'l], recorded in *gyrlgyden* [gheerl'-gheeden], virgin goddess. Perhaps akin to the Old English word is the Low German *gōr* [gher] or *göre* [gher'e], a young person of either sex, but that doesn't take us very far. The semantic approach may help, because one basic sense – as in *lad* and *boy* – appears to be 'young person, growing person, of either sex', and another, still more fundamental, sense appears to be 'growing thing' (the generalization or abstraction would be 'growth'). If, for the purposes of discussion, we admit that semantic premiss, we look for lexical and phonetic evidence: and, looking, we find, in Old English, the rare word *gyr* [gheer], a fig-tree, and, in Southern English dialect, *girlopp* [gher'-lop], a lout, and, even more revealing, *girls* [gherls], primrose blooms. For those three terms, as for the semantic suggestion, I am indebted to *Webster's New World Dictionary of the American Language* (College Edition, 1952), which also put me on what seems to be the right track for *lad*. I used to think, nor am I convinced that I was wrong in thinking, that *girl* might be ultimately kin to Greek κόρη, *korē*, pronounced *ko-ray*, a young girl, the root being *kor-* and the word being merely the feminine of κόρος, *koros*, a child, an adolescent; the apparently later sense 'a shoot, a sprout' may, in fact, have been the earlier. The Indo-European root has been postulated as *ker-*: compare the poetic κέλωρ, *kelōr*, son, for *κέρωρ, *kerōr*; the suffix -ωρ, -ōr, is akin to Latin -er, as in *puer* [poo'-er]. The words *koros* and *korē* would mean 'young *grow*-er', respectively male and female. Suppose we grant the Indo-European stem **ker-*, to grow, can we link it to our *girl*, Old English *gyrl-* [gheerl]? The final *l* is a suffix, probably here, as so often elsewhere, short for *-el*, fundamentally a diminutive, but with the diminutive force either lost or exceedingly vague. That still leaves us with the necessity of equating **ker-* with *ger-*: but is that more difficult than equating, as better philologists than I have equated, **ker-* with Armenian *ser*, lineage, posterity, and *serim*, I am descended from? And with Latin *crĕ-* or *crē* [cray], as in *creare*, to create, (fundamentally) to cause to *grow*? Why not also the *ser-* of Latin *serĕre*, stem *ser-*, to show, a root occurring in several other languages for both 'to sow' and 'to plant'? Now, Latin *crĕ-* or *crē* [cray] may be a metathesis of Indo-European *ker-*. The letter *k* is phonetically equivalent to hard *c*; and what is *g* – that is, hard *g* – but a thickening of hard *c*, hence of *k*? Admit that and you will, however reluctantly, admit the transition, from **ker-* to *ger-* [gher], hence from *kor-*, as in *korē* [ko-ray], a young girl, to *girl*. The vowel-change is, at first thought, a violent one; yet several great philologists, as we have seen, do admit it in Greek *korē* [ko-ray] and Indo-European **ker-*.

But the etymology of *girl* – a word unrecorded before the late thirteenth century – is so obscure that there exists yet another possibility. The late appearance of the word renders unlikely an origin in Greek or Latin.

A famous dictionary calls the pronunciation *gal* 'dialectal and vulgar'; yet it has always been, predominantly, an educated and even a society pronunciation. To show you how untrustworthily my mind works I confess that my attention strays to Irish simply because of the Anglo-Irish *girleen*, apparently a blend of the English *girl* and the Anglo-Irish *colleen*.

Now, *colleen* represents Irish *c-a-i-l-ī-n* (pronounced roughly *că-leen*), diminutive of Irish *c-a-i-l-e* (roughly *că'-'l'ay*), from Early Middle Irish *c-a-l-e* (roughly *că-lay*) – stem *căl*. *Căl* to *gal* presents an easy and frequent mutation. Perhaps *ca-lay* was, by English ears, apprehended as *cah'-lay*, and then *cah* as *cahr*: which would explain the intrusive *r*. The vowel *ah* might easily, in a period of phonetic and scriptural chaos or, at best, indecision, have been thinned to 'the neutral vowel': which would explain the variants g-e-r-l-e, g-i-r-l-e, g-u-r-l-e.

That, however, is a mere suggestion.

The simple truth is that we lack the evidence to decide upon one of those three theories about the etymology of *girl* at the expense of the other two; nor am I trying to be ingenious. So please regard my disjointed remarks on *lad-lass* and *boy-girl* as what it is the fashion to call an 'interim report'. I've done no exhaustive work upon any of them. Indeed, I am almost content to say 'I don't *know*'.

I shall, however, be well content if I have said enough to insinuate into your minds a partial sympathy with my intolerant attitude towards a statement attributed – wrongly, I feel sure – to Skeat of the still extremely useful etymological dictionary: 'If I cannot solve an etymology in twenty minutes, I give it up'. Many of Skeat's own etymologies must have taken him very much longer than that. He was not impatient: no philologist should be, no etymologist can afford to be. In etymology, it is better to travel than to arrive – not that the arrival fails to bring one a lively gratification.

Yet, because of the fascination of these journeys – a fascination that can be shared at second hand – and the very lively satisfaction, likewise shareable, caused by the arrival, I feel it my solemn duty to warn you, as emphatically as courtesy permits, against etymology. Without cataloguing you into boredom, I shall mention only a few of the very real, and very grave, dangers of engaging in etymology: beside which, Cleopatra was a quickly fading harridan, too soon agèd, for the fascination of etymology *can* never stale, let alone die.

Etymology, you see, calls for the exercise of mind, but also of will: for cool judgement, but also a warm heart: for knowledge of books, but also of mankind: for research into books, but also into life: for a bed-rock of philology, but also a deep top-soil of general culture: for a knowledge of, or at least an unfailing tact in, psychology, but also a wide reading in history: for a combination of well-ordered general knowledge and of well-directed specialized knowledge: that specialized knowledge falling into two parts, a general knowledge of language and its operations, and a particular knowledge of all those branches of philology upon which etymology, if it is not to degenerate into ingenuity on the one hand or into fancy on the other, must be based. Advisedly I say 'fancy', not 'imagination'. In etymology, imagination, if carefully controlled, will occasionally solve problems that phonetics cannot touch; it must, however, be imagination exercised, not in defiance of philology but within the vast horizons available to even the most formal philology; the trouble is that some people shrink from marching to the horizon, for fear (an early medieval fear) of falling over the world's edge.

Etymology is a perilous subject: for, reach one horizon, you find another equally distant, if not still more remote. One clue leads to another, which yields to another, which *ad-infinitums* from days to months to years; and often one has to retrace one's steps.

'This way madness lies.' But – to oneself always; to others occasionally – it's a remarkably pleasant madness.

(Delivered, on October 19, 1953, as a paper to the English Seminar of the University of Liverpool.)

PART II

Word-Levels

―――

6

Slang

———

Winged words: ἔπεα πτερόεντο. Homer.
'Words are the very devil!' Australian officer on receiving, in
August, 1916, at Pozières, a confusing message.

Slang is language which takes off its coat, spits on its hands –
and goes to work. Carl Sandberg.

Definition, Etymology, Synonyms, Range

SLANG is easy enough to use, but very hard to write about with
the facile convincingness that a subject apparently so simple
would, at first sight, seem to demand. But the simplest things are
often the hardest to define, certainly the hardest to discuss, for it
is usually at first sight only that their simplicity is what strikes one
the most forcibly. And slang, after all, 'is a peculiar kind of vaga-
bond language, always hanging on the outskirts of legitimate
speech, but continually straying or forcing its way into the most
respectable company.'* Circumstance conspires to complicate the
issue, for – as we read in the Encyclopædia Britannica – 'at one
moment a word or locution may be felt definitely as slang, but
in another set of circumstances the same word or locution may
not produce this impression at all.'

In *The Oxford English Dictionary*, that *monumentum ære perennius*
which is almost insolently cheap for the large amount of 'brass'
that it costs to buy, Sir William Craigie gives four separate
headings to *slang*, and this is for the noun alone. He implies that
these headings probably represent four separate groups and
origins but adds that, in the one strictly relevant class, 'some of

---

* Greenough and Kittredge, *Words and their Ways in English Speech* (1902). (An
excellent, very readable book.)

[103]

the senses may represent independent words'; on the other hand he does not rule out the possibility that certain of the many senses of *slang* may be interrelated either etymologically or semantically. The five senses approximating to that in general use since about 1850 – to the free and easy, 'shirt-sleeves', essentially spoken language with which we are concerned – are Cant (i.e., thieves' slang), other very low and vulgar speech, the jargon of a trade or profession, abuse or impertinence, and – as in Foote's play, *The Orators*, 1762 – humbug or nonsense. The Oxford definition of slang in our sense is, despite Professor G. H. McKnight's doubt 'if an exact definition of slang is possible', admirably clear: 'language of a highly colloquial type, considered as below the level of standard educated speech, and consisting either of new words or of current words employed in some special sense.' A rather different definition, which is also to some extent complementary, is that of Mr H. W. Fowler: 'the diction that results from the favourite game among the young and lively of playing with words and renaming things and actions; some invent new words, or mutilate or misapply the old, for the pleasure of novelty, and others catch up such words for the pleasure of being in the fashion.' In this specific sense – as indeed in that of a vocational jargon – *slang* is not recorded before the early nineteenth century; as meaning cant, whether noun or adjective, it occurs about 1750. The etymology of *slang* – that prize-problem word – is dubious, for whereas *The Oxford Dictionary** considers any connexion with certain Norwegian forms in *-sleng* to be unlikely, Dr Bradley and Professors Weekley and Wyld† think that cognates are furnished by *slenja-ord*, a new slang word, by *slenja-namm*, a nickname, and *slenja-kjeften*, to sling the jaw, i.e., to abuse. The 'sling' sense gains probability from two sides: the *OED*'s quotation, dated about 1400,

> But Eneas be war he abyes
> The bolde wordes that [he] dede sclyng;

---

* After this, referred to as *OED*. The debt to the *OED*, in my second and third paragraphs, is too obvious to be laboured.

† In future references, Weekley, Wyld. So with other authorities.

and low colloquial* usage. The latter has *sling language* or *words*, to talk, and *sling the bat*, to speak the vernacular, especially to speak the language of that foreign country (the Tommy in 1914–18 often used it for 'to speak French, Arabic') where one happens to be; but, although with both of these we should certainly compare the even more highly colloquial *sling off at*, to taunt, to jeer at a person, which approximates to the less familiar *slang*,† to scold, to address very abusively, we must not allow ourselves to be will-o'-the-wisped into taking any notice of *spin the bat*, which, popular with the Tommies in India during the nine-teenth century, represents a deliberate variant of *sling the bat*, but has a rather different meaning – to speak with great gusto, con-siderable vividness, and remarkable vigour – obviously analogous to *spin a yarn*, to tell a story. We can, however, indulge ourselves to the extent of finding the theatrical use, in the eighties, of *slanging* to mean singing, relevant to our purpose, for singing in music halls was so called because of the quantity of spoken slang inserted – often by way of a 'gag' – between the verses of a song.

    Slang has, from about 1850, been the accepted term for 'illegiti-mate' colloquial speech; but even since then, especially among the lower classes, *lingo* has been a synonym, and so also, chiefly among the cultured and the pretentious, has *argot*. Now *argot*, being merely the French for slang, has no business to be used thus – it can rightly be applied only to French slang or French cant: and *lingo* properly means a simplified language that, like Beach-la-Mar and Pidgin-English, represents the distortion of (say) English by coloured peoples speaking English indeed but adapting it to their own phonetics and grammar. *Jargon*, originally – as in Chaucer – used of the warbling of birds,‡ has long been employed

---

  * Hotten, whose evidence from Crabb's *Gipsies' Advocate* (1831), I find unsup-ported elsewhere, asserts that *slang* is pure Gipsy, whereas it was merely adopted by the Gipsies. Another theory is that *slang* is an argotic corruption of the Fr. *langue*, language; too ingenious!

  † Dating, in this sense, from about 1840; *sling off at* from about 1880. *Slang*, to speak in slang, is first recorded in Lytton's *Pelham* (1828).

  ‡ Weekley, *An Etymological Dictionary of Modern English* (1921); a happy hunting-ground for the etymologizing brave.

loosely and synonymously for slang, but it should be reserved for the technicalities of science, the professions, and the trades: though, for such technicalities, *shop* is an equally good word. An earlier synonym is *flash*, which did duty from 1718 until 1850 or so, but even in the eighteenth century it was more generally and correctly applied to the slang of criminals (i.e., cant), not to slang in our wider sense. Before 1850, *slang* meant all definitely vulgar language except cant, or at least this was its prevailing acceptation after 1800, before which (as Grose's invaluable dictionary shows) it served as an alternative to *flash* in the sense of cant. Nor, after 1850, was *slang* accepted with general good grace, for in 1873, we find Hotten protesting against the restriction of the term to 'those lowest words only which are used by the dangerous classes and the lowest grades of society'. As slang is used by every class, and as this fact is now everywhere recognized, the stigma once attached to the word has long since been removed; in 1911, indeed, a foreign research-student at Cambridge could rightly say: 'It is impossible to acquire a thorough knowledge of English [or of any other language, for that matter] without being familiar with slang and vulgarism. Whoever is uninitiated . . . will be at a loss to understand many of the masterpieces of English literature. Nay . . . he will scarcely be able even to understand an English newspaper.'*

Origin, Uses, and Reasons for Use; Attitudes towards Slang

Slang, being the quintessence of colloquial speech, must always be related to convenience rather than to scientific laws, grammatical rules and philosophical ideals. As it originates, so it flourishes best, in colloquial speech. 'Among the impulses which lead to the invention of slang,' Dr Bradley remarked some years ago, 'the two most important seem to be the desire to secure increased vivacity and the desire to secure increased sense of intimacy in the use of language.' The most favourable conditions

---

* Olof E. Bosson, *Slang and Cant in Jerome K. Jerome's Works* (1911).

are those of 'crowding and excitement, and artificial life. . . . Any sudden excitement or peculiar circumstance is quite sufficient to originate and set going a score of slang words', as John Camden Hotten, a publisher and lexicographer, more sinned against than sinning, noted in the excellent Short History that prefaces his valuable collection of mid-Victorian and other slang. Its origin and usage are lit with interest if we remember one of the primary laws: slang is not used merely as a means of self-expression: it connotes personality: 'its coinage and circulation comes rather from the wish of the individual to distinguish himself by oddity or grotesque humour.'* Another aspect is presented by Mr Earle Welby† when he says: 'Some slang originates in an honourable discontent with the battered or bleached phrases in far too general use', this fresh slang being further described by him as 'the plain man's poetry, the plain man's aspiration from penny plain to twopence coloured'.

But the most interesting pronouncements on the origins and uses of slang are those of Mr Mencken and M. Niceforo. The former is so illuminating that to paraphrase him were an impertinence. 'What slang actually consists of,' he says,‡ 'doesn't depend . . . upon intrinsic qualities, but upon the surrounding circumstances. It is the user that determines the matter, and particularly the user's habitual way of thinking. If he chooses words carefully, with a full understanding of their meaning and savour, then no word that he uses seriously will belong to slang, but if his speech is made up chiefly of terms poll-parroted, and he has no sense of their shades and limitations, then slang will bulk largely in his vocabulary. In its origin it is nearly always respectable [comparatively!]; it is devised, not by the stupid populace [what about the Cockneys?], but by individuals of wit and ingenuity; as Whitney says, it is a product of an "exuberance of mental activity, and the natural delight of language making". But when its inventions happen to strike the popular fancy and

* Greenough and Kittredge, op. cit.
† *The Week-end Review*, 25th April, 1931.
‡ *The American Language* (3rd ed., 1923), p. 374.

are adopted by the mob, they are soon worn threadbare and so lose all piquancy and significance, and in Whitney's words, become "incapable of expressing anything that is real". This is the history of such slang phrases as ... "How's your poor feet?" ... "Have a heart!", "This is the life".'

M. Alfredo Niceforo, a widely travelled Italian, notes that, as in general speech, so inevitably in slang, one speaks as one judges – and one judges according to how one feels. His opinions on this subject, together with its relation to the influence of groups, are of first-rate importance.* 'Every social fact – and the language of a group is a social fact,' writes Niceforo, 'is the result of two classes of cause: personal (or biological) causes, represented by the physiological and psychological characteristics of the individual; and external (or mesological) causes, represented by the great accumulation of the social pressures, economic and geographical and other factors, which so powerfully influence mankind.' He shows how language varies in passing from one social group to another and even in the different situations in which any one person may find himself. He indicates the further distinction that sometimes it is feeling or sentiment, sometimes one's profession or trade which determines the nature of one's speech, whether it be standard or unconventional. For instance, children and lunatics speak very much as their emotions dictate; soldiers have a multitude of words and phrases that reflect their daily existence in barracks, on the march, in bivouac, or in the front line. The specialization that characterizes every vocation leads naturally to a specialized vocabulary, to the invention of new words or the re-charging of old words. Such special words and phrases become slang only when they are used outside the vocational group and then only if they change their meaning or are applied in other ways. Motoring, aviation, and the wireless have already supplied us with a large number of slang terms. But, whatever the source, personality and one's surroundings (social or occupational) are the two co-efficients, the two chief factors,

* *Le Génie de l'Argot* (1912).

the determining causes of the nature of slang, as they are of language in general and of style.

Why is slang used at all? That question, like a small child's, is a natural one to ask, but a difficult one to answer. Reasons have occurred to the writer, who, however, is not quite so fatuous as to consider that they account for every slang expression used in the past, much less every slang expression that will be used by the bright lads, sprightly lasses, and naughty old men of the future. That all the following reasons why slang is used are either actually or potentially operative he is nevertheless as sure as a mere man can be, and he would like to add that the order in which they are set down is not so haphazard as it may seem.

Slang, he believes, is employed because of one (or more) of fifteen reasons:

(1) In sheer high spirits, by the young in heart as well as by the young in years; 'just for the fun of the thing'; in playfulness or waggishness.

(2) As an exercise either in wit and ingenuity or in humour. (The motive behind this is usually self-display or snobbishness, emulation or responsiveness, delight in virtuosity.)

(3) To be 'different', to be novel.

(4) To be picturesque (either positively or – as in the wish to avoid insipidity – negatively).

(5) To be unmistakably arresting, even startling.

(6) To escape from clichés, or to be brief and concise. (Actuated by impatience with existing terms.)

(7) To enrich the language. (This deliberateness is rare save among the well-educated, Cockneys forming the most notable exception; it is literary rather than spontaneous.)

(8) To lend an air of solidity, concreteness, to the abstract; of earthiness to the idealistic; of immediacy and appositeness to the remote. (In the cultured the effort is usually premeditated, while in the uncultured it is almost always unconscious when it is not rather subconscious.)

(9a) To lessen the sting of, or on the other hand to give additional point to, a refusal, a rejection, a recantation;

(9b) To reduce, perhaps also to disperse, the solemnity, the pomposity, the excessive seriousness of a conversation (or of a piece of writing);

(9c) To soften the tragedy, to lighten or to 'prettify' the inevitability of death or madness, or to mask the ugliness or the pity of profound turpitude (e.g., treachery, ingratitude); and/or thus to enable the speaker or his auditor or both to ensure, to 'carry on'.

(10) To speak or write down to an inferior, or to amuse a superior public; or merely to be on a colloquial level with either one's audience or one's subject matter.

(11) For ease of social intercourse. (Not to be confused or merged with the preceding.)

(12) To induce either friendliness or intimacy of a deep or a durable kind. (Same remark.)

(13) To show that one belongs to a certain school, trade, or profession, artistic or intellectual set, or social class; in brief, to be 'in the swim' or to establish contact.

(14) Hence, to show or prove that someone is *not* 'in the swim'.

(15) To be secret – not understood by those around one. (Children, students, lovers, members of political secret societies, and criminals in or out of prison, innocent persons in prison, are the chief exponents.)

Such critics as Hotten, Mencken, and Niceforo are almost genial in their attitude towards slang, but others are scornful. As early as 1825 J. P. Thomas, in *My Thought Book*, inveighed thus: 'The language of slang is the conversation of fools. Men of discretion will not pervert language to the unprofitable purposes of conversational mimicry. . . . The friends of literature will never adopt it, as it is actively opposed to pure and grammatical diction.' In our own century the authors of *Words and their Ways* condemn slang on the ground that, being evanescent, vague, and ill-defined, slang has a deleterious effect on those who use it often, for it tends to remove all those delicate shades of meaning which are at the root of a good style; they point out that it is a lazy man's speech; and assert that when a slang word becomes definite in meaning it has almost ceased to be slang. Perhaps a fairer conception is that of the Merton Professor of English Language at Oxford: 'While slang is essentially part of familiar and colloquial speech, it is not necessarily either incorrect or vulgar in its proper place,' which, as the Fowlers say, 'is in real life.' That is, in conversation – for, the Fowlers continue, 'as style is the great antiseptic, so slang is the great corrupting matter; it is perishable, and infects what is round it.' The same thought is conveyed from a different angle by Professor McKnight,* who remarks that, 'originating as slang expressions often do, in an insensibility to the meaning of legitimate words, the use of slang checks an acquisition of a command over recognized modes of expression ... [and] must result in atrophy of the faculty of using language.' This applies mainly to authors and orators. But no real stylist, no one capable of good speaking or good writing, is likely to be harmed by the occasional employment of slang; provided that he is conscious of the fact, he can even employ it both frequently and freely without stultifying his mind, impoverishing his vocabulary, or vitiating the taste and the skill that he brings to the using of that vocabulary. Except in formal and dignified writing and in professional speaking, a vivid and extensive slang is perhaps preferable to a jejune and meagre vocabulary of standard English; on the other hand, it will hardly be denied that, whether in writing or in speech, a sound though restricted vocabulary of standard English is preferable to an equally small vocabulary of slang, however vivid may be that slang.

The same contradictoriness applies to the various attempts to set forth the primary characteristics of slang. Greenough and Kittredge, at the beginning of their thoughtful if somewhat reactionary chapter on Slang and Legitimate Speech, say that 'slang is commonly made by the use of harsh, violent, or ludicrous metaphors, obscure analogies, meaningless words, and expressions derived from the less known and less esteemed vocations or customs', and, twenty pages further on, admit that 'it is sometimes

---

* *English Words and their Background* (1923). (Whence all later quotations.)

humorous, witty, and not seldom picturesque'. A much neater thumb-nail sketch* is that of Niceforo: 'concrete terms, vivid metaphors, brilliant turns of phrase, contrasts, ellipses, and abbreviations.' In fairness, however, to the two American professors, it is to be added that they note that slang, so far from being a novelty, is the most vital aspect of language, the only speech in which linguistic processes can be observed in unrestricted activity; as they remark, there is no primary difference between the processes of slang and those of standard speech. Slang may and often does fill a gap in accepted language; as J. Brander Matthews had observed in 1893,† 'in most cases a man can say best what he has to say without lapsing into slang; but then a slangy expression which actually tells us something is better than the immaculate sentence empty of everything but the consciousness of its own propriety.'

But there is a decided hint of 'It isn't done' in a few of the general accounts of slang. After reading Hotten's famous justification – 'the squeamishness which tries to ignore the existence of slang fails signally, for not only in the streets and in the prisons, but at the bar, on the bench, in the pulpit, and in the Houses of Parliament, does slang make itself heard, and, as the shortest and safest means to an end, understood too' – it is diverting to arrive at the opinion that the word associations of this 'pariah' branch of language are 'low, or at least, undignified, and perhaps disgusting'; if they obtain the franchise of respectability by becoming accepted, for other than trivial or frivolous purposes, by the users of standard speech, then their lowly origins will probably be forgotten and they will become pure as driven snow. This view smacks of the year in which it was expressed – 1902; but the Fowlers‡ are almost as severe. 'Foreign words and slang are,

* These opinions are recorded here in order to establish a point of departure for the ensuing consideration of the 'components' of slang; the real discussion of the essentials of slang is held over till Chapter IV [of *Slang Today and Yesterday*. Ed.].

† In Harper's Magazine (reprinted in the collected essays, *Parts of Speech*, (1901)): an important contribution.

‡ *The King's English* (3rd ed., 1930). A mine, withal a trifle conservative here and there, of dicta on good writing and correct speaking.

as spurious ornaments, on the same level . . . The effect of using quotation marks with slang is merely to convert a mental into a moral weakness.' But they are very sound on the quarters from which slang may come. Taking the averagely intelligent middle-class man as the norm, they show that he can usually detect with ease such words as come from 'below' and add that these constitute the best slang, for many such terms assume their place in the language as 'words that will last', and will not, like many from 'above', die off after a brief vogue; from the same direction, however, derive such colourless counters as *nice, awful, blooming* (this last, by the way, is on the wane). Words from above are less easily detected: *phenomenal, epoch-making, true inwardness, psychological moment, philistine* 'are being subjected to that use, at once over-frequent and inaccurate, which produces one kind of slang. But the average man, seeing from what exalted quarters they come, is dazzled into admiration and hardly knows them for what they are.' The slang from 'the sides' or from 'the centre' consists of those words which, belonging at first to a profession or trade, a pursuit, a game or sport, have invaded general colloquial speech – and very often the printed page. 'Among these a man is naturally less critical of what comes from his own daily concerns, that is, in his view, from the centre.' These two lexicographers and grammarians acutely caution us that, in any collection of slang words and phrases, the degree of recognizability will depend largely upon whether the occupation, for example, is familiar or not, 'though sometimes the familiarity will disguise, and sometimes it will bring out, the slanginess.'

7

Slang and Standard English

FOR OVER A CENTURY, there have been protests against the use of slang and controversies on the relation of slang to the literary language or, as it is now usually called, Standard English. Purists have risen in their wrath and conservatives in their dignity to defend the Bastille of linguistic purity against the revolutionary rabble. The very vehemence of the attack and the very sturdiness of the defence have ensured that only the fittest survive to gain entrance into the citadel, there establish themselves, and then become conservatives and purists in their turn.

Some of the contestants, however, are uncertain what they are fighting for – and even what they are fighting about. They have no very clear ideas as to what constitutes Standard English, and only the haziest ideas of what slang is. Even in many esteemed dictionaries the definitions are unsatisfactory. For instance, in a certain dictionary of acknowledged merit the definition of slang is: 'Expressions in common colloquial' – i.e., spoken – 'use but not regarded as standard English'. Now, that does not go far enough; and even in so far as it commits itself it is misleading.

To make himself clear, the quickest and easiest way is for the present writer to be at first arbitrary or even autocratic, and then explanatory.

In every civilized language, there is a hierarchy. That hierarchy consists, in English, of the following ranks, in ascending order of dignity and respectability:

cant;
slang;
vulgarisms (in both senses);
colloquialisms;
Standard English, with its three ascending varieties:
  Familiar English;

ordinary Standard English;

Literary English.

(Dialect stands rather to one side; it cannot fairly be placed in the hierarchy at all, for it is primitive and regional. Nevertheless, it forms one of the sources from which Standard English is recruited.)

Cant, more generally known as 'the language of the underworld', is the special vocabulary – rather is it a set of interconnected vocabularies – of criminals and tramps and beggars, of their hangers-on and associates, and of racketeers.

Slang may be replenished, indeed it often is replenished, by recruits from the underworld, but usually it stands self-dependent and self-sufficient, until it dies of inanition or weariness or a change in fashion or, on the other hand, so strongly survives that it is adopted and becomes a colloquialism and is subject to the conditions affecting and governing colloquialisms.

Colloquialisms stand midway between slang and Standard English: they are felt to be more respectable, more permanent than slang, but less respectable, less dignified than Standard English. They are called colloquialisms because they are general and fitting enough in conversation but hardly fitting in serious writings, speeches, sermons. They are used by a larger proportion of the population than is slang.

Standard English is such English as is held to be proper and respectable, fitting and dignified, in all conditions; moreover and especially it consists of all such language as is both adequate and seemly on all serious occasions and in communication with foreigners. The best, the predominant variety of Standard English is that which is neither homely (Familiar English) nor elevated (Literary English). Familiar English is that which is suitable and natural in the ordinary commerce of speech and writing; Literary English is that which is used upon solemn or very important occasions, in sustained and deliberate eloquence, in the most philosophical or aesthetic writings or wherever else the writer may feel that, to do justice to the theme, he must employ only the finest language. Obviously the borderlines between Familiar

English, ordinary Standard English, and Literary English are often ill-defined; and the distinctions between these three varieties are much less important than the differences between cant and slang, between slang and colloquialisms, and between colloquialisms and Standard English.

But what of vulgarisms?

Vulgarisms are of two kinds: illiteracies and low language. Illiteracies are, as their name indicates, words and phrases used only by the illiterate; that is, they are words and phrases used incorrectly. Low language, again obviously, consists of expressions avoided by the polite and the decent, at least in polite or decent company. These expressions are not illiterate, they may even be good English – but such good English as, by the association of ideas and by social habit, has come to be avoided in polite company. For instance, *pluck* was once both slang and a vulgarism; at first, the synonymous *guts* was likewise both slang and a vulgarism. In the hierarchy, vulgarisms may be adjudged co-equal with slang or, at lowest, lying somewhere between cant and slang.

But these generalities remain vague and high-handed unless examples are adduced. Without examples, they are as nothing; more, they are nothing. When Dickens speaks of *cracking a crib* (breaking into a building in order to steal certain contents) he is using cant; it is, by the way, obsolete cant. When a twentieth-century novelist or journalist uses the phrase *wide boys*, he also is using cant. If we allude to someone as *a queer fish* or *a rum fellow* we are using slang, for either expression is understood by almost everyone – it is not confined to the underworld, is in fact no longer used by the underworld. When an airman refers to himself as a *penguin*, he is resorting to the specialized slang of the Air Force; all he means is that he is a member of the ground staff and therefore does not fly; a New Zealand airman would call himself a *kiwi*. Neither a penguin nor a kiwi is a flying bird. If someone calls you *a good chap* or *a decent fellow*, he is employing a colloquialism; for some years, the latter phrase has been qualifying for, though it has not yet achieved, the status of Familiar English. *A nice* (or *decent*) *man* is Standard English. If I say, 'Come, lass', I am using Familiar English; if I address her as 'Dear girl', I am using ordinary Standard English; and if I say, 'Come, sweet maid', I am using Literary English. If, however, I allude to the girl as *a dame* or a *Jane*, I am employing slang; if as *a moll*, I am employing cant; if as – but perhaps I had better not particularize the vulgarisms for 'girl' or 'woman'.

It will be noticed that some of these words and phrases have undergone a change of status since first they were used. This change of status, this shift of sense and values, is something that affects the entire language, every language, in general and slang in particular; moreover, it exemplifies or, at the least, implies a fact and a factor that affect, even govern, the whole question of the admissibility of slang into Standard English and the related question of the influence of slang upon Standard English. Language, like Life itself (of which it is at once the mirror and the chief means of communication), should not – except for the purposes of philosophical or dialectical convenience – be compartmented, for such compartments fail to correspond with the facts. The overlappings are numerous, and inevitable. Every new word either dies or lives; if it lives, it tends to become dignified, therefore acceptable, and therefore part of Standard English. Even a new word that is neither cant nor slang nor colloquialism, neither dialect nor vulgarism, even a new word that, in short, is Standard English – that is, absolutely every new word, even if it starts off as Standard English, is regarded with suspicion or distrust or distaste. At best, it is a neologism; or it may be stigmatized as a technicality – a piece of jargon, of scientific terminology: and only by the passage of time does it become generally accepted and indubitable, unquestioned Standard. A word begins its career as a *parvenu*; if it be cant, as a disreputable intruder; if slang, as 'not quite the thing, don't you know!' But once a word achieves the status of Standard English, a status conferred by its acceptance as the predominant word for the object, activity, process, or condition designated, even the purist, if honest, can decently do nothing but record it; he should no longer judge it or adjudge it.

Let us take an extreme case – the case of words that have risen from the lowest status (cant) to the highest. Let us also take the less extreme case of words that from slang have either slowly and gradually become Standard English or leapt the transition with an astonishing – yet circumstantially inevitable – speed. 'That's a *queer* thing' or 'He's a *queer* person' is Standard English as it has been for a century. Yet in the sixteenth–eighteenth centuries, *queer* formed part of the language of the underworld; *queer*, in the sense of counterfeit money, is still a cant word. Originally, *queer* meant 'worthless, inferior, cheap; bad'. In its rise in the social scale and in the linguistic world, it has somewhat changed in its sense, with the result that it normally signifies 'odd, strange', yet almost always it contains an implication of 'unconventional' or even 'not good'. In the sixteenth to mid-eighteenth century, *queer* was the exact opposite of *rum*, which then, i.e. while it was still cant, signified 'valuable superior, expensive; excellent'. *Rum*, however, is still no better than slang. The reason why both *queer* and *rum* now mean 'odd, strange' is another story, a delightful semantic tale. *Booze*, 'drink, liquor', for several centuries a part of the underworld's vocabulary, is now both slang and a vulgarism.

Whereas *queer* took centuries to change from cant to slang and at least a generation to rise from slang to Standard English, *blitz* was promoted within three years. In German, the word means 'lightning'; a *Blitzkrieg* is mobile warfare conducted at lightning speed. As a noun, *blitz* soon came to be English slang for a 'bombardment from the air', and by 1942 it was a colloquialism, which, in this sense, it has remained. But *the Blitz* has, since early in 1943, been accepted – that is, Standard English – for the German bombing of English cities in 1940–41; *the London Blitz* for the bombing that, there, lasted from early September 1940, until the end of May 1941. What, then, of *blitz* as a verb, in the sense 'to bombard from the air, to bomb (a place)'? To *blitz* a place means no more than to bomb or air-bombard it; because it is not felt to be a necessary or, at the least, a useful addition to the English language, 'to *blitz*' is not yet, nor likely to become, Standard English; at present it is slang; within a few years it may become a colloquialism, which it will, I think, remain.

The purists have protested against the use of the word *blitz*. These protests have been useless, in respect of the noun; in the respect of even the verb, these protests have probably effected less than has been done by the good sense of the British people.

The sensible person opposes the adoption by Standard English of an unnecessary or comparatively useless word; welcomes a necessary word, irrespective of its origin. But the casting vote, the final approval lies with the general feeling of the people as a whole. Yet sometimes there is no vote, no decision: a word or a phrase may gain a place in Standard English as though by stealth; by being consonant with and appropriate to the genius of the language. It just drops into its place.

8

The Language of the Underworld

O R, for short, *cant* – the technical name, and the convenient. The noun derives from the verb. In the underworld of the sixteenth–nineteenth centuries, *cant* meant simply 'to speak; to talk'; hence, 'to speak the language of the underworld', a sense that has the same ultimate origin as the better-known one, 'to speak hypocritically or with an implied though baseless piety': a plea for alms sung or rather chanted by religious mendicants, with an allusion on the one hand to the whining tone and on the other to the assumed piety. The word itself presumably comes rather from the Latin noun *cantus*, 'a song, a chant', than from the Latin verb *cantare*, 'to sing; in Ecclesiastical Latin, to chant', itself a frequentative of *canere*, 'to sing', with which compare the Greek *kanakhë*, 'a sharp, ringing or shrill sound', *kanassein*, 'to gurgle, as of – or with – water', *kuknos*, 'a swan', and Sanskrit *kôkas*, 'a duck' (English *cock*), although *kuknos*, *kôkas* and *cock* are cognate rather than identical with the stem *kan-* ('to sound') of the preceding words; German *Hahn* and English *hen* are much closer to *kan*.

To define *cant* as 'the language of the underworld' falls short of clarity, as I know who have so often been asked, 'What *is* the underworld?'

The underworld consists of crooks, i.e. professional burglars and pickpockets, cardsharpers, confidence men, swindlers (including the commercial), racketeers, Black Marketeers, and such hangers-on as fences and spivs; of drug traffickers and white-slavers and prostitutes; of professional tramps and beggars.

Certain words and phrases are common to all or nearly all these classes; some to only one class or to allied classes – for instance, beggars and tramps, or white-slavers and prostitutes. Beggars link with crooks, in that the former sometimes act as look-out men for the latter; tramps may easily, in their search for free or very cheap food and lodging, come into contact with crooks; prostitutes are notoriously and generously kind to beggars and tramps; white-slavers often work hand in hand with drug traffickers; Black Marketeers have contacts among thieves and fences; and so it goes on.

Cant, it must never be forgotten, is a vocabulary, a glossary; not a language with a syntax of its own. It does not trouble to find words for 'a' and 'the', 'to' and 'from', 'is' and 'have' – the small, insignificant coin of speech. Cant is a secret language, but its secrecy extends only to such things, actions, processes, ideas as are, to the underworld, important. For instance, 'to speak, steal, take, murder, hide, kidnap, counterfeit, run away; sentence, electrocute'; 'policeman, detective, prison warder, beggar, burglar, counterfeiter, kidnapper; man, woman, child; prison, cell, house, window, door, staircase; food, drink, clothing; dog, horse, country; moon, road; gold, silver, jewellery, plate, gems; theft, burglary, blackmail; dark, bright, white, hidden, lost, dangerous, rapid, beautiful, ugly, valuable; yes, no, not, very'; and so forth. Only certain words need be secret – only a few.

What, in brief, is the history of cant, whether in the world as a whole, or in Britain, the Commonwealth of Nations, the United States of America? In brief, for to tell the story adequately would require a book.

In France and Germany, cant seems to have existed in the fourteenth, certainly it flourished in the fifteenth century. Italy and Spain possessed a considerable body of cant by the sixteenth, as also did Britain; it may easily have arisen in those three countries as early as the fifteenth century and probably it did, but, for England at least, we have no irrefutable recordings earlier than the 1530s. In North America, it doubtless existed in the seventeenth century, for not all the early emigrants were as respectable as the Pilgrim Fathers: yet our earliest unimpeachable record for the United States is valid for only so early as 1794, after which there is extremely little recorded until the 1840s. To Australia cant travelled with the First Fleet, but lacks an indigenous character until about the 1820s; for New Zealand, South Africa and even Canada our earliest records are astonishingly late – the last quarter of the nineteenth century.

In the English-speaking world, therefore, Britain, so far as the documents go, had by far the most prolific cant until the 1840s; the American corpus has been formidable only since that time, but in the twentieth century it has considerably influenced British cant and is, in itself, numerically larger than the British. Since the War of 1914–1918, the cant inter-influence among all English-speaking countries has been considerable; nor had it from (say) 1850 onwards been negligible. For instance, the Sydney Ducks were teaching the Americans something in the Californian Gold Rush days: and the Americans have been teaching the Australians something ever since. Although the English hardly less than the Americans have teen telling everybody how great is the British debt, both in slang generally and in cant particularly, to the United States, yet ever since the 1850s the American debt to Britain has, in cant at least, been equally noteworthy.

But whereas the American and the Dominion cants have always been, in the main, uncultured though not necessarily illiterate, and although the same is true of British cant since early in the seventeenth century, British cant of the sixteenth century had a large element of learnèd words. 'Once upon a time [cant] was called "Thieves' Latin", a term which is more accurate than would at first appear. At the time of the Reformation many thousands of priests lost their livings, and [some few of them] drifted into the bands of robbers and highwaymen that invested every country at the time. These ex-priests taught Latin (the language with which they were most familiar) to their confederates so that they could communicate with each other with very little danger of having their plans discovered by the ordinary public,' as Detective-Sergeant (in 1943) Alexander Black has written; a passage that needs only these modifications, that cant existed before the Reformation and that almost as important in the early development of the European cants was the coming of the Gypsies to Eastern Europe in the fourteenth century, to Italy and Western Europe early in the fifteenth and to Britain late in the fifteenth. There have always been educated, cultured elements in British cant, whether words adopted from Latin and occasionally from Greek or from French or Italian or Dutch or German, or allusions to art and literature, but it is safe to say that, after 1620 or 1630, the learnèd element has been small.

Moreover, the native element in all cants has naturally been much larger than the foreign, though no less naturally the total number of words derived from foreign languages has been rather more impressive. Then, too, the British element ceased, *ca.* 1850, to be predominant in the cant of the USA, and in the Dominion cants *ca.* 1870.

There have been numerous books and newspaper articles dealing with the underworld, and a considerable number of these contain examples of underworld speech. To give an account of that 'literature' is no part of my intention, but one or two facts may have their interest. The most important British source of underworld speech has never (before my own researches) been consulted; the most important source of post-1920 American cant has (thus far) been ignored. The most valuable dictionary for British cant had, until 1937, been Farmer & Henley's (1890–1904); and until 1942 the best dictionary for American cant was Godfrey Irwin's, 1931. The three greatest American authorities upon the subject of American cant are Godfrey Irwin, Joseph Fishman and David Maurer; there is, too, a mass of cant in Lester V. Berrey & Melvin Van Den Bark's *The American Thesaurus of Slang*, but it is insufficiently differentiated.

Among non-lexicographical twentieth-century users of cant the most notable have perhaps been, in America: Josiah Flynt, Jack London, Jim Tully, Glen Mullin, for tramps; Hutchins Hapgood, A. H. Lewis, Donald Lowrie, George Bronson-Howard, Arthur Stringer, Jack Black, Jack Callahan, 'Chicago May', Charles G. Booth, Charles F. Coe, Edwin H. Sutherland, Lee Duncan and Don Castle, for crooks.

And in Britain, W. H. Davies, the Rev. Frank Jennings, George

Orwell, Matt Marshall, for tramps and beggars; Edwin Pugh, Edgar Wallace (mostly trustworthy), Arthur Gardner, George Ingram, James Curtis, Jim Phelan, Val Davis for crooks.

At this point, a cautionary remark might well be interposed. Rather too many writers upon the underworld are ludicrously ignorant of the speech of the underworld. Some years ago, a very successful play contained the phrase *cracking a crib*, which, used for 'burgling a house', was suitable in Charles Dickens's or even in Charles Reade's day; but throughout the twentieth century the predominant phrase has been *screwing* (or *busting*, now obsolescent) *a joint*; *cracking a crib* has been obsolete since at least as early as 1905. A certain popular novelist employs a cant all his own – some of it genuine, some invented, much of it inaccurately assorted, 'No names, no pack-drill!'

But one can talk, far too long, about something without clarifying what that something is: and so I propose to quote four examples, two British and two American, of cant since 1870.

In the October, 1879, number of *Macmillan's Magazine* there is, edited by the Rev. J. W. Horsley, Chaplain to H.M. Prison, Clerkenwell, London – one who knew much about cant – an 'Autobiography of a Thief in Thieves' Language'. In this brief excerpt the parenthetical explanations are Horsley's; the comments, mine.

I took a ducat (ticket) for Sutton . . . and went a wedge-hunting (stealing plate). . . . I piped a slavey (servant – the term has since become slang) come out of a chat (house), so when she had got a little way up the double (turning of the road), I pratted (went) in the house. . . . I piped some daisy-roots (boots – already slang in 1879). So I claimed (stole) them . . . and guyed to the rattler (railway) and took a brief (ticket) to London Bridge, and took the daisies to a sheney (Jew – already slang) down the Gaff (Shoreditch), and done them for thirty blow (shillings). . . . I got in company with some of the widest (cleverest) people in London. They used to use at (frequent) a pub in Shoreditch. The following people used to go in there – toy-getters (watch-stealers), magsmen (confidence-trick men), men at the mace (sham loan offices), broadsmen (cardsharpers), peter-claimers (portmanteau-stealers), busters and screwmen (both names = burglars), snide-pitchers (utterers of false coin), men at the duff (passing false jewellery), welshers, and skittle-sharps. . . . I went on like this for very near a stretch (year) without being smugged (apprehended). One night I was in the mob (gang of thieves – often called a *push*), I got canon (drunk) . . . I got smugged. . . . They asked me what my monarch (name) was. A reeler (policeman) came to the cell and cross-kidded (questioned) me, but I was too wide for him. . . . I was sent to Maidstone Stir (prison) for two moon (months).

This passage shows that, originally, most rhyming slang was cant; and that much cant has a very long life.

.   .   .   .

In 1938 Don Castle succeeded in getting his grim, moving story *Do Your Own Time* published in England; the Americans had – one can't blame them – refused to print it. *Do Your Own Time* deals with the great prison of San Quentin in about 1934. From this remarkable book I take an incident narrated by a convict.

Th' joke was on me . . . Th' beak (judge) was a Hebe (Jew), an' th' dicks (detectives) knew he was wrong (a crook); so they kep' him on th' spot (in a difficult position) long enough t' make him promise t' give the broad (girl) a five spot (a sentence of five years) in Walla Walla (a penitentiary for women).

Y'see, th' skirt (girl) was th' cutor's lay (prosecutor's or judge's mistress), an' t' hand her a fin (five years' term of imprisonment) like that set pretty tough with him (went against the grain); so he gets me t' tommy-gun (to machine-gun) the tecs. I was in a creep-joint (a gambling-establishment that moves every night) when they comes in f'r a pay-off (share of graft or bribe-money) on a load of M (consignment of morphine), an' I let 'em have it – fas'. They knock off (die) without a whisper (without speaking). I scrams (hurried away) an' am batting up the stem (driving my car up the street) at about sixty when a dumb flat-foot (uniformed policeman) yanks (forces) me t' th' kerb. He makes the bus (searches the car), an' pipes (sees, finds) th' Tommy (Thompson sub-machine gun), an' a coupla quarts o' alky (alcoholic liquor), so what does the nob do but bury me f'r the night (hold me in detention overnight).

Th' nex' mornin' they try t' hang th' torpedoin' (killings) on me, but th' beak gets th' office (warning, notice), an' comes down. He goes (arranges an alibi) f'r me, puts me on th' bricks (has me released), an' hands me two grand ($2,000) an' tells me t' breeze th' burg (get out of town); which I does.

Well, when I hits (arrive in) Frisco th' bulls (police) know me. They frisk (search) me an' pipes (see, discover) the case dough (money reserved against a trial). I tries t' tell 'em it's square jack (honest money), but they don't fall (believe me), an' th' nex' thing I knows I'm doing a ten-spot in college (serving a ten-year's sentence in prison).

Almost every one of those words is still current – and most of the survivors are still cant. Cant is much more conservative, tends to last far longer, than slang; usually, cant words and phrases long remain unknown, except to a very few outsiders; also the under-world is slow to perceive that a word has become familiar to detectives, even to journalists, and therefore dangerous.

Apart from its sociological value, which is immense, cant is particularly notable for its word-histories. Among the most fasci-nating of these are the etymologies of underworld terms that have gained a general currency in colloquial and slangy speech, much as *bloke* and *cove*, *chum* and *cully* and *pal*; *hobo* and *spiv*; *booze* and *grub*; *bingo* (now *binge*) and *stingo*; to *doss* and to *snooze*; to *nab*, *nail*, *snaffle*; to *bump off*; a *mug* and a *hick*; *queer* and *phoney* and *rum*; to *bilk* and *do* (swindle); to *lope* and to *hike*; to *go west*; a *bob* and a *tanner*; *racket* and *stir*; and certain others.

But to examine the etymologies of the thirty named terms would verge on excess. On the other hand, to consider less than (say) ten would be extremely misleading. The chosen ten cover a period of over four centuries: *queer* and *rum*, constituting an in-separable pair; *booze*, which oils the ideological wheels; *racket*, surprisingly early and not solely American; *to go west*, even more astonishingly early; *tanner*; *stir*, not only American; *hobo*, entirely

American; *phoney*, less American than you might suppose; and *spiv*, almost offensively English.

Queer (in the sixteenth century, often *quire* or *quyer*; in the seventeenth, sometimes *quier* or *quere*) has always, in cant, signified 'bad, inferior; cheap, base, counterfeit; criminal': and in the sixteenth–seventeenth centuries was constantly being opposed to *rum*, 'excellent, superior; valuable, expensive; genuine; handsome; great, important, extremely skilful or intelligent'. In the nineteenth century, *queer* assumed the slang senses 'tipsy; ill; unfavourable; slightly mad' and in the twentieth, 'homosexual'; in the nineteenth century (though recorded in isolation in 1774 and 1777: the *OED*), *rum* assumed the slang senses 'odd, eccentric, strange; questionable, disreputable; inferior'.

Why has *rum*, from meaning 'excellent', come to mean the opposite – come, in short, to be synonymous with *queer*? Ponder these phrases: *rum bite* or *rum fun*, a clever swindle; *rum blowen*, a beautiful prostitute; *rum cull*, a man very generous to a woman, a rich man easily duped; *rum diver*, a very dexterous pickpocket; *rum mizzler*, a thief clever at escaping; *rum padder*, a 'superior' highwayman: in these terms, the criminal skill or cleverness is anti-social and, by honest citizens, regarded not as good but as bad, not as profitable but as harmful or damaging; what is *rum* or 'excellent' to the criminal is *queer* or 'very bad' for the rest of society. Now, the early Scottish use of *queer* is probably independent of the underworld use, but both usages probably have the same origin; certainly the underworld *queer* derives from the German *quer*, 'across, athwart, transverse; oblique, crooked': compare the noun *crook*, the adjective *crooked* (dishonest), and the underworld *on the cross*, adjective and adverb for '(by) living dishonestly, especially by theft'.

Rum is a much more difficult word: neither Ernest Weekley nor the *OED* essays an etymology; 'Webster', on the basis of the sixteenth–seventeenth-century variant *rome*, tentatively suggests derivation from Romany *rom*, 'a husband, a Gypsy', presumably on the assumption that, to a Gypsy, anything gypsy is good. There is something to be said for Webster's suggestion; nothing for the suggestion that *rum* derives from dialectal *ram*, 'strong' – for *ram* appears to be, certainly it is recorded, much too late. But I believe that Hotten was right when he derived the adjective *rum*, 'excellent', from *Rome*, presumably in its Italian form *Roma*, which, according to Ernout & Meillet, is 'd'origine sans doute étrusque': Ernout & Meillet omitted to indicate what the Etruscan word was – and what its literary meaning. *Roma* may be cognate with the root that occurs in German *Ruhm*, 'fame' – that old Teutonic radical *hruod*, 'fame', which appears in *Roderick* and *Roger*; or perhaps – less probably? – with Greek, *rhuma*, 'shelter, refuge'. Rome – Tibullus's *Roma aeterna*, Catholics' 'The Eternal City', Edgar Allan Poe's 'the grandeur that was Rome' – Rome in the fifteenth and sixteenth centuries was a monument of architectural grandeur and beauty, a mausoleum of almost mythical power; to the Gypsies, who, either from the Balkans or direct from Egypt, came to Italy in the 1420s and again, more numerously, in the late fifteenth and early sixteenth century, Rome must have seemed, must have been, a miracle of material splendour and a vast museum of history, a storehouse of riches, a notable field for the exercise of their nimble fortune-telling tongues and their adeptly 'conveying' fingers. This fact alone, or this fact conjoined with the fact that in Turkey (a country to which the Gypsies early repaired and where they founded a Turkish Gypsy dialect) 'Roman' was *Rum*, would suffice for the equation of the ideas in 'excellent, splendid, rich, superior, exceedingly clever or skilful' with the Italian *romano* ('Roman'), re-shaped to Gypsy linguistic needs. That is not something I assert, merely a possibility I tentatively suggest.

Booze, like *queer*, is recorded in normal speech long before it appears in cant: but *booze*, like *queer*, owes its nineteenth–twentieth century currency to its presence in cant; and its first appearance in cant may be, probably is, quite independent of its earlier existence. *Booze* is the eighteenth–twentieth-century form of sixteenth–twentieth-century *bouse, bouze, bowse*. The noun apparently derives from the verb: the verb derives from Middle Dutch *bûsen*, 'to tipple': compare Low German *busen*; indeed, *booze* resembles *carouse* in its geographical origin. Kluge obtains the German word from Middle High German *bûs*, 'swelling, tumidity, inflation'; yet I cannot prevent myself from thinking that, but for the missing links, we should take *booze* as being, in its earliest form, cognate with Latin *bibere*, Greek *pinein*, Sanskrit *pibati* (he drinks), and Latin *potus* (adjective), 'having been drunk, having drunk'. The Aryan stem for 'to drink' seems to have been *pi-* or alternatively *po-*: and I suspect that *booze* may ultimately be proved to descend from the *po-* alternative of that stem, rather than from a stem meaning 'tumidity'.

Racket, which so many regard as an Americanism for 'an illicit activity, an illegal trade or enterprise', was English long before it became American. Moreover, it was late eighteenth–mid-nineteenth-century cant before, *ca*. 1860, it became low slang. James Hardy Vaux, who was transported to Australia as a convict, records it in the glossary, compiled in 1810–12, to his *Memoirs* – as a synonym of *lay* (another cant term become slang), a dodge, trick, plan, occupation, 'line' of business, especially when they are illegal or at the least 'shady'. In Pierce Egan's recension (1823) of Grose's *The Vulgar Tongue* we find *be in a racket*, to be privy to an illegality. As *row* (originally cant), a quarrel, derives from *row*, a noisy disturbance, so *racket*, an illegal activity, derives from *racket*, a noise or disturbance; the latter *racket* is probably echoic and comparable, although only semantically, with Greek *thorubos* and perhaps with Latin *clamor*.

To go west, popularized during the War of 1914–1918 in the sense 'to be killed, to die', may owe something to pioneering in North America and certainly owes much to the idea of the sun dying in the west. But not everything. In 1592, Robert Greene, in his *Coney-Catching*, Part II, has this pregnant passage, 'So long the foists (pickpockets) put their vilanie in practise, that Westward they goe, and there solemnly make a rehearsall sermon at tiborne'. From Newgate Prison in east London, condemned criminals *rode up Holborn (Hill)* – compare Ben Jonson's *the heavy hill . . . of Holborn* (1614) – to the gallows at Tyburn, the place of execution for Middlesex from the late twelfth to the latish eighteenth century, the gallows standing at the point where the present Bayswater and Edgware Roads join with Oxford Street: in short, *west* London, the West End.

9

Clichés

═══

IN THE YEAR 1910, O. Henry's *Whirligigs*, a collection of short stories, contained one with the title 'Calloway's Code', based on the 'fact' that one H. B. Calloway, covering the Russo-Japanese war, sent to New York a cablegram written in code. The code was broken by an up-and-coming reporter named Vesey, who had the good sense to remember that newspapermen, like the rest of us, tend to fall back on those well-worn phrases which possess two remarkable virtues. They are readily *understood by even the meanest intelligence* and they cause the writer no pain at all.

Vesey deciphered the cable thus:

Foregone – conclusion	Existing – conditions
Preconcerted – arrangement	Great – White Way
Rash – act	Hotly – contested
Witching – hour of midnight	Brute – force
Goes – without saying	Select – few
Muffled – report	Mooted – question
Rumour – hath it	Parlous – times
Mine – host	Beggars – description
Dark – horse	Ye – correspondent
Silent – majority	Angel – unawares
Unfortunate – pedestrians*	Incontrovertible – fact:
Richmond – in the field	

upon which Vesey comments: 'It's simply newspaper English . . . I've been reporting on the *Enterprise* long enough to know

---

* Mr Vesey afterwards explained that the logical journalistic complement of the word 'unfortunate' was once the word 'victim'. But, since the automobile became so popular, the correct following word is now 'pedestrians'. Of course, in Calloway's code it meant infantry.

it by heart. Old Calloway gives us the cue word, and we use the word that naturally follows it just as we use 'em in the paper. Read it over, and you'll see how pat they drop into their places.' The managing editor playfully jollied Vesey in a few self-chosen words: 'Mr Vesey . . . you have cast a serious reflection upon the literary standards of the paper that employs you. You have also assisted materially in giving us the biggest "beat" of the year.'

Of the ensuing success, O. Henry remarks: 'It was wonderful. And Calloway was wonderful. . . . And Vesey was wonderful. And most wonderful of all are words, and how they make friends one with another, being oft associated, until not even obituary notices do them part.' The ingenious Mr Vesey, hearing that his salary has been raised, ends the story in this satirical manner: 'All right. . . . Every little helps. Say – Mr Scott, which would you say – "We can state without fear of successful contradiction," or, "On the whole it can be safely asserted"?'

Not even Frank Sullivan, in his delectable *New Yorker* skits on clichés, has done better than O. Henry did so many years ago. It's a pity that comparatively few contemporary journalists and authors have read O. Henry – and that so many glibly belittle him without the formality of reading him.

A year after O. Henry came out of prison, Edmund Gosse – who usually talked sense, but who occasionally pontificated – fulminated *in no uncertain terms*, as one might expect of *a citizen of no mean city*, and, *believe it or not*, for the good of consulters of *The Encyclopædia Britannica*: 'All but the obvious motives tend to express themselves no longer as thoughts but as clichés.' Fifty-two years earlier than that, Tennyson had referred to the contemporary literary scene in the effective lines:

> And common is the commonplace
> And vacant chaff well meant for grain.

And almost a century after Tennyson, that well-known London editor James Bone delivered himself of this ambiguous aphorism, 'To make a cliché is to make a classic', which I take to mean, 'Only something wise or witty or otherwise notable can end by

becoming a cliché': a statement demonstrably true of certain kinds
of cliché. (*Of which more anon.*)

The truth, I suspect, lies midway between Frank Binder's
'There is no bigger peril either to thinking or to education than the
popular phrase' (*Dialectic*, 1932) and Frank Whitaker's verdict on
clichés: 'Haste encourages them, but more often they spring from
mental laziness' (an address to the Institute of Journalists, London,
in 1938).

Observant readers will have noticed that I have encroached
upon the domain of suspense-novelists by cheerfully quoting men
either famous or, at the least, distinguished without having
defined the term *cliché*. Let me still further abuse those readers'
patience by mentioning the origin of the word. A *cliché* is 'something stereotyped', from French *clicher*, to stereotype, in the literal
printing sense; it is an echoic word, related to French *claque* and
to English *click* and *clack*.

That this elementary piece of etymology has not been thrown
in for effect or as a jest will appear from the definitions given
by the world's two best dictionaries of English: *The Oxford
English Dictionary* and *Webster's New International Dictionary*.
Whereas the former dismisses a cliché as 'a stereotyped expression,
a commonplace phrase', the latter permits itself a more leisurely
definition, 'A trite phrase that has lost precise meaning by itera-
tion, a hackneyed or stereotyped expression'.

So now you know! – Or do you? Here I must compromise.
Unless you're already authorities upon the subject of clichés – in
which case you won't, unless you're very, very wise, be reading
this article – you will not, for you cannot, have formed more
than a vague idea of the nature and uses of clichés, for I have
neither conscientiously shown the various types nor cited such
examples as would have enabled you to form your own opinions.
(I certainly do not expect you to accept mine.)

But before I can 'go all serious' I must yet be serious. After
more years than I care to remember of noticing British and American
clichés, I have been reluctantly forced to conclude that the addiction to clichés is far commoner than addiction to drugs and that

the immense stock of clichés is common to both the United States and the British Commonwealth. Some clichés are less used in America than in Britain, some less in Britain than in America; but ninety-nine per cent of genuine, indisputable clichés are used in both countries. Indeed, the only All-American cliché I can put my pen on – and even this one isn't all that common in the USA – is the fairly recent *let the chips fall where they may*, which, by its very form, is clearly an educated specimen.

If one passes to the vogue-phrase, one can single out, here and there, a phrase employed in the one, not in the other, country. But these aren't strictly clichés, as may be gathered from the fact that they embody a turn, or a kind, of phrase rather than an expression. For instance, *came the dawn* – used in New York before appearing in London – initiated a group (*came the pay-off, came this, came that, came the other*) best exemplified perhaps by *came the reckoning*, which I've always suspected to be the earliest of them all. The *came the* . . . vogue has gone the way of all such vogues, thank heaven! It was a tiresome, too-literary, rather arty form, but it was worth mentioning, for it indicates one of the main differences between vogue-phrase and cliché: the majority of clichés last for generations, many for a century or even longer. Another difference is that the cliché is more 'human' – easily understood by all. Yet another, the cliché springs from the true, deep soil of language, the vogue-phrase from the top-soil. The cliché, in short, is natural, the vogue-phrase artificial.

But enough of dalliance by the wayside, pleasant though the wayside be, delightful though the dalliance. Consideration of the kinds of cliché will help us to understand its essential nature.

We may roughly classify clichés as belonging to one or other of four groups. It is worth noting that the second group often overlaps the first and that the fourth occasionally overlaps the third; also that the first two groups comprise at least four-fifths of the aggregate. All the same, it is the third and especially the fourth groups which offer the most interest and provide the most fun.

Group One consists of idioms that have become clichés; Group

Two, of other hackneyed phrases. Group Three is formed of stock phrases and familiar quotations from foreign languages, and Group Four of quotations from English and American literature.

'Always define your terms' is a truism in logic, a truism applicable to all discourses and discussions. Do I hear someone ask, What exactly is an idiom? Nobody can give an exact definition. On the one hand, it may safely be stated that an idiom is a turn of phrase, a form of speech, peculiar to a people or a nation; on the other, and in a more particular sense, that it is always a form or a phrase approved by usage, and that sometimes it is a phrase with a total sense different from that of the sum of its parts and not always deducible from an understanding, even a weighing, of those parts. Idioms form an extremely important – an inseparable – part of a language; its very core, its essence, its last resort. But certain idioms have been so widely and so much used, often so indiscriminately used, that they have lost their freshness, their picturesqueness, their point; from being vivid metaphors they have become mere counters, a source of confusion, a recourse of sloppy thinkers. These idiom-clichés are familiar to and understood by everybody whose IQ is higher than that of a moron. They form the stock-in-trade of the morons, who, as often as not, don't firmly grasp their precise general meaning and thus debase them still further. Morons have nothing to say – but how persistently and ardently they say it! Although they propagate a pernicious type of cliché, yet one should charitably forgive them, for they have only one way – a means at once sole and pitiable – of 'making a noise in the world' and that is by making a hell of a lot of noise.

Idiom-clichés themselves are of various kinds: sub-species, as it were. One of the largest is that of the doublets: *dust and ashes* – and *sackcloth and ashes; far and wide; for good and all; by leaps and bounds; much of a muchness* and *six of one and half a dozen of the other; null and void; heart and soul* and *tooth and nail* and *by hook and by crook; ways and means; to pick and choose.*

Then there's the repetition of a word, originally to secure

emphasis, a purpose still vestigially visible in most of these clichés; *again and again* or *time and time again; through and through; share and share alike.* Often the device is more crafty or more literary, as in such alliterations as *bag and baggage, to chop and change, rack and ruin, safe and sound, slow but sure* (or *slow and sure*) – *with all one's might and main;* as in such rhymes as *fair and square* and *high and dry;* and as in such alternatives or complements or opposites as *ever and anon, fast and loose, for love or money, kill or cure, neither here nor there, the long and the short of it.*

Battered similes assault our sensibilities. From the multitude of such similes milling around us, we choose these few: *as steady as a rock* and *as old as the hills* – *as large as life* (occasionally elaborated to . . . *and twice as natural,* which Cuthbert Bede gave us as long ago as 1853) – *as fit as a fiddle* – *as cool as a cucumber.* But among the outworn metaphors, some are almost acceptable, perhaps because they derive either from trades and professions or from domestic life: witness *to know the ropes* and *leave the sinking ship; to stick to one's last; to set one's hand to the plough; to take potluck* and *lead a dog's life* and *to darken* (someone's) *door.*

Group Two consists of non-idiomatic hackneyed phrases: so exhausted with over-use that they can barely hold up their heads for shame. To allow oneself one of these, whether in writing or even in speech, is tantamount to resigning from the human race and to allying oneself with the monkeys and the parrots. Occasionally it may be not merely expedient but wise to heed the cynical dictum, 'If you cannot beat them, join 'em'; but that dictum certainly does not apply to the worst of all four kinds of cliché; here, if anywhere, looms *a fate worse than death.* Somewhere along the way, everyone must *call a halt* and *make a stand* and *resist to the bitter end. Death cometh soon or late,* and usually it comes quickly: but who could bear to live with himself after perpetrating and perpetuating such inanities, such trivialities, such approximations as those in the following list, deliberately drawn up in no particular order and kept mercifully brief – yet not so brief as to encourage the guilty to think they can 'get away with anything'.

[136]

To treat this, the most numerous, group proportionally would be to drive my readers to drink and me to despair. None of us would wish that. Here are a few, with a comment where necessary: *add insult to injury*, which may originally have been a bad pun committed by a good etymologist; *any port in a storm* (nautical); *baptism of fire* (military); *at the eleventh hour* (reprieve); *explore every avenue* (almost the silliest cliché) and *leave no stone unturned* – two of the commonest; *fall on deaf ears; grow no younger; halcyon days* (from an Ancient Greek myth); *imagination runs riot* and *imagination boggles; a moot point* (properly, one for discussion); *nip in the bud* (frosts); *the open road; the picture of health; at the psychological moment* (via French from German; horribly misunderstood and misused); *runs in the blood* (hereditary); *the salt of the earth* (from the New Testament); *sick at heart; skate on thin ice; the (very) soul of honour; the staff of life* (not quite so nauseatingly overworked as it used to be); *a superhuman effort* (compare the candidate *superhuman energy*); *twelve good men and true* (but sometimes not very bright); *venture an opinion* (one of the least offensive); *welcome with open arms* and then *speed the parting guest; you could have knocked me down with a feather* – a fate much too good for the perpetrator.

Some of the political and sociological clichés are so revolting and so often mouthed with such intolerable unction that no conscientious castigator should fail to list a few. Perhaps the following are as objectionable as any: *to leave a* (or *the*) *door open* for further futile committees; *the march of time* (compare the general *How time flies!*); *laying heretical hands upon our imperishable constitution* (far more American than British); *maintain the status quo* (slightly more British than American); *learn from a reliable source*.

Thus we pass, *not without a sigh of relief*, to the Third Group: phrases and quotations from either dead or foreign languages. Only by very well-read people are any Greek phrases used as clichés. But a few Latin phrases do qualify; for instance, *ceteris paribus* (other things being equal) – *de mortuis*, followed by a most eloquent pause that indicates the remainder, *nil nisi bonum*, Of the dead, speak charitably – *deus ex machina* (theatrical in origin) – *in flagrante delicto*, caught right in the act – *longo intervallo*, after a long interval – *mutatis mutandis*, allowing for the necessary changes or modifications – *persona grata* and *pro bono publico*, both familiar to even a Philistine. Of the French, the best known are these: *bête noire* (far too often misspelt), a bugbear; *carte blanche*, a free hand; *cherchez la femme; fait accompli; (un) je ne sais quoi*, something indescribable; *toujours la politesse*.

Of the French quotations properly so called, these two clamour for inclusion: *Nous avons changé tout cela*, as 'way back in 1666, Molière declared, only to be contradicted, in 1849, by Alphonse Karr, *Plus ça change, plus c'est la même chose*, usually misquoted as . . . *plus ça reste la même chose*.

Naturally, the clichés that consist of quotations from British and American authors are so numerous that one *simply doesn't know where to begin*. Fortified by that profession of faith, I list, with a random nonchalance that will very properly infuriate the righteous, a few quotations that stand very high in any right-minded scale of popularity.

Probably the most famous quotation, not only in our two countries but throughout the literate world, is that Shakespearean passage from *Hamlet* which commences: 'To be or not to be: that is the question.' But then, as an enlightened schoolboy once remarked, *Hamlet* is full of quotations. (Nearly as full are *Lear* and *Macbeth* and *Othello*.) But the quotation that deserves to be the best known of all comes, not from English or American literature, but from an English translation from Hebrew. In the Authorized Version or King James's Bible, it reads: 'Be still, and know that I am God' – which lies at the heart of all religion and which has not become a cliché. Another very famous Biblical quotation, this time a notorious cliché, is *Their name is Legion*, utterly misunderstood by nine hundred and ninety-nine in every thousand. Almost as tattered and battered are Milton's *dim religious light* and Keats's *A thing of beauty is a joy for ever*. The oddest quotation-clichés are those which have turned into clichés only in misquotations, such as – to select but one – *When Greek meets Greek*, often completed . . . *then comes the tug-of-war*; what

Nathaniel Lee wrote in 1677 was 'When Greeks joined Greeks [that is, engaged them in battle], then was the tug-of-war'.

Perhaps the only American rivals of those English quotations are several occurring in Longfellow. (We have to omit Benjamin Franklin's proverbs, because proverbs cannot fairly be called clichés.) Clichés in Britain no less than in America are these two from *A Psalm of Life*:

> Tell me not, in mournful numbers,
> Life is but an empty dream!
>
> Life is real! Life is earnest!

Line for line, this Longfellow poem contains more passages that have become clichés than any other poem – than, indeed, any other literary work.

'That's all very well! But are we never to use clichés at all? Aren't they sometimes – well, perhaps not justifiable, but at least excusable?' A fair question.

> To cleesh or not to cleesh: that is the question:
> Whether it is nobler in the mind to suffer
> The dread commonplaces of outrageous morons,
> Or to take pen against a sea of clichés,
> And by opposing end them?
> For who would bear the quipping, boring fools. . . .
> When he himself might his defiance make
> With a bare '*No!* no!'?

To begin with, I'd declare that clichés are never necessary, for nobody is either ethically or legally or, come to that, logically obliged to employ them. I should prefer not to be found dead with one, although I probably shall be; but that doesn't mean to say that I'm such a dim, dull, dedicated, desperate pedant that I won't admit that very often the primary consideration is not stylistic nor even linguistic. Clearly there arise situations, precisely as there exist conditions, in which, whether confronted by peril or some other extreme urgency or harrowed by horror or stricken with grief, one has to say *some*thing: when the sheer need for utterance far outweighs the merely secondary advisability of elegant, or even of lucid, speech; when, indeed, the latter becomes an impropriety, an irrelevance, a stupidity – or worse, an inhumanity. Politicians and other public speakers have been known to justify the cliché by saying that they naturally wish, that they are even bound to, employ phrases that will – or so the optimistic fellows hope – be understood by the entire audience, the implication being that clichés are familiar to everyone. Now and then, warnings have to be given promptly and emphatically; obviously there's no time to search either for the right word and the best phrase, or for clarity and precision, however desirable clarity and precision may be. The clear-minded man, like an able speaker, succeeds better than the man who is neither; yet the latter is at least putting *first things first*, always an admirable rule. Sincerity, after all, is what is needed most: to the sincere, we can and should excuse much.

Perhaps we might summarize the pros and cons for and against clichés in some such way as this. In the interplay of conversation, a cliché is often redeemed by a moue or a shrug or an accomplice-smile: 'There! I've used a cliché. Very careless and humdrum of me, I suppose. But at least you know what I mean.' Intonation, pauses, emphasis, these and other means can invest a cliché-ridden sentence, or set of sentences, with humour and wit, and with realism and trenchancy. In writing, we lack these dramatic, these theatrical, these extraneous aids: we *stand or fall alone*. In writing, the battered simile and the forgotten metaphor may well be ludicrous or inept or repellent; the hackneyed phrase so commonplace that it offends, the idiom so weak that it enfeebles the argument or dulls the description or obscures the statement; the foreign phrase either so inadequate or so out of place that it sets up a misgiving, a doubt, a dissent; the quotation so mauled by the maudlin, so coy in the mouths of the prim, so bombastic in the speech of the pompous, as to be risible, so very common as to lose all distinction, so inept as to fail.

If in doubt, don't!

10

Euphemism and Euphemisms

Substitution of mild or vague expression for harsh or blunt one; expression thus substituted. H. W. and F. G. Fowler.

OF THE NUMEROUS WRITERS who have dealt with this subject, I shall take an assortment chosen for their different nationalities and their varying points of view: an Englishman, an American, an Italian, a Frenchman and a Belgian. They all assume that we know the etymology of the word, which derives from a Greek verb meaning 'to speak favourably'. Greek provides what is perhaps the most famous of all euphemisms: *Eumenides*, the Kindly Ones, for the Furies or Avenging Gods.

Professor Weekley, in *The Romance of Words*, speaks of euphemism as 'that form of speech which avoids calling things by their names' and observes that it results from 'various human instincts which range from religious reverence down to common decency' and, he implies, a good deal lower. He cites two interesting examples of that modesty which leads to much euphemism: 'In 1829 the use of the word *mouchoir*', a handkerchief, 'in a French adaptation of *Othello* caused a riot at the Comédie Française. History repeats itself, for in 1907, a play by J. M. Synge was produced in Dublin, but "the audience broke up in disorder at the word "shift".' *Handkerchief* itself is a euphemism, with the ludicrous literal meaning of hand-cover-head, while *shift* is an earlier euphemism (literally, a change of raiment) for a smock.

Among Americans, Greenough and Kittredge in *Words and Their Ways in English Speech*, Mr H. L. Mencken in *The American Language*, and Professor George McKnight in *English Words and Their Background* have written both thoughtfully and entertainingly on the subject: where so much is good, the last will serve. Professor McKnight stresses the fact that the Greeks and many other races believed – many people still do believe – that 'there is a direct relation between a thing and its name': this belief links intimately with religious and other superstition. He points out that, contrary to a rather general impression, 'one of the most distinctive features of sophisticated speech, as distinguished from unsophisticated speech in our time' – his book appeared in 1923 – 'is the absence of squeamishness and the ready courage to name things directly': since the War of 1914–1918, in fact, it is only the semi-educated and the uneducated who have persisted in consistent euphemism, and, since civilization began, it has always been the 'half-baked' who practise euphemism the most.

The Italian selected is Niceforo,* who relates all ancient euphemism to superstition of some kind or other and implies that a modern, sincerely disclaiming such an origin and alleging modesty or respect or kindness, is nevertheless traditionalist; that, in other words, he unthinkingly preserves what was once either pure superstition or a social usage based on superstition. The Frenchman is M. Henri Bauche, author of that somewhat technical but interesting work, *Le Langage populaire* (1920). He has contributed to the subject chiefly by pointing out that the distinction between the harsh or the gross word and that which is not condemned as such is somewhat arbitrary in all languages; that the harshness or the grossness does not correspond exactly to the picture evoked by the word; that different peoples and different social classes vary considerably, not only at different but at the same periods, on the question of *which* things, as well as *which* words, are to be regarded as objectionable; and that in one restricted but significant group (that of physical intimacy and the sexual parts) the euphemisms are accountable by the fact that, whereas the anatomical terms would be both misplaced and pompously ridiculous, the 'old Roman words' have, by the power of usage, become too gross to be used by the respectable.

Professor Carnoy, of the University of Louvain, in an even more technical and even more readable work, *La Science du Mot*

---

* Alfredo Niceforo: *Le Génie de l'Argot* (1912). His early books were written in his native language; his later, in French.

(1927), has a very important chapter on euphemism and its opposite, dysphemism. Euphemism he neatly defines as discretion,
which does, after all, account for almost every example of euphemism – if we understand 'discretion' in its widest sense. He
shrewdly notes that euphemism is employed not to hide the truth
or the fact or the thing (silence is best for that) but merely to
minimize the painful impression on the listener or the unpleasant
results for the speaker, this latter aspect having never been
adequately treated until Carnoy took it in hand; related to this
latter is the speaker's desire to make a favourable impression. All
this appears in the Professor's classification of the direct causes of
euphemism and the particular reasons for its use, a classification
that I cannot forbear reproducing, though I modify it somewhat.

1. *The desire to adapt oneself to the general sentiment suitable to the
time, place, and other circumstances.* This desire will take one of two
forms: Carnoy notes only the anxiety not to depart from an
elevated or a beautiful style in poetry, oratory, etc., by introducing unseemly or trivial words or metaphors. But, either in very
lowly or very friendly circles, or in addressing children, one may
try to avoid technical or literary words by employing synonyms
that are definitely euphemistic; in conversation with children,
euphemism frequently arises from a modesty that would be
wholly our of place between adults, or a wish to spare children
knowledge that might, to them, be either painful or meaningless.

2. *The effort to enhance the value of what one possesses or of what one
gives.* This is hyperbole, and the relation of hyperbole to euphemism is nowhere so well treated as in McKnight's book already
mentioned. As in *saloon* for a bar, *university* for a technical school,
professor for a teacher or simply an exponent.

3. *Respect for the person addressed, or the desire to impress or please
the person addressed.* Under this heading come titles, the stereotyped
politeness of the professions and of commerce, the calling of a
Jew a *Hebrew,** a negro *a coloured man* (even *gentleman*), any

---

* This is a particularly glaring example, for no decent Jew wants to be called
anything other than *Jew*: why on earth should he? for he has nothing of which to
be ashamed and much to make him proud of his race.

woman a *lady*. Some of the most ridiculous of euphemisms are caused by this desire and this practice; it is, however, to be noticed that such instances of euphemism result not from a desire to impress or to please but from an often mistaken reluctance to offend either the person addressed or perhaps somebody within hearing, as in the ridiculous *dark gentleman* for an Indian of India and in *charlady* for a charwoman. If one is speaking to a person less directly concerned, the avoidance links up with the next group.

4. *The need to diminish, to tone down a painful evocation; to soften tragic news.* That, among civilized peoples and especially in refined circles, is the most frequent of all reasons. Death, above all; but also sickness, madness or idiocy; ruin. *To pass away* or *over, be no more, leave this world, be asleep in the Lord, expire, go west,* and many other terms instead of the simple 'to die'. This tendency has spread to undertakers, their functions, their subjects: *funeral director, obsequies, the loved one* and other atrocities.

5. *Social and Moral Taboos.* In every class, there are actions and objects that are either blameworthy or very intimate, and therefore not mentioned directly in good company. A mild example is drunkenness, which prompts all sorts of euphemisms: *half seas over, elevated, lively, a bit on, happy.* The 'inferior' physical processes and functions afford a stronger and better example. For these, delicacy, reticence, and politeness devise euphemisms as discreet as *to retire* or *pay a visit* or *powder one's nose.* All that relates to sex is heavily veiled: a pregnant woman is *in an interesting condition*; a person lacking in restraint is *fast*; a mistress is a *friend*; the intimacy of marriage becomes *conjugal relations*; 'obscene' becomes *blue* or *hot* or even *frank*.

6. *Superstitious Taboos and Religious Interdictions.* The word is *God*; speech has a mysterious power; the name evokes the thing. These three points of view explain many ancient and modern euphemisms: and the same emotion or attitude, at different stages, is represented by the philosophic concept of the *Logos* and the popular belief implicit in *speak of the devil.* The latter is seen in the old superstition that one must be particularly careful how

one speaks of God, the gods, important persons, the dead; especially with regard to the Deity, this belief survives in such terms as *by golly!*, *by gad!*, *gee-whiz!*, *the deuce!* Superstition may, however, become pure reverence, and reverence of another kind is felt by those truly in love, to whom it dictates a euphemistic vocabulary of intimacy.

These six reasons could be reduced to three: fear, kindness, delicacy, as anyone can see if he examines a list of euphemisms. That point need not be laboured. Yet in euphemism and euphemisms there are certain important features that cannot be ignored.

The need for euphemism is one of the chief causes of synonyms, though it is far from being the only one. Any very general act – to eat, to drink, to walk, to sleep – has a rich synonymy; so has any very usual object – a head, a hand, a house. But when, further, that act or object or condition is not thought respectable or when it is very intimate, then the synonymy becomes richer still. The need – sometimes real, sometimes imagined – for euphemism has led to much verbal ingenuity, rarely beautiful, often clever, sometimes amusing, occasionally morbid.

Euphemism may cause the word it displaces to be forgotten or to become obsolete. Frequently it renders successive synonyms suspect, displeasing, indelicate, immoral or blasphemous. This we see in such words as *lover* and *mistress*, *simple* and *silly*, and, in certain contexts, *weak* and *strong*; an excellent example in French is *fille*. As Weekley has said, 'a euphemism is doomed from its very birth', and as Carnoy has expatiated: 'la vertu adoucissante des termes euphémistiques n'est naturellement pas de très longue durée. Dès que les gens se sont pour de bon habitués à comprendre *B* quand on dit *A*, *A* exprime aussi clairement *B* que le symbole propre à ce dernier. Il faut donc recommencer et aller chercher un nouveau mot qui puisse voiler *B* sans l'obscurcir tout à fait. Dans l'entretemps, *A* s'est définitivement infecté du sens défavorable de *B* et s'est donc *dégradé*.'

Euphemism may be achieved by directing the thought in the desired direction as in *honorarium*, *convey* (to steal), *spend the night with*; by using an extremely vague phrase as in *she made a slip*; by mentioning a significantly concomitant circumstance, as in *remove* (to kill); by being enigmatical or elusive as in *lose the number of one's mess* (to die); by understatement and the negative litotes, as in *have had a glass* (to become drunk) and *it's not too good*; by irony; by employing another language; by reticence, as in *you know where to go*, i.e. 'go to hell!'; and by abbreviation, as in *w.c.* and *T.B.* (more properly *Tb*).

It was in the nineteenth century that euphemism in England and America reached its height. It had gradually increased from the time of the French Revolution until about 1837, and at that pitch it remained for some forty years; nor did a freedom comparable with that of the eighteenth century re-appear until the War of 1914–1918. We have not yet returned to such an absence of euphemism as characterized the Restoration and the late Elizabethan and early Jacobean days. There are few to desire such a return.

All in all, as Mencken observes, 'the Englishman . . . is more plain-spoken than the American, and such terms as *bitch, mare* and *in foal* do not commonly daunt him, largely, perhaps, because of his greater familiarity with country life. . . . The Victorian era saw a great growth of absurd euphemisms in England, but it was in America that the thing was carried farthest. Bartlett* hints that *rooster* came into use in place of *cock* as a matter of delicacy, the latter word having acquired an indecent anatomical significance, and tells us that '. . . even *bull* was banned as too vulgar for refined ears.' (One shudders to think of the repressed dirtiness of mind implicit in these substitutions.) 'In place of it the early purists used *cow-creature, male-cow* and even *gentleman-cow*. *Bitch, ram, boar, stallion, buck* and *sow* went the same way.' Bache† tells us that *pismire* was also banned, *antmire* being substituted for it. *To castrate* became *to alter*. In 1847 the word *chair* was actually barred out and *seat* adopted in its place. Those were the palmy days of euphemism, 'when table-legs were draped'. Women, who became

---

* In his *Dictionary of Americanisms* (1848; revised edition, 1859).
† Richard Bache, *Vulgarisms and Other Errors of Speech* (2nd edition, 1869).

females, were shielded from anything resembling evil: one authority informs us that to mention the word *shirt* in her presence was to insult her; another that *corset* was banned; a third that '*decent* was indecent in the South: no respectable woman was supposed to have any notion of the difference between *decent* and *indecent*'. It was at this period that a wife became *lady*, a leg *limb*, a breast *bosom*,* and *stomach*, as Mencken caustically notes, 'was transformed, by some unfathomable magic, into a euphemism denoting the whole region from the nipples to the pelvic arch'.

The parts of the body, indeed, have suffered gravely from this false modesty; the good English word *belly* is still called stomach; and other instances have just been cited. Moreover, the lewd-minded persons of refinement transferred this abhorrence of anything so unseemly as legs (male or female), belly (likewise), buttocks (likewise), and breast (especially the female breasts) to the garments that lay next to them. For *smock*, as we have seen, *shift* was substituted; when *shift* became indelicate, the French *chemise* was adopted. *Drawers* (women's) became *knickers* or *panties*, and chemise and knickers, considered together, are often termed *lingerie* or *undies* instead of underclothes or underwear: in 1900, apparently, the term was *flannels* or *linen*. So with men: *shirt*, before ladies, was banned; *breeches* became small-clothes or knickerbockers. The male trousers, indeed, had generated a droll synonymy. *Irrepressibles* is the earliest of the genteel euphemisms for breeches (properly coming to just below the knee) or trousers (full length): it dates from 1790. It was shortly followed by *indescribables*, 1794; thirty years later came *ineffables*. In the 1830s arose *unmentionables*, used in America before being brought to England by Dickens, who in the same year (1836) coined *inexplicables*; and, a year later, *unwhisperables*. During 1840–43 three other euphemisms were coined: *innominables*, *indispensables* and

---

* Weekley, in *The Romance of Words*, quotes from Marryat's *Peter Simple* (early 1830s): 'Fate had placed me opposite to a fine turkey. I asked my partner if I should have the pleasure of helping her to a piece of the breast. She looked at me indignantly and said, "Curse your impudence, sar; I wonder where you larn manners. Sar, I take a lilly turkey *bosom*, if you please." '

unutterables. Of all these,* the two that have worn best are *inexpressibles* and, above all, *unmentionables*.

Death, madness, suicide, hanging, prostitution, all have numerous synonyms, mostly euphemisms. Death has already been treated, suicide and hanging we shall omit as being rather too grim. Disease of any kind – the word *disease*, literally discomfort, is itself a euphemism – is nearly always glossed over, especially if it be mental. *Mad* became *crazy*, which became *insane*, which became *lunatic*, which became (*mentally*) *deranged*; *crazy* is now almost as harsh as *mad* and is more harsh than *lunatic* or *insane*; but all these terms have had a long life. Slangy and colloquial euphemisms are (*to have*) *apartments to let, a screw loose, bats in one's belfry,*† *a tile loose, a bee in one's bonnet*, and (*to be*) *batty, cracked, crackers, dippy, dotty, barmy, loopy, loony, strange* or *queer, touched, scatty, not all there, wrong in one's head, off one's rocker* (more usually in the form *go off one's rocker*), *off one's chump* or *head*: slang, it will be observed, is not quite so sensitive on the subject as standard English, but it is rarely cruel.

In Victorian days, prostitution was banned as a theme, and 'to this day', wrote Mencken in 1923, 'the effects of that old reign of terror' (the Comstock Postal Act of precisely fifty years earlier) 'are still with us. We yet use ... such idiotic forms as *red-light district, disorderly house, social disease* and *white slave*. . . . The vice crusaders, if they have accomplished nothing else, have at least forced many of the newspapers to use the honest terms, *syphilis, prostitute* and *venereal disease*.' That holds rather more of the United States than of England, but it is true of both. Since the War of 1914–1918, however, it has been yearly becoming more permissible to speak of *brothel, prostitute, procurer, pimp* and *syphilis*, not that they are ever likely, in Britain or America, to be made general subjects of conversation. The euphemisms for a prostitute are illuminating, and I leave it to my readers to seek the full details in Wyld's *Universal Dictionary*, or in *The Shorter Oxford Dictionary*. Here are

---

* I have collected the terms from Hotten and from Farmer and Henley; the dates from the *OED*.

† Now, *to be bats*.

a few: *anonyma, incognita,* and the obsolete *quaedam; lady of easy virtue* or *accommodating morals* or *more complaisance than virtue; sister of the night* and *street-walker; courtesan; Columbine; gay woman* and *pretty lady* and *perfect lady;* an *unfortunate.* This last is very frequent, and Hotten remarks that whereas Tom Hood used the term 'in its widest and more general sense', this 'modern euphemism' derived from his famous poem *The Bridge of Sighs:*

> One more unfortunate,
> Weary of breath,
> Rashly importunate,
> Gone to her death.

Looking back, I conclude that although it may be weak-minded to employ a euphemism for drunkenness, madness, disease, death (and its analogues), and prostitution, it is a lack of either tact or kindness to force these subjects on those who feel a genuine shrinking, not merely a guilty or sadistic thrill, at their mention; that sexual intimacy is all the better for being respected; that religious matters require no euphemisms; that euphemisms for garments are ridiculous, as are those for non-sexual parts of the body; that perversion is so distasteful to the normal that they naturally avoid talking of it and, if forced to discuss it, are somewhat reticent.

11

What's in a Catch Phrase?

———

B UT WHAT, exactly, is a catch phrase? The standard dictionaries, even the best of them, are singularly inadequate and vague, perhaps because it is easier to define one, not directly but by saying what it is *not* and by offering a few cunningly diversified examples. I sympathize with the lexicographers, for it's extraordinarily difficult to define a catch phrase satisfactorily.

One definition is 'a phrase designed to catch the public fancy' – for instance, a political or an advertising slogan. But I exclude such phrases, unless, as occasionally happens, they achieve a much wider application and a change in significance. As I see it, a catch phrase is roughly – very roughly indeed – a unit of conversation; a phrase originating as a smart or forcible or ironic repartee or comment and becoming an emotional counter with the affective element gradually diminishing. A catch phrase has something in common with a proverbial saying but only rarely anything in common with a fully qualified proverb; a few proverbial sayings began as catch phrases, and a few catch phrases as proverbial sayings. A very famous quotation, provided it be brief, will sometimes lose its quality of quotation and be applied in contexts and senses remote from those of the original. Occasionally a catch phrase becomes a cliché or, if the sense or the application drastically changes, a cliché becomes a catch phrase. Only in a historical dictionary will these nuances and transitions emerge at all clearly. But, in the main, 'once a catch phrase always – until, that is it disappears – a catch phrase'.

From a general consideration of such phrases, three characteristics show up, one being how idiomatic and pithy most of them are; another, how very English, how Anglo-Saxon, the best of them are – they eschew 'fine language' with its Greek and Latin polysyllables; and how very much longer-lived than most people, including the majority of scholars, suppose (or seem to suppose) they are, although, of course, many catch phrases are comparatively short-lived. Only a very few can be classed as ephemeral.

The third feature being the most easily demonstrable, I select three phrases, which are necessarily British, not American: *black's your eye*; *I'll have your guts for garters*; and *hay is for horses*. *Black's your eye* is included in the best dictionaries of proverbs and proverbial sayings. Obviously it isn't fully and properly a proverb, but that it may, either originally or at some later stage of its long history, have been or become a proverbial saying, I shouldn't care to deny; on the other hand, it was certainly, at some period and perhaps always, a catch phrase. Dating from the fifteenth century, or perhaps the fourteenth, it is well attested up to the year 1828, as the late Professor F. P. Wilson's admirable third edition (1970) of *The Oxford Dictionary of English Proverbs* makes clear. The quotations in that and other dictionaries suggest that until some time in the eighteenth century *to say black is your eye* was genuinely a proverbial saying, and that *black's your eye* derives from it and is, no less genuinely, a true catch phrase. The general sense of the saying is 'to imply an adverse criticism of someone' and that of the catch phrase is one of contemptuous defiance or accusation. The phrase is now, I think yet would not swear, obsolete; I do, however, remember its being used as late as the 1920s.

I'll have your guts for garters has probably been current, especially among Cockneys, since the late seventeenth century, for in Robert Greene's *James the Fourth* (c. 1591), at III, ii, occurs the threat, 'I'll make garters of thy guts, thou villain', and an early seventeenth-century parish register records what must be the original form: *I'll have your guts for garter points*, where a *point* is 'a tagged lace or cord' (*OED*) for fastening or attaching one part of clothing to another. The sense ranges from dire to comically ironic threat, and the phrase is now seldom used by those who do not belong to the linguistically privileged world of Cockneys.

A third example of longevity among catch phrases is afforded by *hay is for horses*. In Swift's wonderful recording of educated colloquialism, *Polite Conversation*, published in 1738 but commenced some thirty years earlier, a footman calls to a visitor, '*Hey,* Miss' and witty Miss retorts, '*Hay* is for horses'. The reproof – one of the domestic catch phrases (compare '*she*' *is a cat's mother*) – is still current, although perhaps slightly obsolescent. In the present century, the variant '*ay is for 'orses* – where '*ay* has been prompted by *eh* (in place of exclamatory *hey*) – is very frequent; for instance, it forms the first letter of the Comic Phonetic Alphabet, which, if you remember, continues as '*B* is for honey, *C* is for fish . . .'

Interesting historically, yet still more interesting for other reasons, is *does your mother know you're out?* – dated by Sir Gurney 'Quotations' Benham at *c.* 1840. This predominantly British catch phrase seems to have crossed the Atlantic at tremendous speed, for it occurs, 1840, in one of Thomas Chandler Haliburton's 'Sam Slick' books, *The Attaché*, where the brash young salesman, in New York for the first time, goes to the theatre and is invited behind the scenes; a saucy girl of the chorus line, spotting him for the 'hick' he is, asks him, 'Does your mother know you're out?' Theories about the origin vary, but at least it's almost certainly *not* obstetric. Although undoubtedly obsolescent, it is not, especially among those over sixty, obsolete.

A few further, not too carefully selected, catch phrases will provide enough material for everyone to hit upon a definition satisfactory to himself. *I couldn't care less* became popular in, if I remember correctly, 1940. Its most significant feature is its semantic origin, in that catch phrase of the 1930s, *I couldn't agree more*, for it exemplifies a tendency of such phrases to fall into, and therefore, to follow, a pattern.

Catch phrases of agreement are expectably numerous. One may note the enthusiastic *I'll say it is!*; the synonyms, *you can say that again* or *you can say that twice*, the latter adopted from America but the former perhaps suggested by the much earlier English *say it again!*; the derivative elaboration, *you can say that in spades*, which, because of its specialism and comparative artificiality, was already, in Britain at least, obsolescent by 1970, even though it was adopted only *c.* 1945; and *that makes two of us*, predominantly and originally British, dating from *c.* 1940 and addressed to someone who has just expressed either complete ignorance or considerable bewilderment.

The irony detectable in several of the preceding phrases recurs in, for instance, *that'll be the day*, where *that* is heavily emphasized. It was coined, I believe, late in 1918, and it had, at first, the variant *that'll be the bloody day*; it arose as a soldiers' exclamation and may have been satirical of *der Tag*, the day Germany would conquer Britain or, more generally, that on which Germany would attain her dream place in the sun. The mild and humorous doubt it expresses is no less civilized than endearing.

From these somewhat haphazard comments the intelligent could – and the amiable will – deduce or, at worst, admit that catch phrases, in the mass, may reflect a people's thought-ways and speech-ways and, in many particular examples, possess sociological and historical, as well as linguistic, value.

12

Business English and its Confederates

NOT ALL business English is bad. Far from it. I know a publisher, an editor, a business man, all of whom write admirable
business letters: concise, lucid, pertinent, yet neither so detached
as to be cold nor so dispassionate as to be forbidding. Business
English is gradually improving; the standard is far higher now
than even thirty years ago. The same applies to what I have called
'its confederates' – journalese on one side, officialese on the other.

This improvement in all three branches is due to two main
factors. These are the general movement of all writing, whether
literary or journalistic, official or commercial, the letters of the
educated or those of the semi-educated, away from the pompous
and the ponderous, the elegant and the genteel, a movement in
accord with the changing tempo of civilization; and the particular
advice of certain public benefactors. Of these benefactors the
most influential have perhaps been Sir Arthur Quiller-Couch,
who in 1913 at Cambridge delivered a witty lecture on 'Jargon',
reprinted in 1916, and still available, in *On the Art of Writing*: the
late and much lamented H. W. Fowler, in *A Dictionary of Modern
English Usage*, 1926: A.P., now Sir Alan, Herbert, in *What a
Word!* published in the middle 1930s and often reprinted: Sir
Ernest Gowers in *Plain Words*, 1948, and in *The A.B.C.* of the
same subject, 1951: myself, in *Usage and Abusage*, 1947, and
British and American English since 1900 (in collaboration with John
W. Clark), 1951.

Sir Arthur Quiller-Couch attacked officialese, journalese and
commercialese, as also did H. W. Fowler, Sir Alan Herbert concentrated upon commercialese, with side-glances at the other two
enemies. Sir Ernest Gowers, addressing his fellow Civil Servants,
naturally deals, in the main, with officialese. I have treated of all
three vices.

[154]

But, before considering these three forms of wrongdoing, let us settle the question of nomenclature.

Commercialese, a term formed, like officialese, on the analogy of journalese, has also been called officese, to be avoided because of its similarity to officialese. Commercialese is likewise called business English. Strictly, business English should mean the English used in the transaction of business, but in practice it is mostly regarded as synonymous with commercialese, which is the worst kind of English used in business.

Journalese, itself perhaps on the analogy of Johnsonese (the style of Dr Samuel Johnson when writing in his more ponderous manner), is journalistic English of the worst kind; obviously much journalistic writing is good, some of it very good indeed – good, that is, for its purpose. All writing, whether prose or verse, is to be judged by its suitability to the purpose. A lyric poet does not write like a business man, nor a business man like a poet. A style eminently suitable for one subject may be not merely unsuitable but ludicrous for another. One does not expect an official letter to be written with the wit and charm of a letter by Cowper or Lamb, Wilde or Meredith, Walter Raleigh (the scholar) or George Gordon. The historical style of Gibbon or Macaulay, Froude or Trevelyan, transcends the needs of a reporter describing a street accident.

Officialese is often called official jargon or simply jargon; simply not confusingly, for both journalese and commercialese are equally jargon. In America they call it either Federal prose, humorously Washington Choctaw, that weighty sort of official English which is issued from Washington, and which corresponds to Whitehallese, or gobbledygook, the language of lesser officials and of politicians. Then there is that shocking abortion of English which is perpetrated by official economists: economese.

To generalize about officialese, journalese, commercialese is almost fatally easy. I could write this article without once touching earth. 'Example is better than precept.' Let us look at a few brief examples of each kind of writing before we examine business English in some detail.

When a journalist or an official speaks of *information emanating and transpiring at the highest level* he is using both journalese (*emanating and transpiring*) and officialese (*at the highest level*). He is also very conveniently illustrating a *significant*, or important, and *sinister*, or dangerous tendency: the tendency of journalese to infect the language of officials, and that of officialese to impress journalists. When an official uses *ult.*, *inst.*, *prox.*, he has been contaminated by commercialese. If a business man speaks of *incidents* when he means quarrels, he has been influenced by journalism, and if he says that a certain matter can be decided only *at a higher level* he too has borrowed from the vocabulary of officialdom.

All three classes of person – the official, the journalist, the business man – tend to be influenced by the other two, whichever the other two happen to be. If they all wrote Standard English they would run no such risk. But then, if they all wrote Standard English, there would exist, there could exist, no such things as officialese, journalese, commercialese. This inter-influence is unavoidable. The most we can, in an imperfect world, ask, because the most we can expect, is that the terms proper to officials be left to officials; that journalists should use no more officialise and journalese than their duties oblige them to use; and that business men should ape neither officials nor journalists. Heaven knows, every one of these three classes of person has quite enough to do to keep its own house clean!

Journalese may be exemplified by a quotation that I have used elsewhere. It occurred a little over a century ago, yet it could easily have been written today and will probably be written tomorrow.

'Not withstanding the genuine literary productions that have sprung out of' – at least not, we thankfully notice, *emanated from* – 'the haunts of cotton mills and weaving sheds, they have only here and there penetrated far beyond the immediate neighbourhood that called them into existence' (a Manchester journalist, 1850). Put into ordinary English, the sentence might read: 'Despite the literature that has come from the industrial areas, it has seldom been noticed outside them.'

Officialese we have, every adult of us, encountered at some time or other, especially in the fascinating pages of *How to Fill up Your Form*, the engaging leaflet sent to all those who are so fortunate as to pay income tax: after all, the one thing worse than paying it is *not* having any to pay. This annual bringer of glad tidings has improved both its manners and its English: the same improvement has, I'm told, been remarked in the United States about the corresponding form. But *How to Fill up Your Form* could be further improved. For instance, 'How Profits Are to Be Calculated' is inferior to 'How to Reckon Profits'. Among the 'Expenses which cannot be allowed include' (why not 'Taxable expenses include'?) we find 'Cost of maintaining yourself or your family or payments for any other domestic or private purposes', which might perhaps be rewritten 'Your or your family's living expenses and amusements'. 'No deduction can ordinarily be claimed for the cost of travelling between your residence and your place of employment' might advantageously be changed to 'You cannot claim allowances for the cost of travelling to and from work'. Without being pernickety or hypercritical, a good writer – in short, a clear thinker – could simplify the form and reduce its 'wordage' by at least one-fifth.

Thus, by easy transition, we arrive at commercialese. To list the monstrosities permitted – nay, encouraged – by many business men would be out of place in an essay or even an article. Instead, I shall give an example of the sort of thing still far too common.

Dear Sir,
We are in receipt of your esteemed favour of the 31st ult. with regard to the estimate you require for the packing and removal of your books and other personal effects from your residence at 17 The Willows, Arcana, to your prospective residence at 19 The Oaks, Refuge, on the 20th inst. We take great pleasure in asking you to confirm an arrangement whereby our representative would call on you, on the 4th inst. at 3 p.m., in order to make an inspection of the above mentioned books and effects preliminary to calculating the number of cases we shall need to effect the packing and subsequent removal of same. We trust that the suggested time will suit your

convenience and that we may then be entrusted with the required estimate and enjoy the favour of undertaking this work for you. We shall then issue our quotation and hope to receive an early reply from your good self. The time you suggest for the removal, 8.30 a.m., would be entirely convenient.

    Assuring you of our best attention at all times,
               We beg to remain,
                   Yours faithfully,
                         Burble & Burble, Ltd.

That letter could have been written more briefly and pleasingly in several ways. The following amendment should be taken, not as the best, but merely as preferable to the removers' letter.

Dear Sir,
    Thank you for your letter of May 31. Shall our man call, at 3 p.m., June 4, to estimate the cost? If the quotation suits, our van will call at 8.30 a.m., June 20.
                   Yours faithfully,
                         Burble & Burble, Ltd.

The trouble with much business English is that it is so very inefficient: excessively and exasperatingly wordy; addicted to un-English activities; using an outmoded jargon; unnecessarily obsequious. Be polite, yes! Politeness oils the wheels of trade and commerce. But not grateful for something that may never happen.

To write as these removers did is to waste time and paper, to obscure the salient needs and facts, and to insult the English language, which can be as brief, polished, clear as any other language, French included. Such a letter seems to imply that the writer thinks the other fellow a blithering idiot. For instance, the inquiry must have been received; an estimate has to be made; only if the inquirer approves the estimate and therefore, in effect, confirms the removal, will the van call for the goods.

It is easy, far too easy, to write a letter in which occur all the well-worn terms, all the long-winded phrases, all the substitutes for thinking. Only rarely is it possible, for the circumstances usually need to be detailed, to achieve the brevity that a business acquaintance and I, fired by his example, once achieved. I had overlooked an account long overdue. He sent a dated statement and the accompanying note:

Dear Mr Partridge,
Please!

By return of post I sent a cheque, with a note:

Dear Mr ——,
Herewith.
E— P—

By return, he wrote:

Dear Mr Partridge,
Thanks!

That exchange of notes was, I maintain, business-like; my note admittedly a shade less courteous than his. At the time, he was at the head, as he still is, of a very large business.

Translated into commercialese, the correspondence would have gone something like this:

Dear Sir,
The enclosed statement will show that this debt was incurred almost three years ago. If it is not paid immediately, we shall be forced to take action.
Yours faithfully,
Managing Director.

Dear Sir,
I regret exceedingly that this oversight should have occurred. Herewith please find enclosed my cheque for the amount involved.
Yours faithfully,

Some days later, the cheque having been cleared at the bank:

Dear Sir,

Your favour of the —th received. Please find our receipt enclosed herewith.

Now that the matter has been satisfactorily settled, we should be glad to do business with you again.

We are, Sir,

Yours faithfully,

_____

A fitting reply to that letter would be——. But no, perhaps not.

It is so much easier to use all the well-known conventional phrases and stopgaps – *the matter is receiving our best attention, in due course, with the minimum of delay*, etc. – than to think; so much easier to pad than to prune; so much easier to gorge than to diet. Almost before one realizes it, a letter has got itself written: but that is no way to write a letter of any kind whatsoever. On a busy day, one perhaps shrinks from the effort needed to write one clear, helpful, strictly relevant, comprehensive letter after another. With a little practice, however, one finds that the pleasure derived from writing well lessens the fatigue. Soon, too, the fatigue decreases; soon, indeed, there will be no fatigue.

Admittedly one can hardly be expected to correct faults if one does not know what they are. The chief faults in bad business English are these: 'Passing the buck' – whether directly or indirectly. Blaming general conditions instead of admitting faulty organization within the firm as a whole or one's own particular mistake. This cowardice shows itself also in using such indirect expressions as *it would seem that*, owing to an oversight, a mistake was perhaps made. If the writer of a letter is responsible, let him take the responsibility: ultimately, someone has to take it. Business men are not expected to be supermen. Honesty and sincerity will usually outweigh an error.

Allied to such cowardice is the preference of the passive – *it is believed that*, for *I believe that* – to the active. This tendency often goes so far that a writer uses two or even three passives in one sentence. For instance: '*It is thought* by the management that the work *could not possibly be carried out* in the time *stipulated by you*', instead of 'We think that we could not complete the work in the time you stipulate'.

The preference of long words to short. 'We do not *contemplate* the *possibility* of such an *eventuality*', for 'We do not think that such a thing will happen' or, better, '. . . that this will happen'. *After prolonged consideration* rarely means more than *after much thought*.

The preference of long sentences to short. 'When you have given the matter the attention which we feel it deserves – and we urge you to consider it very carefully indeed, for its importance can hardly be exaggerated – we shall, if you wish to pursue the matter further, be happy to afford you all the assistance within our power' could take the form: 'Please consider the matter carefully. Then, if you wish to go ahead, we shall help as best we can.'

Abstract or, at the best, very vague instead of concrete words and phrases. '*National circumstances* are such as to *necessitate* a comprehensive *alteration* of financial policy and a consequent *reduction* of *capital expenditure* in both the *domestic* and the *foreign market*' – 'Events force us to spend less both at home and abroad'.

And perhaps the worst and most frequent of all faults: the tendency to think that one's correspondent has no memory, doesn't know what he is doing, needs to have every 'i' double-dotted and every 't' double-crossed, and is, in short, a fool.

The remedy is easy. Write as if you believe your correspondent to be intelligent; write as compactly, briefly, simply and directly as you can; keep closely to the point; write as if you are not only responsible for what you write but also responsible for what you do; be polite and pleasant.

13

The Shaggy Dog*

THE 'shaggy dog' story has developed from an idea recorded in literature some 2,400 years ago. As you might expect, the Greeks had a word for it – at least, for the idea: *para prosdokian*, contrary to expectation. The most important feature of 'shaggy dogs' is the unexpectedness of their endings, although that in itself is not enough to make a story 'shaggy'.

The Roman comedy-writers carried on the idea, which forms part of a tradition almost as old as the human race. But to call it a tradition is to understate: the origin of this sort of thing lies in that spirit of mischief which characterizes all such human beings as take neither themselves nor others too seriously. From this spirit of mischief have sprung the catch-story, the epigram, and the tall story. In one sense the 'shaggy dog' forms a special aspect of the catch-story; in another, of the ordinary witty story, exemplified perhaps first in the very ancient Greek example: A pert youth, meeting an old crone driving a small herd, cried, Good morning, mother of asses! – Good morning, my son.

The Greeks were masters of the epigram; the Romans took it from them and, in their turn, passed it to the medieval European scholars. Among the inheritors were Britons. Alexander Pope, another master of the epigram, caused to be engraved on the collar of a dog he presented in 1736 to His Royal Highness, this couplet:

> I am his Highness' dog at Kew;
> Pray tell me, Sir, whose dog are you?

---

* My *The 'Shaggy Dog' Story* – its origin, development and nature, with a few seemly examples – appeared several months after this article was published in *The Sydney Morning Herald*. The book was deliciously illustrated with line-drawings by V. H. Drummond and remains in print.

Another factor in the gradual development of the 'shaggy dog' story was the catch-poem, as written by Oliver Goldsmith, Tom Hood and later practitioners. It was Goldsmith who sang of the mad dog that bit a man, a very touching poem with its mordant conclusion. 'The dog it was that died'. That poem has, with variations, passed into folklore and has even originated the journalistic advice, handed by every conscientious editor to every cub reporter: If a dog bites a man, it's a very ordinary occurrence: if a man bites a dog, it's news.

Passing to the latter half of the nineteenth century, we come to a good example of the folk story, a funny story current the whole world over. I have heard the following story in Australia, New Zealand, England, Scotland; it is, I'm told, known in Canada and South Africa; and wherever it is told it has the proper local setting and is claimed as indigenous. After a long, tiring day, two drovers halted for the night. The simple meal having been eaten in silence by these two strong, silent men, one of them gazed into the starlit distance. 'Horse,' he remarked. Joining him, the other gazed even harder. 'Cow,' he said. The next morning, the first speaker packed his few things. 'Going somewhere?' asked the second. 'Yes; too much so-and-so talk around here.'

Other contributions to the evolution of the catch-story towards the 'shaggy dog' were provided by such diverse literary forms as the limerick:

> There was a young lady of Riga
> Who smiled as she rode on a tiger:
>   They returned from the ride
>   With the lady inside,
> And the smile on the face of the tiger;

as the clerihew, a verse-form invented by Edward Clerihew Bentley:

> What I like about Clive
> Is that he is no longer alive,
> There is a great deal to be said
> For being dead;

and as the tall story, not indeed invented by Americans but certainly perfected by them:

A farmer kept a cow and calf out at pasture. If he wanted them for anything, he rang a bell to call them home. One day he heard a loud noise in the farmyard. Hastening outside, he saw an unusual sight. A swarm of mosquitoes had eaten the cow – and were ringing the bell to call the calf.

A factor even more important was the peculiar twist imparted to catch-stories early in the present century, as in that of the two strangers on a train. One looked up from his newspaper and said, 'Very interesting article here. About ghosts.' – 'All rubbish! I don't believe in that sort of nonsense.' – '*Don't* you?' said the other – and vanished.

Somewhere about 1906 arrived the earliest of all genuine 'shaggy dog' stories. During World War One it was put into uniform and told of a young officer on leave in Paris. It has since received yet other forms, but the essential feature is that a man picks up a letter he cannot read, gets into all sorts of trouble when others read it for him, and finally, just when he is about to solve the mystery, finds that he has lost the letter.

From January 31, 1924, the date of his first broadcast, until shortly before his death in 1941, A. J. Alan, whose real name was Leslie Harrison Lambert, entertained radio listeners with his seemingly artless stories, many of which had something in common with 'shaggy dogs' and one of which, 'The Diver' (broadcast on Christmas Day, 1925), contained the earliest 'shaggy dog' to achieve a vast audience and reputable print; it appeared in *Good Evening, Everyone!* 1928. 'A. J. Alan', a king among broadcasters, did more than anyone else to set the scene for the 'shaggy dog' as we know it today, and his own stories in this kind, embedded within his radio stories, did much to popularize the kind itself. Alan's 'shaggy dogs' had a tremendous influence, despite their fewness; I can remember only two – that of the disgruntled shark in 'The Diver' and that of Hilarion the Goldfish.

The next man to endow the 'shaggy dog' with literary merit was the distinguished American dramatist, novelist and essayist,

Christopher Morley, who in *John Mistletoe*, 1931, told a delightful story of 'a small hairy dog': a story that clearly has influenced the very name of this art-form.

Since those days, the 'shaggy dog' has attracted less of literary, more of public attention. It has strengthened its position in the United States and invaded the British Dominions, where, by the way, the harrowing tale of the young army officer and the mysterious letter had, since 1918 or 1919, been heard from time to time. Its widespread currency and popularity, attested by the fact that highbrows and exclusives try to obtain a reputation for superiority of mind and taste by affecting to despise it and, when they think they can get away with a pose, by pretending to know none, have resulted in an improvement of quality. A good 'shaggy dog' possesses a wittily sudden and unexpected ending, all the more unexpected that the 'lead-in' and the 'lead-up' have had to be leisurely, almost diffuse, and deceptively factual and matter-of-fact; narrative and dialogue mingle skilfully but unnoticeably; no matter how absurd, a 'shaggy dog' must never be silly; and it is clean.

Asked for an example, one is at a disadvantage. So many stories clamour for attention; some are too long; yet the longer are usually – and very naturally – the better. The following stories, though short, do not lack merit.

Travelling by train to London from one of its outer dormitories, a businessman got into a compartment and was amazed to see a middle-aged passenger playing chess with a handsome Newfoundland. The players moved the pieces swiftly and surely. Just before the train pulled in at the London terminus, the game ended, with the dog victorious. 'That's an extraordinary dog, beating you like that – and obviously you're pretty good yourself.' – 'Oh, I don't think he's so hot; I beat him in the two games before that.'

Which reminds me of the American story about a dog carrying on a long and animated conversation with a parrot. It happened in a saloon, and the bartender congratulated the owner of these two gifted creatures. 'Aw, well, I think I ought to tell you, the act's not on the level.' – 'Not on the level! What do you mean?' – 'I mean, not on the level. You see, the dog is a ventriloquist.'

Which resembles the story of that mouse which, standing on the counter in an American bar room, gaily sang 'Annie Laurie'. When another customer offered to buy the mouse, the owner exclaimed, 'You don't have to buy him. Buy me a drink and I'll *give* him to you.' The other man hastily did so, hastily pocketed the mouse, hastily departed. The bartender exclaimed, 'Why did you do a crazy thing like that? Parting with a gold mine!' – 'Don't you believe it. "Annie Laurie" is the only song that mouse *can* sing.'

Which seems to be a suitable note on which to conclude.

PART III

Words

14

The Real McCoy and the Real Mackay

IF YOU WANT to pick a fight in Chicago, just tell a member of either the sporting or the 'sporty' community that the American phrase, *the real McCoy*, originated, as *the real Mackay*, in Britain: if you prefer to be knocked out in Scotland, you have only to tell almost any Scot that the British phrase, *the real Mackay*, is merely an adaptation of *the real McCoy*.

As a repentant sinner, I should like to set forth the evidence available to both parties in this dispute. So far, the case has been rather one-sidedly stated, not only by Americans. I shall examine first the American claims and then the British.

Although *the real McCoy* did not win a place in the main body of the great 1934 recension – known as the second edition – of *Webster's New International Dictionary*, it will be found in the 'New Words' added to later impressions of that edition, thus: '*McCoy, the*. Also, *the real McCoy*. The genuine person or article, the real thing. *Slang, U.S.*' Apparently the original form is *the real McCoy*, and the other a convenient shortening. An earlier lexicographic recording occurs in Godfrey Irwin's *American Tramp and Underworld Slang*, 1931, thus: '*McCoy*. – Neat; good-looking; unusually excellent or genuine.'

In his *Phrase Origins*, 1936, Alfred H. Holt says that *the real McCoy* 'appears to be a ringing tribute to some honest and dependable Irishman of that name, but no candidate for the honor has, I believe, come forward'; there had, in fact, been two claimants proposed, both of them some five years earlier. 'Of course,' he continues, 'it may be ephemeral, but if it should persist, in the sense of something genuine and wholly admirable, people will be asking why we didn't locate Mr McCoy before it was too late.' Well, Mr McCoy is still very much with us. In *A Hog on Ice and other Curious Expressions*, 1950 in Britain but 1948 in America,

Dr Charles Earle Funk has, like Godfrey Irwin before him, attributed the origin to the name of a boxer – whom, in a round or two, we shall meet.

American glossarists and others have variously discovered the origin of *the real McCoy* in the fame of a notorious bootlegger, in that of a cowboy and, especially, in that of a boxer. If the term arose early in the 1920s, it almost certainly owed its existence to the bootlegger; if about 1898–1901, then almost certainly to the boxer. Only if it had arisen later than 1925, would the cowboy have been a serious contender.

In *The Real McCoy*, written in 1930 and published in the following year, Frederick Van de Water has told the story of Bill McCoy, who, 'the founder of Rum Row off New York', was the liquor-running trade's 'most daring and successful exponent' at least, during the period 1921–25; McCoy's illicit career ended in the latter year. What Van de Water has to say is important. Having veraciously remarked that 'the liquor McCoy's ships carried to Rum Row was always the best', the biographer continues, 'His erstwhile associates have epitomized his square crookedness in a phrase that has become part of the nation's slang: "The real McCoy" – signifying all that is best and most genuine. Eventually dictionaries may pick it up' – Godfrey Irwin's book appeared in April, 1931 – 'a verbal monument to one who played a hazardous game daringly and, after his lights, fairly and honestly. I knew the slang long before I met the man'; knew it, apparently, from 1922 or, at latest, 1923; author met subject some time after 1925. It is to be noted that, in the underworld of the 1920s, *the McCoy* denoted genuine distilled spirit (especially whisky) – neither adulterated nor diluted.

That theory, propounded in 1930, has much to be said for it; yet Godfrey Irwin, writing in the same year as Van de Water, had no doubt of the pugilistic origin of the phrase, and he too had been a newspaper man. But let us here interpose a few words about the least probable progenitor, the cowboy. In *The Glasgow Herald* of 27 July 1950, the Editorial Diarist has, under the provocative heading 'The Real Mackay', written: 'We have always felt a peculiarly Scottish resentment when in American films we have heard something referred to as "the real McCoy". Indeed, our admiration for that notable cowboy hero, Tim McCoy, has been shadowed by the feeling that somewhere near Reay he has ancestors who are turning under gravestones engraved "Mackay", restless at the distortion of their honourable patronymic' – a passage that has prompted the well-known columnist Ian Mackay to corroborate his brother Scot thus: 'The fact that the Real McCoy the American cowboy came from Reay suggests that his name is a corruption of Mackay'.

What then of the boxer? In his *American Tramp and Underworld Slang*, Godfrey Irwin attributes *the McCoy* to 'the pugilist, "Kid" McCoy, who was for some time at the head of his class'. 'Kid McCoy' was the boxing name of Norman Selby (1873–1941). He began as a welterweight and in 1896 won the title from Tommy Ryan; outgrowing that weight, he became a middle-weight – one of the best that ever lived; then he fought equally well as a 'cruiserweight' or light-heavyweight; and even as a heavyweight he proved to be formidable. 'Kid McCoy was not really a Heavyweight, although he succeeded in building up until he just exceeded the Cruiserweight limit,' says Robert Haldane in *Giants of the Ring* (1948) – to which I owe most of my information about McCoy.

McCoy, who was at his best *ca*. 1895–1901, owed part of his fame to his reputation of being 'a smart guy', an exceptionally good card-player, notoriously cunning in business, and unscrupulous; he knew what a gaol looked like from the inside. A shrewd judge of men but less shrewd about women – his matrimonial adventures were hardly less notorious than his cunning – he used his wits: and when he retired from the ring, he made good as a film actor. In short, a character.

An oblique tribute is this, paid by Robert Haldane: 'Perhaps the best thing [Tom] Sharkey ever did was to beat Kid McCoy, which, his weight advantage notwithstanding, was a remarkable feat'. Not in the least oblique, however, is this passage, from the same book: 'As a boxer he was unquestionably very good; as a

Heavyweight, his greatest achievement was perhaps to batter Gus Ruhlin to defeat . . . in 1898; he also beat . . . Joe Choinski, Nick Burley and Peter Maher. One of his last fights as a Heavyweight was his defeat by Marvin Hart in 1903; but by then he was past his best'. In 1903, he also lost his light-heavyweight title to Jack Root. His decline as a heavyweight – not, it must be repeated, his true weight – began in 1900, when he lost in five rounds to Jim Corbett after 'a match full of science' (Haldane).

'McCoy,' as the same writer reminds us, 'has a particular claim to our attention, for he was the inventor of the Corkscrew Punch, in which the fist is twisted at the moment of impact. Like Fitz-simmons' Solar Plexus Punch, it requires a practised hand to use it, and, like so many "special inventions", it is rarely seen to-day. But it made McCoy a formidable fighter and a dangerous hitter.'

Between the boxer and the bootlegger lies the claim of being the originator of *the real McCoy*, for the cowboy is not a serious candidate. Frankly, I don't know to which the award should be made: yet, salutarily aware how long a word or a phrase may exist in the vernacular before it attains to the printed page, I should guess that *the real McCoy* arose *ca.* 1899 and therefore from the fame of that picturesque fellow, Kid McCoy. (But I shouldn't feel in the least surprised if that guess were to be proved wrong: we do not possess quite enough lexical evidence to justify an assertion.)

It must have become clear 'to even the meanest intelligence' – as it used to be the very rude fashion to say – that I assume *the real McCoy* to be, in itself, American. It is. But I suspect it to be an American adaptation, suggested by the fame and notoriety of either Kid McCoy or Bill McCoy or possibly both, of the British *the real Mackay*. The adaptation may have been unconscious or, otherwise regarded, an example of folk-etymology.

For some years, I took it for granted that the original phrase was *the real McCoy* and that *the real Mackay* was a British adaptation of the American – an opinion I recorded in the first edition (1937) of *A Dictionary of Slang and Unconventional English*. Then I found that *the real Mackay* had been current in Australia from well before 1903, when Joseph Furphy's novel, *Such Is Life*, appeared, that novel dealing with the last thirty years or so of the nineteenth century – a fact I mention in the third edition (1949) of my dictionary. The Furphy quotation is perhaps worth recording here. 'There was an indescribable something . . . which made us feel that [sheep] station aristocracy to be mere bourgeoisie, and ourselves the real Mackay.'

What clinched the matter – the detail that definitively proved the phrase to have existed much longer than I had thought – was the fact (communicated to me by the Rev. Robert Whyte, M.A., B.D., of Cape Town) that, on December 14, 1886, Robert Louis Stevenson ended a letter thus, 'My dear Colvin, ever yours, The Real Mackay'; and on August 11, 1894, in a letter to James Payn, whom he and Henley had, many years before, confused with John Payne, he referred to Payn as 'the real Mackay'. That Stevenson could, in 1886, use *the real Mackay* as a phrase so familiar that the allusion had no longer to be explained – this points to an existence long antedating the year 1886. The Rev. Robert Whyte, born 1873, in Scotland, recalls it as a childhood memory, a schoolboy memory (George Watson's College), an undergraduate memory (University of Edinburgh); the Editorial Diarist of *The Glasgow Herald* states that the phrase amounts, in his family, to a tradition; Ian Mackay thinks that, in Scotland, 'it has been in use for over 100 years'.

In Scotland, the phrase has long – perhaps always – been associated with whisky. (By the way, convention speaks of *Scotch whisky* and *Irish whiskey*.) The precise reason for that association remains obscure, for the association existed long before any Scotch whisky received the brand-name *the real Mackay*; but it may be noted that, north of Inverness, lies the Mackay country, which is also whisky country. Several Scotch whiskies did receive that name; for instance, the firm of Mackay & Company (established, 1903, in Guernsey) gave it to a whisky in 1908 or 1909, and at least two other firms have bestowed it upon brands of theirs. But the application of *the real Mackay* as the name of a brand of

Scotch whisky, whether as the registered trade mark or informally, was caused by the widespread use of the phrase to mean 'the real thing, the genuine article'; the phrase did not originate in the brand. The popularity of the various *The Real Mackay* brands, however, has probably helped to perpetuate the phrase *the real Mackay*.

After that necessary digression, let us see whether we can establish – at least, as a probability, for in these matters certainty can rarely be achieved – the origin of the phrase itself. Whereas in the United States the contenders are a boxer, a bootlegger and a cowboy, in Scotland they are a bandit, an actor, and the chief of the Clan Mackay.

The least convincing of the three Scottish claimants is a certain bandit who, named Mackay (or MacKay), was on the run. He sheltered with the clan, whose members, individually asked their names, replied 'Mackay', only to be told that they were not the Mackay wanted by the pursuers – not, in fact, the real Mackay. That is a Scottish folk-tale and not, I think 'the real Mackay'.

The actor's claim arose thus. There is, in many parts of Scotland, a tradition that during the 1860s and 1870s the part of the bandit hero, Rob Roy McGregor, in the play or pantomime *Rob Roy*, exceedingly popular in Scotland, was played by a famous, well-liked actor named Mackay. My informant, Mr Alan Mackay of the Guernsey firm of wine merchants, goes on to relate that 'one night he was ill and to the intense indignation of the audience his part was played by an understudy. The audience rose and, amongst other things, shouted at him, "Ye're no the real Mackay" '; Mr Mackay adds, 'It was from this incident the expression came in time to be associated in Scotland with all that is good, genuine and authentic'.

The actor's claim is certainly superior to the bandit's – every intelligent person will, of course, have perceived the possibility that a fusion of folk-tale and anecdote may have taken place – and it is perhaps the one that merits the adjudication *the real Mackay*. I, for one, should not dream of flatly denying its validity; that claim may be correct. But I do ask whether the theatrical incident occurred early enough to have originated the phrase. Historically considered, the chief of the Clan Mackay has, I believe, the soundest claim – a claim set forth, thus concisely and undogmatically, by Mr Ian Mackay ('the real Ian Mackay') in modest, good-natured answer to my not impertinent inquiry.

'I am afraid I don't know much about the famous phrase. . . .

'There is a tradition, however, among the Mackays that the phrase arose from the fact that there are two branches of the clan, the Black Mackays and the Red Mackays, and they were always disputing priority.

'It may be significant also that for many years the chief of the clan Mackay, who is Lord Reay, has lived in Holland and is a very prominent leader of the Dutch nobility. In Holland he is known as the Baron Ophemert. . . . Just before the war he came back to this country and has, I believe, resumed the chieftainship of the clan. He is in fact the Real Mackay, and it is possible that the dispute as to who was the Real Mackay, arose long long ago when his ancestors left Caithness.'

They left Caithness in 1627; or rather, Donald Mackay of Far did so. During a brief visit to Britain in 1628, Donald Mackay was elevated to the peerage with 'the title Lord Reay, to him and his heirs male for ever, bearing name and arms of Mackay' *(Dictionary of National Biography)*. The family name of the 13th Baron Reay of Reay – in Holland, the Baron Mackay van Ophemert – is Aeneas Alexander Mackay; born in 1905 in Holland, he is indeed Chief of the Clan Mackay, a title he resumed before 1938, as we see by *Scottish Biographies*, 1938.

The case for the chief of the clan, with its turbulent early history (see, for example, Robert Mackay's *History of the House and Clan of Mackay*, 1829), is reasonably cogent, without being infallible. If that be the origin, the phrase may go back to the 1620s or 1630s.

We can now draw a tentative pedigree. *The real Mackay* was originally Scottish and is still used more by the Scots than by even the English, who were using it at least as early as the 1880s; it went to Australia, apparently in the 1870s or 1880s, and it probably travelled to North America at the same period. At first it was applied to men; by 1880 at latest, also to things, originally and, in Scotland, still predominantly to Scotch whisky. Such a firm as that of Messrs A. & M. Mackay of Glasgow – a firm that was founded in 1865 – exported its whisky to the United States, its liquor being uncontestably real Mackay; and the numerous Scottish settlers in the USA and Canada kept both the whisky and the phrase very much alive. But whereas in (say) Australia that phrase retained its original form, *the real Mackay*, in the United States it was transformed to *the real McCoy*, first under the impact of the hero-worship that, in the late 1890s, accrued to boxer Kid McCoy and then under that which, in the early 1920s, accrued, at least in New York State, to bootlegger Bill McCoy. Ignorant of *the real Mackay*, certain Britons – but no Scots – have, since about 1930, adopted *the real McCoy*. Recently, however, I have noticed that *the real Mackay* is, in England, gaining ground at the expense of *the real McCoy*; throughout Britain and the Commonwealth of Nations, *the real Mackay* is, in short, the predominant form.

As Americans have an iconoclastic yet unassailable right to *McCoy*, so Britons have a traditional, equally unassailable and almost immemorial right to *Mackay*. To Americans *McCoy*, to Britons *Mackay*, is *the real* form: usage has made them so.*

(Written in August, 1950. A considerably shorter version served as my Christmas card for 1951.)

* Since I wrote this article, Dr M. M. Mathews's scholarly and exciting *Dictionary of Americanisms* has appeared. 'He consulted scholars and experts, from H. L. (*The American Language*) Mencken down to a lifer in a federal prison who told him about *the real McCoy*, from the real Macao – the uncut heroin smuggled in from the Portuguese island colony of Macao': *Time*, 2 April 1951. If one had no other evidence, this plausible theory would be seductive; and, as a guess, it is worth recording. Dr Mathews, however, gives this origin a less whole-hearted support than the writer in *Time* might lead one to suppose.

15

The Etymology of Medicine

'... AND for the purposes of this Act, *medicine* is to be taken in its widest meaning, with no nonsense about medical and surgical wards.'

From its very nature and supreme importance, medicine has a vocabulary rich in words with long and fascinating etymologies or histories, perhaps none more notable than that of *medicine* itself, which came into Middle English from Old French *medecine*, from Latin *medicina*, an *-ina* derivative from *medicus*, a physician, an *-icus* derivative (originally adjectival, from Greek *-ikos*, the commonest of adjectival suffixes) from *medēri*, to heal, a doctor being primarily a healer: and *med-* is that Indo-European base or root *med-*, variant *met-*, which, meaning 'to measure, hence to consider', appears in L *meditari*, to meditate (literally to measure in one's mind), L *metire*, to measure, Old English *metan*, to measure: a doctor can heal a sick person only after he has *measured* the nature and extent of the complaint and then *considered* what is to be done about it. L *medicus*, physician, becomes Italian *medico*, adopted by English as an endearing term of familiar reference, and acquires the adjective *medicalis*, our *medical*.

The general practitioner of medicine has long been known as *doctor*. This sense has triumphed over the two that, in the Middle Ages, co-existed on equal terms: 'doctor of philosophy' and 'doctor of theology', which survive only in academic circles. *Doctor* has come through French from L *doctor*, a teacher, from *docēre*, to teach; among the most famous European physicians, surgeons, professors of medicine, have always been those of Paris. Nowadays, a doctor concerning himself with medicine as opposed to surgery is a *physician*, Middle English – from Old French – *fisicien*, from L *physica*, from Gr *phusikē*, short for *phusikē tekhnē*, skill (hence art and science) in or of Nature, hence natural science, from *phusis*, Nature, from *phuein*, to produce, to cause to emerge into existence and to grow. Like *doctor, physician* has become specialized.

The doctor concerning himself with the treatment of either injury (or deformity) or disease by manual or instrumental – strictly, manual and instrumental – operations, is a *surgeon*, Middle English *surgien*, a contraction of Old French *serurgien*, a variant of *cirurgien*, an *-ien* derivative (compare Old French *fiscien*) from *cirurgie*, variant *serurgie*, from late Latin *chirurgia*, from Greek *kheirourgia*, an *ourgia* (from *ergein*, to work) or working with the *kheir* or hand: a manual skill, indeed the noblest of all manual skills. It is pertinent to recall that the *kheir* is fundamentally 'the grasper' and that *operation*, so ominous a word to many laymen, means simply 'a working', through French from Latin *operatio* ('of an operation' being *operationis*), from *operari*, to work, from *opus*, work, akin to the synonymous Sanskrit *ápas*, probably of religious origin.

All medical *treatment* is designed to *cure* the sufferer. *Treatment* derives from French *traitement*, from *traiter* (whence to *treat*), from Latin *tractare*, to handle, itself the frequentative of *trahere*, to draw or pull along (*tractus*, drawn or pulled); here, as in *surgery*, the emphasis rests upon manual skill. A *cure*, whence 'to *cure*', comes, as the majority of medical terms come, through French: and the Old French *cure* derives from Latin *cura*, anxiety or sorrow, hence care, the trouble one takes, especially for others, from an Indo-European basic word meaning 'to sorrow': *cure*, therefore, expresses that selfless care which characterizes physicians and surgeons alike.

Doctors are often assisted by *nurses*; doctors often work in *hospitals*. Both *nurse* and *hospital* are words possessing a history longer and more interesting and more fundamentally important than that possessed by most of the technicalities of the other professions.

A *nurse*, Middle English from Old French *norice*, or ME *nurice* from OF *nurrice*, draws her name from Late Latin *nutricia*, a nurse, a noun formed from the feminine of the Latin adjective *nutricius*, applied to one who nourishes, especially one who suckles a baby, from *nutrix*, a wet nurse, itself from *nutrire*, to nourish, especially to wet-nurse a baby, to suckle it (compare 'a *nursing* mother)'. The root of *nutrire* is *nu-*, akin to the *na-* of Greek *naein*, to flow, and to the *nau-* of Sanskrit *snauti*, she gives milk, a word containing that prefix *s-* which we see in Greek *stegos*, a roof, a house, as compared with its virtual synonym, *tegos*, and in *snow* (Old English *snaw*) as compared with Latin *niuis*, of snow. Here, then, we find yet another specialization of sense; occurring, this time, so long ago as in Late Latin; that is, during the approximate period AD 180–600.

Hospital has a story rather differently complex from that of *nurse*. In its archaic shortened form *spital*, it occurs in *Spitalfields* and in the now only historically famous *Spital* of London. The word *hospital* came into English from Old French; OF *hospital* represents Medieval Latin *hospitale*, properly the neuter of the Latin adjective *hospitalis*, relating to a *hospes* or guest (in Late Latin, an innkeeper); *hospitale* was apparently suggested by the L *hospitalis domus*, a house for the reception of guests. The medieval monasteries and convents gave food and shelter to travellers and, to the needy, alms and, to the ill, care: the passage from such a 'guest-house' to a hostel for the sick and the aged, thence to a hospital in the modern sense, is linguistically normal and culturally inevitable. In Latin, *hospes* was both the receiver and entertainer of strangers, i.e. the host, and the stranger received, i.e. the guest. *Hospes* (stem *hosp-*, root *hos-*) is intimately related to *hostis* (stem *host-*, root *hos-*), a foreigner or a stranger, hence a guest, with the latter sense gradually ousted by *hospes* and with the equally natural sense 'enemy' simultaneously coming to predominate, so that *hospitalis* means only 'hospitable' and *hostilis* only 'inimical, hostile'. It looks, therefore, as if both *hospes* and *hostis* descend from a remote Indo-European root *hos-*, a stranger. And, by the way, that Medieval Latin *hospitale*, which gave us *hospital*, also gives us, again through Old French, *hostel*, where the 'guest-house' sense has survived, partly because of the 'true hospital' competition set up by *hospital*.

Of the many other medical terms clamouring for inclusion –

one could so easily write a considerable monograph upon medical etymologies! – a few of those for anaesthetics and drugs stand out as perhaps the most generally interesting. *Anaesthetic* (noun from adjective) imitates *aesthetic* and derives from Greek *anaisthētos*, unfelt, hence unfeeling, insensible; *drug*, formerly with a much wider application, comes, through Middle English *drogge*, from Old French *drogue*, itself from Low German *droge vate*, dry vats or casks, in which *droge*, dry, was wrongly thought to refer to the contents. Consequently *drug* is ultimately the same word as *dry* and akin to *drought*.

A very ancient drug is *opium*, a Latin word from Greek *opion*, juice of that poppy which yields opium; from *opos*, any vegetable juice. The more powerful *morphine*, one of those innumerable chemical and medical derivatives in *-ine*, is adopted from French, which takes it from German *Morphin*, which comes, through Latin, from *Morpheus*, the Greek god of dreams (not, as so commonly stated, of sleep), literally 'The Shaper or Fashioner', from the shapes he evokes for the dreamer. *Morpheus* deriving from *morphē*, shape, form. (*Morphia* is a Scientific Latin alteration of the earlier *morphium*, itself from *Morpheus*.) A similarly German-named drug is *heroin*, Ger *Heroin*, properly a trade-name, bestowed, one feels, somewhat arbitrarily in reference to Latin *heroicus*, Greek *hērōikos*, of a hero.

Chloroform merely adapts French *chloroforme*, a compound of *chloro-*, the combining form of *chlorine* (from Greek *khloros*, greenish-yellow or pale-green), and *formyl* (*formic* acid+the chemical suffix *-yl*); *ether*, as an anaesthetic, drastically specializes *ether*, air, the atmosphere, earlier the clear sky, earliest the heavens and derives from Old French *ethere* (modern *éther*), from Latin *aether*, from Greek *aithēr*; *gas*, formerly much quoted as a word made from nothing, first appears, 1670, in a French translation of a work by the Flemish doctor and chemist, Jan van Helmont (1577–1644), who in the original says *Halitum illud gas vocavi, non longe a chao veterum*, 'I have called this exhalation *gas*, not far removed from the *chaos* of the Ancients': Latin *chaos*, from Greek *khaos*, a gaping, empty space.

All those drugs and anaesthetics take their names from Greek. But *penicillin* (chemical suffix *-in*, var. *-ine*) comes from Scientific Latin *Penicillium*, a genus of fungi; *Penicillium* (chemical suffix *-ium*) comes from Latin *penicillus*, an artist's paint-brush, the diminutive of *penis* in its sense 'tail', the fungi being collectively named *Penicillium* from the tufts at the ends of their erect branchlets.

And how better end one's medical troubles than with *penicillin*?

16

Quacks and Quackery

—————

ARLY IN 1931 I strolled into Davis and Orioli's unusual and
E unusually courteous second-hand bookshop in Museum Street,
London, and in a moment of weakness I picked up a little book
with a title that has suggested mine. I really shouldn't have gone
into that shop. . . .

The first edition of this work appeared in 1801; my copy is a
second, dated the next year. The relevant part of the title-page
reads:

THE DETECTOR

OF

QUACKERY;

OR

ANALYSER

OF

MEDICAL, PHILOSOPHICAL, POLITICAL,
DRAMATIC AND LITERARY IMPOSTURE.
COMPREHENDING A SKETCH OF THE MANNERS
OF THE AGE
BY JOHN CORRY.

This descriptive title, of a kind that characterizes the period
1700–1850, quotes from Boileau, the French satirist (1636–1711),
and repeats Addison's famous and invigorating statement: 'I have
endeavoured to make nothing ridiculous that is not in some
measure criminal.'

The general subject of quackery has always been a butt of the
satirists, and much of the best of Juvenal, Pope and Byron deals
with these shameless and impudent pretenders to a knowledge
that, without exception, they claim to be beneficial to mankind.

The very etymology of the subject has a charm. At the heading

'Mountebank' in Professor Ernest Weekley's *More Words Ancient and Modern*, 1927, we find an admirable short article (it reads like a short story), from which I lift some salient facts and which I supplement with a few details gleaned elsewhere. The word *mountebank* reached England in the sixteenth century from the Italian *montimbanco*, which obviously derives from *montar in banco*, to mount on a bench, in the specific sense to mount on the trestle stage at a fair; hence the metaphorical meaning, to play the mountebank. From the beginning, *mountebank* was contemptuous: it was applied to a quack-doctor, who made his mission of healing the more acceptable to the masses by a side-line of conjuring and patter, in which he had the assistance of a clownish servant known as a *zany* (the English form of the pet-abbreviation of the Italian *Giovanni*, John) or as a *merry Andrew*. We now use *mountebank* almost exclusively of a politician who tends to have ideas and is therefore suspect. *Charlatan* is enlisted by modern journalists to describe a doctor, a politician, an inventor, or a preacher. The word is French, and Cotgrave in his famous dictionary of 1611 (which I hope some day to reprint) defines it – I modernize the spelling – as 'a mountebank, a cozening drug-seller, a prattling quack-salver, a tattler, babbler'. The origin in Italian, *ciarlatano*. 'This,' says Professor Weekley, 'has been popularly associated with Italian *ciarlare*, to prattle, which has affected its form. The older word is *ceretano*, originally meaning a vendor of papal indulgences from Cerreto.' Cotgrave used the word *quacksalver*, apparently first printed in 1579 and very common in the seventeenth century; it merely anglicizes the Dutch *Kwakzalver*, which signifies one who disposes of his salves or ointments by his 'gammon and patter', his *quack*, although it is possible that *quack* – or *kwak* – means to work in bungling fashion, as the great *Oxford Dictionary* mentions by way of suggestion. Sewel, the author of an excellent dictionary of the Dutch and English languages in 1708, defines the Dutch verb *quakzalven* as 'to quack as a mountebank', and it is the abbreviated form *quack* which, from 1700 onwards, has been most used of a charlatan doctor and a vendor of bogus medicines and salves.

This word *bogus* was originally American slang, and apparently first in print in 1827; like so many Americanisms, it is an abbreviation: Grose in 1785, in the *Classical Dictionary of the Vulgar Tongue*, has *calibogus*, 'rum and spruce beer, an American beverage'. *Quackery* appears in print first in the title of a book: J. Spinke's *Quackery Unmask'd*, 1709–1711; it is still the best description of an all too frequent abuse, but nowadays *quack medicine* has given way to *patent medicine*, where the sense of *patent* may be compared with that in *patent leather*.

In *The Detector of Quackery* we have a very interesting commentary on the charlatan or quack or mountebank ('itinerant empirics', the author calls them):* 'The mountebank, clothed in green and gold, his sagacious head adorned with a tye-wig, and his beneficent hands filled with boluses [*big pills*] and bottles, ascended the stage, while the merry Andrew, who had collected the people by *sound of trumpet*, approached, and vaulted up beside his master, with whom he entered into a humorous dialogue, and mimicked to the great delight of the surrounding populace. When the witticisms and feats of Mr Merryman† had softened the spectators into universal good humour, the Doctor profited by their hilarity, and dispensed his nostrums to the credulous, who eagerly gave their money for the inestimable *box of pills*, *healing balm*, or *bottle of cordial*, which were indued with virtues not only to cure existing diseases, but even to operate as a kind of *magical preventive* of every ailment.' This reminds us that *nostrum* is from the Latin *noster*, our; that 'our remedy' is always the best is the origin of the word and the cause that, almost from its very inception into English, it has meant a quack medicine or remedy. In eighteenth-century literature one frequently meets with the term *nostrum-monger*; in one of his plays Sheridan asks, 'Will you submit to be cured by a quack nostrum-monger?'

---

* As early as the sixteenth century the word *empiric* designated an untrained 'doctor' or 'surgeon', and it soon came to mean a quack or a charlatan.

† Apparently first recorded by Francis Grose, who, at *Merry Andrew, or Mr Merryman*, reads thus: 'The jack pudding, jester or zany of a mountebank, usually dressed in a parti-coloured coat.'

It is worth noting that John Corry considers that, while there have always been unscrupulous persons preying on the credulity and superstition of the ignorant and the half-wits, the operative origin of quackery, 'which has since been more destructive to mankind than the sword', resides in the theories and writings of Paracelsus, 'who endeavoured to explain the art of healing on chemical principles at once fanciful and illusory'. The celebrated Swiss physician, chemist, and natural philosopher, Paracelsus, who lived from 1490 to 1541, was properly called Philippus Theophrastus von Hohenheim. He had a very large following, both in his lifetime and after his death. His comparatively early death leads Corry to quote an English chronicler, who implies that Paracelsus's claim that he could make man immortal was damaged by his untimely end. In the seventeenth to eighteenth centuries, *Paracelsic(al)* and *Paracelsian* carried a connotation of 'extravagant', 'visionary'; modern writers, beginning with Browning, are more ready to see the good in the man and his doctrines.

Whence *Hogmanay?*

*H*ogmanay, December 31 and notably the evening thereof – a gift made, especially to children, on that day – children's cries of eager demand for or of gratified reception of that gift, hence the joyous celebration of the joyous occasion – this *Hogmanay* (strictly, capitalled only in the calendar sense) has caused, I was going to say more trouble than enough, but that would not be true, for it is the word, not the occasion, which has caused all the trouble among the etymologists in particular, the philologists in general, and among those inquiring laymen (bless 'em) who make the etymologist's life worth living, those unpretentious word-lovers who are welcomed by every true wordman.

In view of the bitter controversies it has caused, we do well to recall that *Hogmanay* was earliest recorded in the following shapes: *Hogmynae*, *ca.* 1680; *Hagmane*, 1693; *Hagmana*, 1694; *Hagman Heigh*, *Hagmenay*, *Hagmenai*, all in 1790; *Hogmanay*, 1792. The variation *hog-*, *hag-*, may be important and is certainly not to be ignored.

The most reputed etymologists have disposed thus of *Hogmanay*: *The Oxford English Dictionary* says 'Of obscure history', makes some valuable comments on earlier theories, and suggests an origin in a dialectal variation of the Old French *aguilanneuf*, New Year's Day, new year's gift; *Webster's New International Dictionary* gives a 'perhaps' support to Oxford's suggestion, which, by the way, owes much to Joseph Wright's proposal in *The English Dialect Dictionary*; and Ernest Weekley, in the 1952 edition of *A Concise Etymological Dictionary of Modern English*, flatly declares, 'Origin unknown'. All three are agreed that the word has not a Celtic origin.

The guesses concerning the origin are so disparate, the material is incongruous and even inconsequent, that, to avoid drowning in a welter of turbulent cross-currents, one is forced to conclude that the simplest way of dealing with the proposed etymologies and of arriving perhaps at a plausible and, pending further evidence, provisional solution, is to ignore the most glaring absurdities and divide the theories into the two main classes: already propounded; only now propounded. The former includes two patently improbable origins, the one in Greek, the other in Spanish, and two French origins, the one all-explanatory but folk-etymological, the other explanatory only in part, but scholarly, and one excellent Latin suggestion; the latter consists of an improbable French and a suggestive Latin origin.

The Greek origin was first put forward in 1694, by Robert Calder in *Scotch Presbyterian Eloquence Display'd*, where he says 'It is ordinary among some plebeians to go about from door to door upon New Year's eve, crying Hagmana, a corrupted word from the Greek Hagia-mana, which signifies the holy month'. Calder probably intends the second element of his Greek word to be phonetic, the usual transliteration being *hagia mēnē* (ἄγια μήνη). One need hardly prove the ineligibility of this guess: to equate an entire month to one day seems, to put it mildly, absurd.

The Spanish guess is of the same low order. The Spanish equivalent, *aguilando* (now *aguinalpo*), has been derived from Latin *calendae*, the first day of the Roman month: but the Spanish probably came from the French and can hardly have originated *hogmanay*. As for the French variant *aguilanleu* and the aphetic *guilanlé* being derived from *calendae*, well . . . !

Of the two French origins already proposed, let us glance at the improbable before passing to the quite probable theory. Even the improbable one has several variants. John Jamieson, in his *An Etymological Dictionary of the Scottish Language*, revised edition, 1880, quotes an anonymous late eighteenth-century philologist as citing a beggars' call '*Au gui menez*, Roi Follet' and a Gaulish Druidic chant '*Au gui l'an neuf*, le Roi vient' and an Aquitaine custom associated with December 31 and emphasizing the cry *Au guy! l'an neuf!* – 'To the mistletoe, the New Year [comes]!' The *OED* has shown the first to be a figment of the imagination and remarked that 'these' and one or two similar 'explanations, with the reference to the *gui* or mistletoe, are now rejected by French scholars as merely "popular etymology".'

The *OED*, however, notes that '*Hogmanay* corresponds exactly in sense and use to Old French *aguilanneuf*'. The form *aguilanneuf* occurs as primary in Godefroy's dictionary of Old French, which gives such variants as *aguillanneuf, aguilleneuf, aguilleneu, aguilanleu, aguillenleu* and the significant *haguilennef* and *haguirenleu*. Godefroy cites also such dialectal forms as the truncated *aguilan* and the aphetic *guilané* and *guilanneu*. *Aguil(l)anneuf* does not occur until 1480; all the early forms end in *-u* or in *-o*; *-f* is probably a learned refashioning.

The *lanneuf* part of *aguil(l)anneuf*, if we accept it, seems clear and constant; it very probably represents *l'an neuf*, the new year, the New Year. 'Although the phonetic difference between *aguillanneuf* and the Scotch word is great, the Norman form *hoguinané* is much closer to *hagmané, hogmanay*, and it cannot be doubted that both the custom and the term are from the French' (*OED*). *Webster* accepts all this; and Joseph Wright's etymology in *The English Dialect Dictionary* antedates and supplements the *OED*, thus: 'Of French origin, Compare Norman dialectal *hoquinano, haguinelo*, cries on New Year's Eve; *hoguilanno* (at Caen), a New Year's gift.'

These three great authorities imply a belief in the validity of the '*lanneuf* (*lanneu*, etc.) = the New Year' solution. Perhaps wisely, they avoid saying anything of the first element *agui* or *hagui*, or *hogui* or *hoqui*. Before dealing with the theory I myself rather fancy, I mention, most apologetically, a momentary idea that came to me: that such forms as *hoguinane, hoquinano*, might possibly point to an origin in *houp à l'an neuf*, which, *houp* being an echoic term (roughly equivalent to *whoop*), might be colloquially translated 'whoops for the New Year!' That, however, is folk-etymology.

Here is a serious proposal.

As we have noticed, the first element of *aguilanneuf*, etc., is *agui-* or *hagui-* on the one hand and, on the other, *hogui-* or *hoqui-*.

These may be combining-forms of the stems *ag-* or, aspirated, *hag-* and of *hog-* or *hoq-*. We may, I think, discard the unaspirated *ag-*: the French dislike aspirates. The conflict between *hag-* and *hog* (or *hoq-*) would disappear if we accepted the supposition that Old French derives the *hag-* forms from the cry: *haec* [dona] *anno novo*, these gifts for the New Year; and the *hog-* (*hoq-*) forms from the alternative or variant cry: *hoc* [donum] *anno novo*, this gift for the New Year. The terminal *g* is merely a thickening of terminal *c*; *hoq-* a mere variant of *hoc-*.

Anyone who knows anything about French, knows that *an neuf* derives, singly and jointly, from Latin *annus novus* (*novus*; not the Classical Latin *nouus*), the new year. The Norman dialectal forms *hoquinano* and *hogilanno* are very important: the latter shows the influence of the *aguilanneuf-haguilennef* type (with medial *l*, probably the *l'* of the French 'the') and both, with their *-an(n)o* ending, indicate at least a possibility of origin either based on or influenced by the Latin dative *anno novo*, for the new year, as we saw it used above in

haec [dona] anno novo,

whence the *hag-*, *haq-* derivatives, and in

hoc [donum] anno novo,

whence the *hog-*, *hoq-* derivatives. There has been an intimate interaction between the Latin *annus novus* and *anno novo* and the French *l'an neuf*. The exact nature and the precise order of such interactions are sometimes impossible to unravel.

That Latin origin may, by some, be preferred to W. W. Skeat's. In his still invaluable work, *An Etymological Dictionary of the English Language* (4th edition, 1910), Skeat includes *hogmanay* in the supplement and closely follows the etymology proposed in 1849 by A. Duméril in *Dictionnaire du Patois Normand*, where, on the evidence of a noted seventeenth-century scholar, Jacques Moisant de Brieux, is quoted an old song, bearing the refrain *hoquinano* (with variant *haquinelo*). Duméril interprets *hoquinano* as *hoc in anno*, in this year. Phonetically that interpretation is fault-less, especially as *hoquinano* could so easily become *hoquinane*, and *hoquinane* become *hoguinane*, which, as Skeat says, would ulti-mately account for *hogmanay*. The sense, however, is inferior. My proposal of *hoc* (donum) *anno novo*, this gift for the New Year, yields better sense; and *hoc anno novo* could develop thus:

> *hocannonovo*
> *hoc'nono; -vo* being naturally dropped
> *hocnano*
> *hognano*
> *hogmano*
> *hogmané*
> *hogmanay.*

On that genial note, I bid such readers as have endured to the end: a bonny *hogmanay* and a happy New Year's Eve and New Year's Day.

18

Familiar Terms of Address

IT IS HARDLY the fashion for Court circles to address one another as *mate, chum, bo,* such terms, except during the War, being confined to the lower classes, if such there be. But almost everybody has read or heard or, if a man, been addressed by one or another of the following: *mate, pal, chum* (English); *bo* or *buddy* (American); *digger* or *cobber* (Australian). Words that mean so much more than the *comrade* and *brother* of internationalism. In fact *comrade* generally indicates that the speaker is envious of the other's position, *brother* that he intends to get some of his money: 'If a man call you "brother", put your hand in your pocket – and keep it there.'

The English terms, naturally enough, are much the oldest, and of these *mate* is centuries the earliest. From either Dutch or Low German, the word at first implied a partaking and sharing of meat. The earliest mention is 1380, when it occurred in a verse romance in the sense of an associate or a companion; in 1440 it is recorded in the invaluable *Promptorium Parvulorum,* the Latin-English dictionary that, since 1840, has attracted two different learned editions; in a chronicle of 1568 we hear that 'the Duke of Yorke and his mates were lodged within the city'. From that date onwards, the word is very general, but in the examples I have given it is not a term of address: in the narrower sense, *mate* is recorded first in 1450 and until about 1600 it was restricted to sailors. In 1859 John Camden Hotten, the lexicographer of slang and the founder of the publishing house of Chatto & Windus, defined it as 'the term a coster or low person applies to a friend, partner, or companion; "me and my mate . . ." is a common phrase with a low Londoner'. Just fifty years later, Dr Henry Bradley remarked: 'now only in working-class use'. In frequent use now in address, but originally equivalent to a dockyard labourer, is *matey*, an elaboration to be found in Marryat a century ago and listed by Hotten in his *Slang Dictionary*. *Mate* itself has had its ups-and-downs. At first dignified, it came, like *companion*, to be used contemptuously; in short, it followed the vicissitudes of its synonym *fellow*. Again, like *companion*, but unlike *fellow*, it has rehabilitated itself, 'always a difficult feat for either a word or a person', as Greenough and Kittredge sagely observe in *Words and their Ways*. Always, however, as *fellow* did at first, *mate* has 'implied friendly association' (Professor Weekley in his delightful *Words Ancient and Modern*). At one time, *messmate* was a variant: 'a companion, a camerade', Grose, 1785. In certain dialects, *mate* has long been a common way of greeting a stranger, and in 1914–18 *mate* and *chum* were, among English soldiers, the most frequent terms of address; in 1914–18 *mate* was also a synonym for friend or comrade, while *be matey* implied 'be a sport, be friendly!'

Both *pal* and *chum* became established in what, roughly, we call the Restoration period. Ultimately cognate with a Sanskrit word for brother, through the Turkish Gypsy *pral*, *plal*, likewise a brother, *pal* comes from the English Gypsy *pal*, originally a brother but derivatively an associate, a mate, hence a friend; it is in print first in 1681–2, in a diocesan record, but it was doubtless used in speech long before that. During the approximate period 1700–1820 the word was under a cloud, for, in the region of cant, it then connoted villainy: an accomplice. In Grose's *Classical Dictionary of the Vulgar Tongue*, we find that *chosen pells* were highwaymen who robbed in pairs, especially in the streets of London; *pell* was a Cockney spelling and pronunciation. In Gypsy also the word had a pejorative meaning in certain contexts, for while, in the glossary of *Romano Lavo-Lil*, *pal* is defined simply as brother and we learn that *pal of the bor* is a hedgehog (literally, brother of the hedge), and while the English Gypsies say *pal* and *pen*, brother, sister, when they address one another, George Borrow remarks on the other hand, that *blowen* signifies 'a sister in debauchery as *pal* denotes a brother in villainy'. As late as Hotten, the word bore the gloss, 'a partner, acquaintance, friend, an accomplice'. It was not until about 1890 that *pal* became respectable. Although it has never been current in dialect, it was common among soldiers during the War to designate a friend or a comrade; but it was rarely used in the vocative except with *old*. Men from Liverpool and Manchester will recall that the four 'city' battalions of those parts were known as *the Pals*, and men from any part will remember that as *matey* connoted a specific act of friendliness, *pally* connoted a temperamental tendency to be companionable or 'chummy'.

Chum attains print for the first time in 1684, when Creech, in his translation of Theocritus, dedicates one of the Idylls 'To my chum Mr Hody of Wadham College'. In 1690 it appears in B.E.'s dictionary of cant. Sir James Murray's pronouncement (1905) that it is 'now chiefly in familiar colloquial use with schoolboys, fellow-students; also with criminals, convicts, etc.', is illuminating when set against Creech and B.E., and piquant when juxtaposed with Dr Johnson's 'a chamber-fellow, a term used in the universities', and Captain Grose's 'a chamber-fellow, particularly at the universities and in prisons'. Although, as *The Oxford Dictionary* says, the derivation of *chum* by abbreviation from *chamber* in *chamber-fellow, chamber-mate*, is unproven, this derivation, as Professor Weekley maintains in his *Etymological Dictionary of Modern English*, is probably correct, for 'this was the age of clipped words (*mob, cit, bam*, etc.)'. By 1860 the word was 'recognised' as meaning an intimate acquaintance. As friend or comrade it was more popular among non-Cockney troops in 1914–18 than either *mate* or *pal*, and it was very frequent indeed as a term of address. (Australians and New Zealanders, in addressing a Tommy, nearly always said *chum*, generally in the Lancashire form, *choom*: apparently the word amused them vastly.) Yet it is not a widespread dialect word. We may however note the pretty Essex custom, not quite obsolete, of calling one's wife *chum* or *oad chum*.

Wholly dialectal is *sorry* or *surry*, which was often heard among Yorkshire and Lancashire troops: 'Give us a light, sorry!', 'Eh, sorry, where are you going?' The word, in various forms, occurs in Irish and in many Northern and Midland dialects. Definitely a corruption of *sirrah* and rarely anything but a vocative. In 1903 the late Joseph Wright, who, greatest of the dialect-lexicographers, was wont to call all his male students (even if aged thirty or more) *lad* and all his girl students *lass*, glossed the word thus: 'A term of contempt or familiarity, especially used to an animal or to a young person of either sex, or by boys among themselves.' But while familiar in tone in War and post-War days, contempt and undue familiarity cannot, after 1914, be laid at its door.

Even among English troops, *digger* came, in 1918, to replace to some extent the typically English vocatives *mate*, *pal*, *chum*, and *sorry*. This was due to the influence of 'the Diggers', the Australian and the New Zealand troops, the former of whom never employed any vocative other than *digger* or *cobber*, the latter than *digger*: that is, among themselves. It is rarely that I can take exception to the comments in Fraser and Gibbons's valuable *Soldier and Sailor Words and Phrases*, but here I must be contradictory and assert that *digger*, though more general, never displaced *cobber* among the Australians. *Digger* dates from the old gold-rush days, but it has not reached *The Oxford Dictionary*;* it is, of course, related to *diggings*, in university slang *digs*, for lodgings, apartment, or house, recorded since 1838. But *digger*, except as a term of address, has never been a synonym of *mate*, *pal*, *chum*, for friend or comrade or companion.

Cobber is much more obscure. In the ordinary way it means a friend, a comrade, and it is used freely in the vocative. It is an Australianism dating from about 1890, but is absent from the dictionaries of Murray, Wright and Weekley, as from the dictionaries of slang, and even from Morris's *Austral English* (1898). There are, however, two possibilities, both offered by Wright's *English Dialect Dictionary*. In Cornish, there is *cobba*, a bungler or a simpleton: this may have migrated to Australia and there, as so often happens with emigrants, have been gradually altered. The other possibility is more likely: that *cobber* has developed from the Suffolk word *cob*, to form a friendship for, to take a liking to. But these theories must, I think, be discarded in favour of the fact that

---

* It does, however, appear in the Supplement (1933), which also admits *cobber*.

both Yiddish and pure Hebrew have the word *chaber*, a comrade, for Australian slang contains a number of Hebrew and some few Yiddish words, for instance *cliner, clinah*, a sweetheart.

No less picturesque are the two American vocatives, *bo* and *buddy*. *Bo* is an abbreviation of *hobo*, a late nineteenth-century Americanism of obscure origin. Most dictionaries define *hobo* as a tramp or a professional tramp, but properly a *hobo* is either 'a tramp who works' or 'a migratory worker, especially one who will work whenever he finds an opportunity', as we see from *The American Tramp and Underworld Slang* of Godfrey Irwin, who suggests a derivation-by-corruption from *homo bonus*; to those who know that many cant words have a learned origin this seems a possibility. In ordinary colloquial use, *bo* is always a term of address; as a non-vocative, it is 'generally applied to all vagrants on railroad property by trainmen, railroad police, and officials' (Irwin).

Buddy is in common use, in reputable as in underworld American slang, for a mate, a companion, a good friend; compare *buddy-up*, to make friends. The word is almost certainly a corruption of the English *butty*, recorded for 1790 in the sense of a fellow-worker or a mate; as a mining middle-man, it comes later; in present-day English, *butty* is a miner's mate and occasionally employed as a vocative, but as a familiar vocative, not confined to miners, it had occurred as early as 1859 in Henry Kingsley's *Geoffrey Hamlyn*. Three derivations have been proposed: *to play booty*, act as confederate, a phrase common enough in the seventeenth and eighteenth centuries (Weekley and *The Oxford Dictionary*); *booty-pal*, Romany for a fellow-workman (Farmer); *buttock*, or rather the shortened *butt* (the latter current in dialect from at least as early as 1800), since in mining especially but also at other jobs men often work back to back (Irwin) – and was not a recent mining novel* called *The Back-to-Backs*? Despite the fact that dialect has the phrase *to play butty*, I 'vote for' the third derivation, for the words are not necessarily identical.

---

* Though here the allusion is not anatomical but architectural.

19

Naming Influences and Fashions

THESE MAY BE incidental and fortuitous, at least in their beginnings; or general and inevitable, although not necessarily more enduring – except in the mass. When I amplify *fashions* as fashions sponsored or unwittingly caused by great persons (saints and kings, mostly) or occasioned by great events (principally wars), and *influences* as influences springing from a widespread movement, religious or cultural, or from a *Zeitgeist*, a 'spirit of the age', a prevalent national atmosphere, I feel – although I know I can cite valid examples – that Ambrose Bierce uttered two profound thoughts when he defined an accident as 'an inevitable occurrence due to the action of immutable natural laws' and logic as 'the art of thinking and reasoning in strict accordance with the limitations and incapacities of the human misunderstanding'.

Wars have given a brief popularity to the names of admirals and generals (see *Arthur*, *Horace*, *Nelson*) and have even originated *Alma* and *Maida* and the happily obsolete *Inkermann*. Important scientific discoveries have resulted in a very few inventors' surnames becoming 'Christians' – but only among the scientifically inclined. Saints, princes, kings and queens have exercised a much wider influence, although often (as with *Albert*) it has been merely a fashion. The saints, as Saints, are revered mostly by Catholics: it is among them that the Saints' names are mainly to be found, though we must except the Apostles' names as being co-extensive with Christianity and therefore hasten to differentiate between religion as such and, on the other hand, creed and theology and hagiolatry, for 'religious' names such as *James*, *John* and *Mark* may fairly be described as 'general and inevitable', whereas *Aloysius* and *Xavier* cannot justifiably be included in that class. Queens and princesses have received due honour, the three best English examples being *Elizabeth, Anne, Victoria*. A very modern instance is *Marina* (q.v. in the dictionary proper). But then, as Professor Ernest Weekley* notes, 'female names are curiously subject to fashion and are apt to "date" their bearers. Just now [1932] nearly all babies of the more important sex are being christened *Jane* or *Ann*, which were decidedly out of fashion a few generations ago. A decade or two earlier *Joan* had a great vogue, a name which, in Shakespeare's time, was equivalent to a kitchen-wench. [*Susan*, to me, is a domestic servant; so also to the poet Gray.] It is symptomatic of the game of general post now being played by the classes and masses that *Susan* is taking refuge, with *Betty, Peggy, Jane* and *Ann*, among the aristocracy, while *Gladys* and *Muriel* reign below stairs. . . . A modern Quarles [early seventeenth century] would be inclined to reverse the names in the line – "Courtly Mildred dies, while country Madge survives".' If princes (Edward the Black Prince, dashing Rupert, brilliant Eugene) have left a lesser mark than kings, they are yet not to be despised. Among kings, we may select, first of all, Arthur and Alfred, both encrusted with legend and patina'd with romance. William the Conqueror's name set a fashion among the aristocracy; as a general name, it belongs to the more permanent class. The kings Edward have added their prestige to that of the princes. The various Henrys,† but especially Henry V (mostly as *Harry*), have so determined fashion that it has become an influence. Charles the Martyr King. The Georges, none more than the two latest of the name: much-loved, quietly effective.

Many of these royal names might, therefore, have fallen into the category of 'general and inevitable', a description that we, in our folly, have reserved for names arising from, or, more accurately, favoured by the time-spirit or by religious‡ and cultural movements.

The embryonic Anglo-Saxon culture was quickened and

---

* *Words and Names*, pp. 83–4.

† See, e.g., Weekley, *Romance of Names*, p. 61.

‡ I have already noted the difficulty of distinguishing between 'religious' names and the names of the Apostolic Saints.

broadened by the Normans. From 1066 to *circa* 1300, England was bi-lingual; the Normans impinged on Wales, Scotland and even Ireland.* Anglo-Saxon and Celtic names were softened or re-shaped by French names, mostly Norman at first but soon Angevin and Provençal as well. The knights and ladies of the Round Table mingled with the paladins and sparse royalties of Charlemagne to introduce a few of their names into the nomenclature of aristocrat and 'learnèd clerk'. Chaucer combined the two cultures as no one before him – and none after.

Chaucer dead, England passed through a very dull period until the sixteenth century, when, for the English, ecclesiastical and legal Latin yielded to Classical Latin; when, in significant addition, the literature of Greece swam, meteor-wise, into the ken of eager Scot and Welshman and Irishman and Englishman. Lydias and Corinnas and Phyllises, Sacharissas and Cecilias and Celias, Chloes and Chlorises sported from the lyric page into the lyric heart; though the Classic males fared badly. Literary influence upon nomenclature has, in the nineteenth and twentieth centuries, been more marked in England, France and the United States than in Germany and even Italy and Spain, but Classical names have thrived less in England than in France and America.

Late in the sixteenth century, there began the Puritan influence, mainly religious – for Milton is half-Classical, half-Puritanical. Biblical names had entered in the wake of the Reformation. The Puritans, however, were not content with *Habbakuk*, *Adam*, *Deborah*, *Sarah*, and other Biblical names: they wanted, and got, such abstractions as *Patience*, *Prudence*, *Faith*, *Charity* and *Mercy*. 'The prominence of a fresh doctrine,' says Charlotte Yonge, 'is shown in . . . the outburst of Scripture names in all Calvinist countries; so that in French pedigrees, Huguenotism may be traced by the Isaacs and other patriarchal apparitions in the genealogy, and Puritanism has in England produced the quaint Old Testament appellations to be found in every parish register.'

* Ireland, by the way, exported certain of her Christian names through those Norwegians who, after settling in Ireland, returned to England. (See especially an article by Dr A. H. Smith in *La Revue Celtique*, vol. XLIV, 1927.)

Whereas the more obscure prophets, judges and kings – and their wives, if any – have fallen into comparative disuse, the abstract virtues have lasted tolerably well.

This usually sober influence was succeeded by a glorified fashion in ambitious names, some of them not a little pretentious. In the eighteenth century and until the late nineteenth, men's names were occasionally portentous (*Adolphus* and other *-us*'es), but it was, as ever, women's names that suffered most, some of them being the sixteenth-century literary prettinesses kept alive beyond their time, others indicating the ravages of such a plague of *-a*'s as went far beyond Classic bounds. *Amelia* and *Augusta* ran riot with others of the same termination.

But, somewhere about 1890, there began a natural reaction towards simplicity, a reaction that became very marked during the war of 1914–18, a reaction that represents something much more deep-rooted than a fashion. We have already seen the reinstatement of *Ann(e)*, *Jane*, *Joan*, *Susan*, *Betty*, *Peggy* and *Madge*. In men's names, the twentieth century shows a marked preference for 'simple *John*, *Henry*, etc., or [for] good old names which were long out of fashion, such as *Roger*, *Michael*, *Peter* and *Anthony*. The hero of the modern novel is usually *Dick*, *Bill*, or *Jim*, the last being almost *de rigueur* in . . . the "thick ear" school of romance. . . . The more ornamental type [of male name] has become derisive' (Weekley, *Words and Names*). *Algernon* and *Archibald*; *Vere* and *Percy*; *Clarence*, *Claud(e)* and *Cuthbert*; *Harold* and *Horace* and *Howard*: these gallant or those stately men, twirling their Regency or Victorian canes, have lost their popularity. But perhaps they have gone to console *Claribella* and *Clarimond*; *Dulcibella*, *Augusta*, *Walburga* and *Wilhelmina*; *Jacintha* and *Josephine*; *Chloris* and *Sacharissa* and *Aminta*; *Malvina* and *Marcellina*; *Euphemia*; *Phyllida* and *Priscilla*; *Robinette*, *Rosalia* and *Rowena*, those fair ladies and beauteous damsels a-languishing that they are ogled no longer, no longer cynosured.

20

Vignettes

===

Burnous, Fez and Turban

ALL THREE WORDS have an Oriental sound; all three words denote headgear, although a burnous is primarily a hooded cloak.

A European woman's turban is an emasculated form of the male headdress worn by Moslems in the Near and Middle East. The word was originally Persian *dulband*, a sash, hence a sash wound into a turban. From Persia it passed to Turkey, where, modified as *dulbend*, it colloquially became *tulbend*, which the French turned into *tulban*, then *turbant*, finally *turban*, soon adopted by the English. From the resemblance of the flower to the headdress, *turban* has given us *tulip*.

The Turks had a headdress of their own, the *fez*, a kind of domed skull-cap made gay with a tassel; not so very long ago, it was often inflicted upon British children. It takes its name from *Fez*, that ancient, both cultural and industrial, Moroccan city which manufactured it.

A *burnous*, often spelt and always pronounced *burnoose*, has a less obvious origin. Speaking of the far-reaching influence of Byzantium, the Grecized eastern capital of the Roman Empire, in the sixth century, A.D., Henry St L. B. Moss, in his fascinating book, *The Birth of the Middle Ages*, says that 'The Berber chieftain was proud to wear the ceremonial *burnous*, the diadems, medals, brooches, and purple boots bestowed upon him in reward for his loyalty'. So the burnous is not originally Oriental, either sartorially or linguistically? Correct! *Burnous* is French for the Arabic *burnus*, but the Arab word merely reshapes either the Latin *byrrus* or *birrus* or the corresponding Greek *burros* or *birros*, credibly related to Latin *burrus*, Greek *purros*, 'fiery red' (from *pur*, fire – whence our *pyre*).

The Latin *birrus* has a diminutive *birrettum*, a cap: and *birrettum* has two notable modern derivatives, the Italian *biretta*, a square cap with three projections, worn by ecclesiastics, and the French *beret*, a round flat cap worn jauntily by all sorts of Frenchmen and tentatively by several sorts of Englishmen.

Pedlars, Palmers, Tramps and Hoboes

These four classes of wanderers 'hit the road'. A *pedlar* or *peddler* is a *pedder*, an itinerant vendor carrying *peds* or baskets: thus the accepted etymology. I suspect that *peddler* is basically identical with *pedestrian*, one who is constantly using his feet (Latin *pedes*). A *palmer* was, medievally, one who, having visited the Holy Land, wore two *palm* leaves, in memory of the palm branches strewn by the multitude in the roadway as Christ triumphantly entered Jerusalem shortly before His crucifixion – an event commemorated by Palm Sunday. Soon *palmer* came to designate any itinerant votary. Some of these votaries, to lessen the expenses of the journey, peddled small goods: hence, *Pedlar* as the inevitable nickname of all men surnamed *Palmer*.

A *tramp* is one who *tramps* about the country; he disdains to work; to beg he certainly is not ashamed; *tramp*, of Teutonic stock, is ultimately akin to *tread*.

What then is a *hobo*? What a *bum*? A *bum* 'bums' or sponges his way through life; the noun comes from the verb, which comes from *bummer*, a loafer, which comes from German *Bummler*, an idler, a loafer; he travels no more than necessary. An experienced American hobo has thus differentiated *tramp, bum, hobo*: 'Bums loafs and sits. Tramps loafs and walks. But a hobo moves and works, and he's clean;' works seasonally, and is usually clean.

The word *hobo* is a mystery. The best-known dictionaries dismiss the word with 'origin unknown'. The four most popular etymologies are: (1) Latin '*homo bonus*', good man; (2) soldiers returning home from the Civil war answered inquiries with '*homeward bound*'; (3) strolling musicians playing the *hautboy* (later, the *oboe*) were the first hoboes; (4) and, as *A Dictionary of*

American English and the present writer think far more likely (Nos 1–3 are patently absurd), *ho, beau!*, later *ho, bo!* in address, where *beau* is an offshoot from *beau*, a dandy, and *beau*, a girl's male escort.

Punctuation and Pugilists

The world's great boxers have not been embarrassingly famous for their punctuation, yet they owe their ability to the same source as that to which we lesser men owe the gentler art of punctuation. And what is more, *pugilist* and *punctuation* derive from the same root or radical or stem: a word meaning 'to sting'. I know that it sounds an unlikely story; yet it's true.

In Latin, 'to sting' is *pungere*; 'stinging' (compare 'a *stinging* blow') is *pungens* (compare *pungency* and *pungent*); 'stung' is *punctus*. Either from *punctus* or from the noun deriving from it (*punctum*, a mark made with a sharp-pointed instrument), comes the Latin *punctuare*, to mark with such dots as can be made with such an instrument, a verb that, by way of its past participle *punctuatus*, yields *punctuatio*, 'such a marking', with the possessive case *punctuationis*, showing how *punctuation* arose. You have only to look at a page of Braille to see the kind of dots I mean.

The Latin for a 'pugilist' is *pugil*, which is akin to *pugnus*, the Latin for a 'fist' and the origin of *pugnacious*: after all, a pugilist or boxer is one who, as his first characteristic, fights – or is supposed to fight – with his fists. A man only *fist*-tall belongs to the fabled race of *pygmies*; the word *pygmy* comes, via Latin, from the Greek *pugmaios*, often written *pygmaios*, itself from *pugmē* or *pygmē*, 'a fist', to which the Latin *pugnus* is clearly related.

The decisive factor common to *punctuation, pugilist, pygmy*, appears in the fact that, in *pugilism* or boxing, the *pugmē* or *pugnus* or *fist* is clenched, so that the knuckles form a ridge, a *pointed* weapon, with which the two opponents act *pugnaciously*, each dealing the other a number of *stinging* blows.

Stormy Weather

Storms, tempests, gales; cyclones, typhoons, hurricanes: such violent disturbances of the weather are picturesquely represented by the very words that denote them.

For instance, a storm sets up a mighty stir: and *storm* is akin to *stir*, both in idea and in sound: they are Germanic. The noun *stir* derives from the verb *stir*; both *stir* and *storm* are related to the Old High German *stören*, to scatter, to destroy – which is precisely what a severe storm will do. *Tempest* has a milder origin, for the Latin *tempestas* originally signified a length of time, hence of weather – good or bad; the bad driving out the good, *tempestas* came to signify bad weather, hence very bad weather, hence stormy weather, hence a storm or tempest. Clearly, *tempestas* derived from Latin *tempus*, time; even in Old French, *tempesté* meant 'time' before it meant 'tempest'.

A *gale*, or tempestuous wind, is admittedly of uncertain origin, but it appears to be related to Old Norse *gala*, to scream, and therefore to *yell*: in a gale, the wind screams and yells, sometimes with a strangely blood-chilling effect.

In 1848, by Henry Piddington in *The Sailor's Horn-Book for the Law of Storms*, a violent rotary storm was named a *cyclone*, either from the Greek *kuklōn*, moving in a circle, or from the Greek *kuklōma*, a serpent's coil. The weather-men's sense of *cyclone*, a system of winds, has given rise to *anti-cyclone*. A tropical cyclone, if it occurs in the China Sea, is called a *typhoon*, strictly from the Cantonese *tai-fung* or great wind, but early influenced by Greek *tuphōn*, whirlwind, typhoon – compare *Tuphōn*, father of the winds – akin to Greek *tuphōs*, vapour or smoke, and therefore, by the way, both to *typhoid* and to *fume*.

But the most interesting of all tempestuous terms is *hurricane*, which, altered from Spanish *huracan*, came from the language of the extinct Tainos in the West Indies; their *huracan* or *hurrican* bore the same meaning, it is true, but also the original meaning 'evil spirit': compare the *hyorcan*, devil, of the Galibis in Northern South America and *Hurakan*, the Guatemalan god of thunder and lightning, a god mentioned in Malcolm Lowry's *Below the Volcano* (1947), one of the three most remarkable novels published since the war. As *typhoon* to *Tuphōn*, so perhaps *hurricane* to *Hurakan*.

PART IV
Dictionaries

Abbreviations

THE FOLLOWING EXTRACTS from dictionaries compiled by Eric Partridge have been reset but retain the editorial style of the original. These abbreviations occur:

A	American	C	century
abbr	abbreviation of	ca	about (the year)
adj	adjective	CanF	Canadian French
adv	adverb	cf	compare
AF	Anglo-French	coll	colloquial(ism)
Alg	Algonquin	contr	contraction
anl	analogous, analogously, analogy	c.p.	catch phrase
anon	anonymous	DAE	Craigie & Hulbert, *Dictionary of American English*
app	apparently		
B.	various works by S. J. Baker, with dates	DAF	*Dictionnaire d'Ancien Français* (1947)
		dial	dialect(al)
B.E.	B.E.'s *Dictionary of the Canting Crew*, ca. 1690	Dor	Doric
B & L	Barrère & Leland, *A Dictionary of Slang, Jargon and Cant*	E	English
		EDD	Wright, *English Dialect Dictionary*
B & P	Brophy & Partridge, *Songs and Slang*	EF	Early Modern French
		EIr	Early Irish
Bu	Bantu	esp	especially
B & W	Bloch & Wartburg, *Dictionnaire Etymologique de la Langue Française*	etym	etymology
		ex	derived from
		extn	extension
		f	female
c	cant (Ch. 30 – about)	F	French

F & H	Farmer & Henley, *Slang and its Analogues*	ML	Medieval Latin
f.a.e.	for anterior etymology	n	noun
fig	figurative(ly)	ob(s)	obsolescent
Fr	French	OC	Old Celtic
freq	frequentative	occ	occasional(ly)
		OE	Old English
Ga	Gaelic	OED	*The Oxford English Dictionary*
gen	generally		
Ger	German	OF	Old French
Gmc	Germanic	OHG	Old High German
Go	Gothic	ON	Old Norse
Gr	Greek	o.o.o.	of obscure origin
Grose	*Dictionary of the Vulgar Tongue*	opp	opposite
		orig	original(ly)
GW	Great War 1914–18	OS	Old Saxon
		o/s	oblique stem
H	Hotten, *The Slang Dictionary*	pa	participial adjective
H & P	Hunt & Pringle, *Service Slang*	para	paragraph
		perh	perhaps
Heb	Hebrew	PGR	Partridge, Granville & Roberts, *A Dictionary of Forces' Slang, 1939–45*
i	intransitive		
IE	Indo-European	pl	plural
imm	immediately	Port	Portuguese
It	Italian	pp(l)	participle
		prob	probably
L	Latin	prop	properly
LGr	Late Greek		
lit	literal(ly)	(q)qv	which see!
Lith	Lithuanian		
LL	Late Latin	r	root
		ref	referring to
m	male		
ME	Middle English	s	slang (Ch. 25 – stem)
MF	Middle French	Sc	Scots
MHG	Middle High German	s.f.	near the end

SE	Standard English	>	become(s)
sem	semantic(s)	=	is equivalent to
		—	(before dates) known
ult	ultimate(ly)		to exist then, and
usu	usually		presumably used some
			years earlier
v	verb		obsolete
var(r)	variant(s)	†	
★	presumed word-		
	form/sense		
	(Chs. 23, 24, cant term)		

D

daily and **diurnal**. *Daily* is 'of or belonging to each day; occurring or done every day; issued or published every day (or every week-day)', as in 'A daily paper comes out call'd The Spectator' (Hearne) and 'The daily labour to gain their daily bread' (Brougham).

In current usage, *diurnal* is the opposite of *nocturnal*, and (of the motion of the heavenly bodies) it = 'performed in or occupying one day', as in 'the planet's diurnal rotation'. *(The O.E.D.)*

dam is incorrect for *damn* (n., v., and interjection); and *damn* ('It's damn cold') is incorrect for *damn'*, short for *damned = damnably*.

damaged is used of things (or, jocularly, of persons); *injured*, of persons and animal life. One should not, for instance, speak of one's teeth as being (or getting) *injured*.

'd and **'ld**. At present, *'d* is used both for *had* ('If I'd only known!') and for *would* ('If he'd only do it!'). Would it not be better to reserve *'d* for *had* and set *'ld* aside for *would*? The adoption of this recommendation (already observed by F. E. Brett Young, who has a sense of style) would at least serve to prevent an occasional ambiguity. According to certain authorities *should* has no shortened form. [American authorities regard *'d* as a colloquial contraction of *had*, *would* and *should*.]

dangerous. See CRITICAL.

dare, misused for *dared* or *dares*. ' "Did you touch the body?" "Oh, no, sir—I daren't" ', John Bude, *The Cheltenham Square Murder*, 1937. 'Fingleton *had* to find a background . . . He dare not appear on an empty stage. Background was essential', Claude Houghton. *Six Lives and a Book*, 1943. 'If she dare, she dare'— for 'If she dare *(subjunctive)*, she dares' *(indicative)*. One would think that, like *must*, *dare* were single-tensed and single-numbered!

data is wrong when it is used for the correct singular, *datum*. 'For this data, much of it routine, it would be sensible to enlist the local authorities'. Milton Propper, *Murder at the Polls*, 1936. [In American English, *data* may be singular or plural. *Webster's*, Krapp, Perrin.]

date back to and **date back from**. Certain newspaper editors, on their style sheets, forbid the former and recommend the latter: actually, both usage and good sense tell us to prefer *date back to* to *date back from*. Style, prompted by economy of words, suggests that *date from* is preferable to either of the phrases under discussion.

daughters-in-law is the correct plural; so *sons-in-law, mothers-in-law, fathers-in-law*, etc.

Day of Rest, the. See SABBATH.

deadly and **deathly**. Both = 'causing death, fatal, mortal', but *deathly* is obsolescent in this sense;

as = 'of or pertaining to death', *deathly* is poetical; indeed, the only general extant sense of *deathly* is 'death-like; as gloomy or still or silent or pale as death', as in 'Poor fellow, he looks deathly; can't last much longer, I fear', 'a deathly silence, stillness, pallor'.

Deadly is a more general word. In addition to the sense noted above, it = (of things) 'poisonous, venomous, pestilential, esp. if to a fatal degree'; in Theology, 'mortal' as opposite to 'venial', as in 'the seven deadly sins'; 'aiming at (or involving an aim) to kill or destroy; implacable; to the death', as in 'The contest . . . becomes sharp and deadly' (Mark Pattison); and 'death-like' ('a deadly faintness'), though in this nuance *deathly* is more usual. (*The O.E.D.*)

deaf and dumb is the adjective; **deaf-mute** the noun.

deal, a, like **a good** (or **great**) **deal,** 'a large quantity or number', is a colloquialism, to be avoided in formal literary language.

deal in; deal with. Weseen neatly epitomizes the distinctions: 'In business we deal *in* commodities and *with* persons, as "They deal chiefly *in* iron products and deal *with* contractors in many cities." In discussion we deal *with* a subject, as "He dealt with all phases of the matter".'

dean and **doyen** are dignified words; therefore do not, as certain journalists use, speak of 'the dean (or doyen) of the caddies', 'the dean (or doyen) of polo-players', and so forth; as applied to a diplomatic corps, they are in place, though *doyen* is here the better term.

dear. See EXPENSIVE.

dear price. See CHEAP PRICE.

deathless, immortal, undying. 'We have not only *immortal*, but also *undying* and *deathless*, expressing different shades of meaning, e.g., we would not speak of *immortal* admiration or affection' (Weekley, *Something about Words*, 1935). Cf. the following examples of correct use from *The O.E.D.*: 'The faith that animals have immaterial and deathless souls', Tyler, *Prim Cult*, 1871. 'The deathless name of Godwina', Freeman, *Norman Conquest*, 1876. 'Our deathlessness is in what we do, not in what we are', G. Meredith, *Rhoda Fleming*, 1865. 'The world itself probably is not immortal', Hume, 1752. 'The undying interest ever felt by kindly women in a question of love or marriage', Mrs Alexander, *Valerie's Fate*, 1885. For *deathless*, see also 'DEADLY and DEATHLY'.

deathlike. See DEADLY.

debar; disbar. The latter is used in only one sense, 'to expel from the bar'; *debar* ('to exclude, prevent, prohibit') is not so used.

debate is misused when it is made synonymous with *doubt, pondering, question,* or *cogitation.* 'He wasted no debates on what had happened, but concentrated on how it had happened, and attempted to guess how his own investigation might be involved', Robert George Dean, *The Sutton Place Murders*, 1936.

decease is the legal synonym of *to die*, which is preferable in every context other than the legal. The same applies to the noun.

decern. See DESCRY.

decimate means only 'to take or destroy one in ten', but is loosely used for 'cut up, wipe out entirely, destroy'.

Name into Word

===

E

eau de cologne (or **Cologne**); **eau de luce** (or **Luce**); **eau de nil** (or **Nil**); or **eau-de-** etc. At Cologne, the commercial centre of Prussia, scent is a favoured industry: the *Kölnische Wasser*, or *eau de Cologne* or 'Cologne water', was originally, as it is still mainly, prepared at Cologne. The German *Köln*, French and English *Cologne*, derives from the Latin *Colonia*, '*the* Roman colony' of Germania.

The second term, *eau de Luce* (a snake-bite antidote, used also as smelling-salts), means 'water—or scent—of Louis', in reference to one of the French kings: compare **fleur-de-luce**. For *eau de Nil*, the colour otherwise known as 'pale green', see the subsidiary list.

Ebenezer. 'How irritating are the janglings of sect against sect, Bethel's cracked note trying to outvoice the plaintive tinkle of Ebenezer,' Ronald Knox, *An Open-Air Pulpit*, 1926. A Nonconformist term, both in this sense 'house of worship' and in the lower-cased sense 'memorial stone' (1 *Samuel*, vii, 12). it springs from the literal meaning of the Hebrew masculine name: *eben-ha-'ezer*, 'the stone of help'.

Cf. **bethel** and **bethesda**.

Hence, in the U.S.A., *set-up (one's) Ebenezer*, 'to make up one's mind firmly'; hence, too, *ebenezer*, 'anger, temper'—slang of ca. 1820–60. (DAE.)

écossaise is short for *danse écossaise*, 'Scottish dance'. But on this tricky subject, it is mere commonsense to cite, not an ordinary dictionary but that eminent musicologist, Dr Percy Scholes, who himself cites a great Scottish musician, Sir Alexander Mackenzie, as saying 'It is difficult to believe that the *Ecossaise* is of Scottish origin, for it bears no resemblance either to the strathspey or to the reel . . . which solely represent the dance music of Scotland,' and himself continues, 'The fact of a French name being used would seem to point to an origin in the ball-rooms of Paris' (in the late 18th Century).

edam. 'The cheese' of Holland 'is made chiefly west of the Zuider Zee, e.g. at Alkmaar and Edam, and the butter chiefly east of it, e.g. at Gröningen and Zwolle,' Lionel W. Lyde, *Man and His Markets*, 1896.

This cheese, yellow-hued (with a dark-red outside) and fine-flavoured, was made originally at, and still in the district around, Edam, a village eleven miles north-east by north of Amsterdam.

Eden. Either as *the Garden of Eden* or simply as *Eden*, the term has come to possess, beside its literal meaning, the sense 'an earthly paradise; a scene, a life, of much felicity; a realized Utopia—with the emphasis on personal happiness rather than on the common weal'.

For a witty commentary, see the first two or three pages of Rose Macaulay's light satirical novel, *Going Abroad*, 1934.

'Here through many an hour of rapt reading of poetry she had returned to Eden', Hugh I'Anson Fausset, *Between the Tides*, 1942.

In Hebrew, *eden* means 'pleasure, delight': 'Paradise is a place lying in the eastern parts, whose name is translated out of the Greek into Latin as *hortus* (i.e. garden)'—some scholars render *eden* as 'orchard'. 'It is called in the hebrew tongue Eden, which is translated in our language as *Deliciae* (i.e. place of luxury and delight). Uniting these two gives us Garden of Delight,' Isidore of Seville, who flourished ca. A.D. 600–36. (With thanks to G. H. T. Kimble, *Geography in the Middle Ages*, 1938.)

Egeria has come to be equated with 'a gracious woman counsellor of much wisdom and not a little charm'. In Roman mythology, she was the goddess of fountains: near the Porta Capena of Rome, she had a sacred spring, where, by night, she met King Numa and gave him much sage advice: there has been among godless moderns, a tendency to surmise that she bestowed more than advice, yet this cynicism may have arisen from the fact that, according to one legend, she was Numa's wife.

The name may derive from Latin *egerere*, 'to bear'; for Egeria was also the goddess of childbirth. More probably Etruscan.

It is worth noting that of the four inspiring mistresses known in legend, history, literature, only Egeria belongs to mythology—Roman mythology; Beatrice is historical—Italy of the 13th Century; Dulcinea is imaginary and Spanish; Aspasia, through Pericles, forms part of Greek history of the 5th century B.C.

Compare **Beatrice** and **Dulcinea**; contrast (and compare) **Aspasia.**

Eldorado (strictly, **El Dorado**); or, as a genuine Common Noun, *eldorado*. 'Four-wheeled wagons . . ., superb stone vessels, golden daggers, spears and axes of electrum (gold-silver alloy), lovely miniature animals of gold, soldiers' helmets of copper, curious inlaid gaming-boards, beads and ornaments of every description are amongst the . . . precious objects yielded in staggering profusion by this El Dorado of the dead' (the Royal Cemetery at Ur), Patrick Carleton, *Buried Empires*, 1939.

Eldorado (Spanish, 'the golden'; strictly, 'the gilded'), 'legendary country of tropical America, which early explorers believed, according to native rumours, to lie in different parts of the vast region between the Amazon and the Orinoco. In the centre of this country stood, according to tradition, a city with roofs of gold, known as *Manoa del Dorado*' (George Chisholm, *Gazetteer*). Some very interesting, though cursory, information on the medieval phase of the El Dorado legends is to be found in G. H. T. Kimble, *Geography in the Middle Ages*, 1938.

elacampane is the plant known also as horse-heal. The word comes by metathesis from Medieval Latin *enula campana*; in Classical Latin, *enula* is *inula*, which means the plant 'elecampane'. Why, then, the *campane* element of *elecampane*? Probably it represents *campana*, which signifies either 'of the fields' or 'Campanian' (of the Campania in Italy).

23

A Dictionary of the Underworld

G

*G. One thousand dollars: 1928, John O'Connor, *Broadway Racketeers.* 'They had me in the bag for nearly ten G's before I pulled the string and let the joint go blooey'; 1930, Burke, who spells it *gee*: 1931, Godfrey Irwin; 1931, Damon Runyon, *Guys and Dolls*; Nov. 18, 1933, *Flynn's*; 1934, Convict; June 6, 1936, *Flynn's*, George Bruce; 1936, Charles F. Coe, *G-Man*; Oct. 9, 1937, *Flynn's*, Fred C. Painton; extant. I.e., '*grand*' (q.v.).

*G(-)guy is synonymous with **G man**: ca. 1925-36, then journalistic s. *Flynn's*, Aug. 24, 1935, Howard McLellan, 'I Am a Public Enemy'.

*g.m. Gone midnight: Jan. 16, 1926, *Flynn's*. 'About three, g.m., we got ditched in some hick burg'; slightly ob.

*G man, 'a Government agent' —a Federal officer, may orig. (ca. 1922) have been c. (Fred D. Pasley, *Al Capone*, 1931.)

*G.O.M. Morphine: drug addicts': since ca. 1925. BVB. 1942. I.e., 'God's own *medicine*': cf. **God's medicine.**

*G rap. 'Charge made by the federal officers,' Edwin H. Sutherland, *The Professional Thief*, 1937: since ca. 1932. Cf. **G man.**

gab, 'mouth', hence 'loquacity', is not c. but orig. and largely dial. It must, however, be admitted that in C. 18-early 19, it was very frequently used in the English underworld; and in 1904, No. 1500, in his *Life in Sing Sing*, claimed it as American c. A variant of **gob.**

gab, blow the. 'To confess, or peach': 1785, Grose; 1834, Ainsworth: † by 1850, the phrase being superseded by *blow the gaff.* Here *gab* = mouth or, derivatively, loquacity.

gab(-)string, a bridle; low s., not c. Grose, 1785.

gabbling dommerar (or **-er**). A pretended *dumb* man who mouths *gabblingly*: 1608, Dekker, *The Belman of London*, 'In another troope are *Gabling Domerers*'; † by 1690. See **dommerar.**

*gabbo. A talkative person: convicts': 1934, Rose: extant. Ex:—

*gabby. 'A gossip; a tale-bearer [in prison]'; No. 1500, *Life in Sing Sing*, 1904; by 1915, s. Ex English dial. *gabby*, 'loquacious; esp., too loquacious'.

gad. A shirt: tramps': C. 20. Jules Manchon, *Le Slang*, 1923. A Romany word; cf. Hindi *gat*, 'apparel'.

gad the hoof, 'to go without shoes', may orig. (— 1839) have been beggars' c., as its occurrence in Brandon's glossary suggests; slightly more prob., however, it was always low s. Perhaps suggested by **pad the hoof.**

gadgie (or **-y**), **gadjie** (or **-y**). A husband; a lover: tramps': C. 20. John Worby, *The Other Half*, 1937.

Adopted ex Romany *gaujo, gauger*, 'a stranger', perhaps via North Country *gadgy*, C. 20 c. or low s. for 'a man'.

gaff, n. A fair: 1753, John Poulter, *Discoveries* (see quot'n at **buss**): 1797, Potter; 1809, Andrewes; 1811, *Lexicon Balatronicum*, 'The drop coves maced the joskins at the gaff'; 1812, J. H. Vaux; 1821, D. Haggart; 1823, Bee; 1848, *Sinks of London*; 1859. Matsell (*Vocabulum*: U.S.A.): 1860, H. 2nd ed.; by 1880, showmen's s. Of obscure origin, *gaff*, 'a fair' (with its noise), is prob. cognate with *gab*, 'much or loud talk'.—2. 'A meeting of gamblers for the purpose of play': 1812, J. H. Vaux; app. † by 1890. Ex sense 1.—3. 'Any public place of amusement is liable to be called *the gaff*, when spoken of in *flash* company who know to what it alludes' (whence Cockney s. *penny gaff*, a cheap theatre or music-hall): 1812, J. H. Vaux; by 1855, low s. Ex sense 1.—4. 'A ring worn on the fore-finger of the dealer' at cards = and used in order to deal specific cards to this or that person: U.S. card-sharpers'; ca. 1830–65: 1859, Matsell. Prob. ex S.E. *gaff*, a steel hook, or the fighting cock's artificial spur.—5. A pretence; an imposture: convicts': 1877, *Five Years' Penal Servitude*; 1889, B & L; 1893. F & H; by 1920, †. Perhaps ex sense 4.—6. 'Mental or physical punishment,' No. 1500, *Life in Sing Sing*, 1904: U.S.A.: by 1929 it had merged with, or rather it had > sense 8.—7. 'Means of making player lose or win at will on . . . a "skin game".' Irving Baltimore, 'About Carnival and Pitchment' in *The Editor*, Dec. 2, 1916: U.S.A. (and Canada): rather showmen's s.

than c.—8. 'Police examination or interrogation,' W. R. Burnett, *Little Caesar*, 1929; extant. Perhaps ex sense 7, but prob. ex the gaff used in fishing.—9. (Prob. ex sense 3.) A house; a room: one's abode, one's 'place': 1932, G. Scott Moncrieff, *Café Bar*; 1934, Axel Bracey, *School for Scoundrels*; 1935, George Ingram, *Cockney Cavalcade*; 1935, David Hume; 1937, Charles Prior, *So I Wrote It*; 1938, James Curtis, *They Drive by Night*; 1939, G. Ingram, *Welded Lives*; 1943, Black; extant.—10. Hence (?), a shop: 1932. Arthur Gardner, 'Any sort of building'; 1935, R. Thurston Hopkins, *Life and Death at the Old Bailey*; 1935, George Ingram, *Stir Train*; 1936, G. Ingram, *The Muffled Man*; 1938, James Curtis, *They Drive by Night*; 1943, Black; extant.—11. (Ex sense 1.) A race-meeting: racecourse underworld: late C. 19–20. Michael Fane, *Racecourse Swindles*, 1936.—12. Synonym of **gimick**, 4: U.S.A.; since ca. 1925. Cf. senses 6, 7, 8.—13. (Ex 9 and 10.) 'A place chosen for a robbery, or the "job" itself,' John Worby, *Spiv's Progress*, 1939: since the 1920's. David Hume, 1935; James Curtis, 1936.

gaff, v. 'To game by tossing up halfpence': 1811, *Lexicon Balatronicum*; 1812, J. H. Vaux, To gamble with cards, dice, &c., or to toss up'; 1823, Bee; 1848, *Sinks of London Laid Open*; 1849, Alex. Harris, *The Emigrant Family* (Australia); 1857, Snowden's *Magistrate's Assistant*, 3rd ed., where it is misprinted *goff*; by 1864 (H. 3rd ed.: *gaffing*), it was low s.; Rolf Boldrewood, *Robbery under Arms* (Australia), 1881. Cf. **gaff**, n., 2.—

. . . .

24

A Dictionary of Clichés

labour of love, a. Work undertaken from affection for, or from a desire to please, another: mid C. 19–20. No longer apprehended as a reminiscence of 1 *Thessalonians*, i. 3 and *Hebrews*, vi. 10.

'labourer is worthy of his hire, the.' A workman is entitled to the money that his work brings him: C. 19–20. *Luke*, x. 7.

lady of the house, the. The mistress of a household: late C. 19–20. An elaboration of the earliest sense of *lady* (C. 9–mid 18).

land of milk and honey, a; and its original, **'a land flowing with m. and h.'** A land rich in natural food: C. 19–20. 'Palestine is often referred to in the Bible as a land flowing with milk and honey' (Dr C. H. Irwin's *Cruden's Concordance*); e.g., *Exodus*, iii. 8.

land of the living, the. See **in the land . . .**

lap of luxury, the; esp., **to live in the . . ., be cradled in the . . .** See **cradled.**

lapse from virtue, a (or **one's**). A moral fall, slip, act of weakness: mid C. 19–20.—Cf. the theological *lapse of Adam*.

*Lares and Penates. Household goods; hence, hearth and home, or, esp., home and household goods: late C. 18–20. In Latin, both *Lares* and *Penates* are gods, metaphorically home or hearth.

*last but not least. C. 19–20. An adaptation (perhaps originally a misquotation) of Spenser's 'though last, not least' (*Colin Clout*, 1595).

last extremity, the. The final state of illness, grief, destitution, etc.; the last stage; hence, *in the last extremity* means also **in the last resort;** late C.–19–20.

last gasp, at one's (or **the**). See **at one's last gasp.**

last legs; esp., **to be on one's . . .,** very frail, near death; hence, of things, extremely dilapidated or worn: C. 20.

last straw, the. From the proverb, 'It's the last straw that breaks the camel's back'. The cliché is of C. 19–20.

late in the day; esp., **it's rather late in the day to . . .,** it is too late to do something if you wish to succeed or profit: C. 20.

late in the field (?). 'He was rather late in the field: many applicants had been interviewed days before he appeared.' Late C. 19–20.

latest intelligence, the. The latest information or news: mid C. 19–20; slightly obsolescent, owing to the obsolescent (but not moribund) state of that excellent word *intelligence*.

laudator temporis acti. One who is constantly praising 'the good old days': C. 19–20. Horace, 'Difficilis, querulus, laudator temporis acti, | Se puero' (*De Arte Poetico*, 173).

laugh in (now often **up**) **one's sleeve, to.** To laugh to oneself; to be inwardly amused: late C. 18–20.

laugh on the wrong side of one's mouth, to. From glad to become sad—from confident, vexed or abashed—from exultant, depressed: late C. 19–20. In C. 18–mid 19, one laughed on the *other* side.

laugh out of court, to. To render (a person, a project) ridiculous by derisive laughter: from ca. 1880; originally, legal.

laugh to scorn, to. To deride; so to laugh at a person as to induce scorn in others: C. 19–20. Recorded for C. 15 and common in Bible: e.g., *Psalms* xxii. 7; *Matthew*, ix. 24.

law-abiding citizen, a; law-abiding citizens, persons submitting to (and upholding) the law: late C. 19–20.

law and order; esp., to be on the side of law and order, to range oneself with those who enforce and maintain the laws and by-laws: mid C. 19–20.

law, is an ass, the, is the usual form of ' "If the law supposes that," said Mr Bumble . . . "the law is a ass—a idiot" ' (Dickens, *Oliver Twist*, Part III, 1839). Mid C. 19–20.

law of the Medes and Persians, the. See **Medes and Persians.**

law to (obsolescently, **unto**) **oneself, to be a.** To be self-willed *and* in some way remarkable; to have one's own way of doing things: late C. 19–20.

*****lawful occasions; esp., to go about one's,** to attend to one's business or affairs, whether official, occupational, or social: very common in C. 17–mid 19; uncommon in late C. 19–early 20; extremely common—a cliché—from ca. 1915.

lay down the law, to. To make arrogant or dogmatic statements, esp. in discussion or argument: colloquial: from the 1880's.

lay (esp., **laying**) **heretical hands on our imperishable constitution.** An American political cliché of late C. 19–20. (Recorded by Stuart Chase.)

lay it on with a trowel, to. To flatter (or eulogize) excessively and/or unsubtly, grossly: mid C. 19–20. Shakespeare, *As You Like It,* i, ii, 112, 'Well said, that was laid on with a trowel'.

'lay on, Macduff.' Strike vigorously!; attack vigorously! C. 19–20. *Macbeth*, v, viii, 33.

lay one's cards on the table, to; show one's hand. To say frankly what one intends to do; to disclose one's resources, confess one's weaknesses: C. 20. From card-playing.

lay the flattering unction to one's soul, to. To be fatuously pleased with praise: mid C. 19–20. From 'Lay not that flattering unction to your soul' (*Hamlet*, iii, iv).

lead a cat and dog life, to. (Of relatives, married couples, associates) to be constantly quarrelling: from ca. 1880. (In C. 16–18, *to agree like cat and dog*.)—Cf. **lead a dog's life.**

lead (someone) **a dance, to.** To hurry a person from place to place; hence, to force or induce him to do a number of troublesome things: from C. 16; a cliché in C. 18–20.

lead a dog's life, to. To cause a person distress and constant trouble; to be caused . . .: late C. 19–20.

25

Origins

M

ma. See MAMA (heading—cf para 1).

ma'am. Cf *madam, madame* at DAME.

Mac in surnames. See FILIAL, para 3.

macabre, adopted from F (1842 as adj), comes from F *danse macabre, macabre* being a scribal error for EF (danse) *Macabré*; cf OF *Macabré*, Macchabaeus, and ML (C15) *chorea Macchabeorum*, a *danse macabre*—lit, of the Maccabees, leaders of a Jewish revolt in C2 B.C. The sem association is obscure. (B & W.)

macadam, whence macadamize; tarmac.

The word *tarmac* stands for the trade-name *Tarmac*, for *tar macadam*, a bituminous road-binder, hence a road or surface thus treated; *macadam* derives from the Sc engineer, John L. *McAdam* (1756–1836), who, ca 1820, invented the process.

macaroni, when ce the C18 fops the Macaronis; macaroon; macaronic.

Tubular *macaroni* re-spells the It pl *maccaroni*, dial var of *maccheroni*, prob (Prati) from the obs It *maccare*, to break, to break up. *Maccheroni* has jocular adj *maccherònico*, applied to verse that intermingles L with other IE languages, either in words only or in entire verse-lines, whence EF-F *maxaronique*: whence E *macaronic*. *Maccheroni* has sing *maccherone*, with

dial var *maccarone*, whence C17– 18 E *macaron*, whence *macaroon*.

Macassar, as in *Macassar oil*, whence (to counteract its effects upon chair-backs) *antimacassar*, is a var of *Makassar*, a district and its seaport in the Celebes.

macaw (cf of the EF *mecou*): Port *macó*; (prob) Tupi *maccaúba*, the macaw palm, for the bird feeds on its fruit: a blend of Arawak *macoya* (from *amaca*, a hammock)+Tupi *úba*, tree. (Webster.) But Dauzat and B & W may be right in saying that the word is African (Bu. to be more precise) and was imported into Brazil by the Portuguese.

mace (1), club. See MATTOCK, s.f.

mace (2), a spice: ME *maces*, apprehended as pl: MF-F *macis*: ML *macis*: scribal error for L *macir*, the rind of an Indian root: LGr *maker* (var *makeir*): 'vox Indica' (Du Cange).

Macedon, Macedonia, Macedonian (adj, hence n), macédoine.

The last, a—usu, culinary—medley, is adopted from F, where it jests upon the diversity of races in *Macedonia*, Gr *Makedōn*, a Macedonian, has adj *Makedonios*, L. *Macedonius*, E *Macedonian*; hence *Makedonia*, L *Macedonia*.

macerate, maceration. See MASON, para 2.

Machiavellian derives from Niccolo *Machiavelli* (1469–1527),

Italian diplomat, ref the political principles enunciated in *Il Principe*, The Prince, 1513.

machicolate, machicolation. See MASSACRE, para 2.

machination. See para 2 of:

machine (n, hence adj and v), whence **machinery** and **machinist** (imm from EF-F *machiniste*); **machinate, machination, machinator; mechanic,** adj (now always in extn **mechanical**), hence 'a **mechanic**'—**mechanics**—**mechanism,** whence anl **mechanistic, mechanize;** cf the element *mechano-*.—Cf ult MAY (v).

1. *Machine,* adopted from MF-F, comes, through L *māchina,* invention, an invention, a machine, a device, a trick, from Gr *mēkhanē,* or rather from Doric *mākhanā,* from Gr *mēkhos,* Dor *makhos,* means, esp an expedient: akin to the Gmc 'may' words: f.a.e., MAY (v).

2. L *māchina* has derivative *māchināri,* to devise, esp to plot, with pp *māchinātus,* whence 'to *machinate*'; derivative LL *māchinātiō,* o/s *māchinātiōn-,* yields MF-F, whence E, *machination;* derivative L *māchinātor* is adopted by E.

3. Gr *mēkhanē* has adj *mēkhanikos,* LL *mēchanicus,* E *mechanic;* Aristotle's(?) (*ta*) *mēkhanika,* (the) mechanical things, becomes E *mechanics. Mēkhanē* has derivative n *mēkhanēma,* an engine, whence app the LL *mēchanisma,* whence E *mechanism,* and derivative v *mēkhanesthai,* to invent, to devise, which perh prompted 'to *mechanize*'.

macintosh. See MACKINTOSH.

mackerel: MF *maquerel* (later *maquereau*): ML *macarellus:* o.o.o.: but cf ML *megarus,* EIr *magar,* a small fish, and Ga *maghar,* a young fish, a shellfish. Being a spotted fish,

it could derive from OC **mac,* to strike, to bruise (Malvezin).

mackinaw, a short, heavy coat, is short for *Mackinaw coat:* CanF *mackinac:* prob from *Mackinac* (Michigan), 'where stores were formerly distributed to the Indians': itself short for CanF *Michilimackinac;* Ojibway (Alg tribe) *mitchimakināk,* great turtle. (Webster; DAF. Mathews notes that this etym has been contested.)

mackintosh, prop but now rarely **macintosh,** a waterproof cape, invented by an A chemist, Charles *Macintosh* (1766–1843).

macrocosm, great world, opp *microcosm,* small world: cf of the element *macro-* and the r of COSMETIC (Gr *kosmos,* world).

macula, maculate. See the 1st MAIL, para 1.

mad, whence 'to **madden**', whence the pa **maddening**— **madly—madness; maim** and **mayhem;** to **mangle.**

1. *Mad* comes from OE *gemaēd,* pp of a lost v from the adj *gemād,* mad: cf OS *gemēd,* OHG *gimeit,* foolish, also Go *gamaidans* (acc pl), crippled, ON *meitha,* to hurt, Lith *apmaitinti,* to wound, Gr *mistullein* (s *mistul-,* r **mist-*), to cut into (small) pieces. IE r, perh **mait-,* to hew.

2. Go *gomaidans* is akin to MHG *meidenen,* to castrate, MHG *meidem,* a gelding, Go *maidjan,* to alter, to adulterate, hence also to ME *maymen,* whence 'to *maim*', whence 'a *maim*'; ME *maymen* is a contr of ME *mahaymen,* from OF *mahaignier* (varr *mes-* and *me-*), to mutilate, to wound, of Gmc origin—perh the Go words cited here.

N

nag. A pejorative for 'a small riding horse'. 'Yon ribaudred nag of Egypt' (i.e. Cleopatra), *A. & C.*, III x 10: Antony is the **rider**: see **ride**; cf. **mount** and especially **hackney** and **hobby-horse**.

Etymology: cf. Middle Dutch *negge*; anterior history obscure.

naked. '*Iago.* To be naked with her friend in bed, An hour or more, not meaning any harm?—*Othello.* Naked in bed, and not mean harm! It is hypocrisy against the devil': IV i 3–6.

Cognate with L. *nudus*, it is of Aryan origin.

naked bed. (Cf. *Othello* quotation at **naked.**) 'Who sees his true love in her naked bed, Teaching the sheets a whiter hue than white, But, when his glutton eye so full hath fed, His other agents aim at like delight?', *Venus*, vv. 397–400: naked in her bed.

naked seeing self. The pudend: for the semantics, cf. **eye** and **O**, qq.v. 'Can you blame her, then, being a maid yet rosed-over with the virgin crimson of modesty, if she deny the appearance of' [Cupid, who is] 'a naked blind boy in her naked seeing self?', *Henry V,* V ii 303–307.

nasty. Sexually dirty or otherwise sexually objectionable. See quotation at **enseamed bed.**

Cf. **filthy, foul, greasy, muddy,** and also **beastly.** Etymologically. *nasty* appears to = dirty.

naughtily. Indelicately. Cressida to Troilus, 'You smile and mock me, as if I meant naughtily', IV ii 37. Cf.:—

naughty. Obscene: inclined to love-making. Pandarus to Cressida, 'Would he not—a naughty man—let it sleep?': *T. & C.*, IV ii 25 and 32–33.

Naughty originally meant 'worthless' (a thing of *naught*).

naughty-house. (Cf. **bawdy-house** and **bad woman.**) A brothel. 'This house, if it be not a bawd's house, . . . is a naughty house', *Measure*, II i 75–76.

See **naughty** and cf. the C.19–20 euphemism, *house of ill fame.*

Neapolitan bone-ache. Syphilis; cf. **malady of France,** q.v. 'Vengeance on the whole camp! or, rather, the Neapolitan bone-ache! for that, methinks, is the curse dependant upon those that war for a placket', *T. & C.*, II iii 19–21; in V i 21, it is called *incurable bone-ache.*

neat. Cattle, in the sense 'horned herd' (see at **horned**). 'Come, captain, we must be neat', says jealous Leontes in *The W. Tale*, I ii 122–123.

As *cattle* and *chattel* are doublets, coming from a L. word meaning 'property', so *neat* probably comes from a common-Teutonic base that means 'to use'.

neck. A woman's bosom. See the quotation at **paddle.** Here, *neck* is used instead of *bosom* for the sake of the metre—not as a euphemism.

needle. (Cf. **prick** and **thorn,** qq.v.) In 'Hostess. We cannot lodge and board a dozen, . . . gentlewomen that live honestly by the prick of their needles, but it will be thought we keep a bawdy-house', *Henry V*, II i 33–36, the term bears its literal sense, then there is a reference to the **eye** of the needle, and there is an allusion to **prick**, n. and v.

ne'er lust-wearied. See **lust-wearied.**

nest of spicery. The pudend and the circumambient hair. '*Elizabeth.* But thou didst kill my children.—*Richard.* But in your daughter's womb I'll bury them: Where, in that nest of spicery, they shall breed Selves of themselves, to your recomforture', *Richard III*, IV iv 424–426.

Semantics: a lark's next. As for *spicery*: well, that olfactory and gustatory allusion hardly requires explanation; but cf. **honey** and **sweetness.**

Netherlands, the. (Cf. **holland** and **low countries.**) The pudend and adjacent area. 'I could find out countries in her . . . Where stood . . . the Netherlands? —O, sir, I did not look so low', *Com. of Errors*, III ii 112–135; cf. *R. & J.*, II i 19, '[Rosalind's] quivering thigh, and the demesnes that there adjacent lie'.

In relation to the nether *trunk* of the human body, for, after all, 'the nether limbs' are the legs.

nipple. The terminal projection on a human breast; especially either teat of a woman's bosom. 'When it did taste the womanhood on the nipple Of my dug, and felt it bitter . . .', *R. & J.*, I iii 32–33.—*Macbeth*, I vii 57.

Origin obscure: but may it not be 'that little thing which the baby *nips* as it sucks the breast'?

nose. Penis. '*Iras.* Am I not an inch of fortune better than she?—*Charmian.* Well, if you were but an inch of fortune better than I, where would you choose it?— *Iras.* Not in my husband's nose', *A. & C.*, I ii 56–59.

This entry must be compared with the next: here, *nose* = proboscis — trunk = dangling projection.

nose-painting. Lechery; (excessive) copulation. '*Macduff.* What three things does drink especially provoke?—*Porter.* . . . Nose-painting, sleep and urine', *Macbeth*, III iii 27–28. The remainder of the Porter's speech makes it clear that lechery, not the nose-reddening that results from over-drinking, is primarily meant, though there may be a pun. (Cf. Othello's 'O, I see that nose of yours, but not that dog I shall throw it to' (IV i 142–143), to Cassio whom he believes to be Desdemona's paramour.)

See **parson's nose** and consider its potentialities: there is, I surmise, a very greasy allusion.

nuptial, n. and adj. Bridal. 'This union stood upon . . . her nuptial vow', *Titus Andronicus*, II iii 125.—*R. & J.*, I v 37.—*M.N. Dream*: see quotation at **desire.**—'Nuptial rites', *The M. of V.*, II viii 6.—'In heart As merry as when our nuptial day was done, And tapers burnt to bedward!', *Coriolanus*, I iv, 30–32.

L. *nuptiae*, ' a wedding', ex *nubere*, 'to become a wife'.

nymph. A girl or young woman, especially if pretty and oncoming. 'To strut before a wanton ambling nymph', *Richard III*, I i 17.—*Titus Andronicus*, II i 22 (see at **siren**).—Favourably in 'Thou gentle nymph, cherish thy forlorn swain!', *Two Gentlemen*, V iv 12.

27

A Dictionary of Forces' Slang, 1939–45

O

oboe. Displaced *orange* as signallers' word for the letter O. See **able.**

observatory. An astrodome—that part of an aircraft from which the navigator observes the stars.

Ocean Swell, the. The late Admiral Sir Bernard Ramsey, because of his sartorial splendour.

Octu. An O.C.T.U., Officer Cadet Training Unit. *Pre-Octu*—a preliminary course intended to weed out unsuitable candidates and to give the others a foretaste of what was in store for them. (Army and Air Force colloquialisms.)

O.D. An Ordinary Seaman. From '*ordinary*'?

odds and sods. Men on miscellaneous duties. Men not classified. Members of other denominations than Roman Catholic, Church of England and Presbyterian. (Army.)

(2) In the Navy, the rank and file—the *hoi polloi*—of the lower-deck.

O.D.'s. Other denominations. Church of England, Roman Catholic and Presbyterian were the three recognized religious denominations. All others were classified as O.D.'s.

(2) Ordinary Seamen.

off caps. When naming anyone of eminence in the Navy or a departed shipmate, *off caps* is sometimes murmured.

office. A plane's cabin or cockpit.

(2) Inside information. 'Do you know what the office is?' implies 'What is the information from Headquarters?' Cf. the civilian *give a person the office*, to inform him or give him a timely warning.

office, up for. To be on a charge. (Army.)

official cuts. Ceremonial punishment held in H.M. training ships; justified only by exceptionally bad conduct.

off net. See **net.**

off the road. See **road.**

oggies. Cornish pasties. Short for *tiddyoggies*. (Navy.)

'oggin, the. The sea. (Lower-deck). 'The skipper's lost his best cap in the 'oggin.' Cf. **gravy** or **ditch.**

ogo pogo, to. Usually in the form of a verbal noun (*ogo-pogoing*). To seek an unidentified plane in order to identify it.

Oh, Miss Weston! An expression of disapproval of any strong language. Dame Agnes Weston was a great stickler for propriety.

oil. Tea. (Army.)

(2) Information; *dinkum oil*, genuine information: Australian and New Zealand troops'. A survival from 1914–18.

oil spoilers. Stokers, R.N.

[222]

oily. An oilskin. When these were first introduced at the Naval Gunnery School they were known as *Excellent's Ulsters*, H.M.S. *Excellent* being the ship name for Whale Island, Portsmouth.

old-and-bolds, the. Naval officers brought back into the Service in time of war.

old Annie. See **Annie** and **limping Annie.** Also *old Faithful*, from its reliability.

Old Black Men. African native troops. Cf. **black chums.**

Old Close-the-Range. Admiral of the Fleet Lord Cunningham. From his habit of getting to close quarters.

Old Faithful. Field-Marshal Montgomery's car in North Africa and Italy.
    (2) A nickname for the Anson aircraft. Cf. **limping Annie.**

old iron. Spare copper coins that an airman doesn't object to hazarding in a gamble—a bet, a raffle, a card game.

old lug. A term of reproach or abuse. (Army.)

Old Man, the. The Commanding Officer. The Air Force gets it from the Army, which gets it from the Navy, which got it from the Merchant Service.

Old Newton. The force of gravity, always tending to bring a plane to earth. From Isaac Newton, the discoverer of the laws of gravity.

old ship. A former messmate. (Navy.)

old soldier. One who, by reason of his long service, claimed to know more about everything military than anybody else. Some old soldiers did, of course, but his interlocutors believed, often with justice, that it was in the scrounging and shirking side of soldiering that his superiority was most marked. To call someone an 'old soldier' was not intended as a compliment, though there may have been a grudging admiration in the remark. *To come the old soldier*—to lie, shirk, malinger or boast.

old sweat. Old soldier. This phrase did not have the same uncomplimentary implication as 'old soldier'. Rather the reverse, in fact.

old tin man, come the. To bluff or 'flannel' or be generally objectionable. (Navy.)

old vets. Royal Fleet Reservemen called out in a National Emergency. The backbone of the Navy.

Old Whittle, the. A Whitley bomber, already obsolescent in 1943. It rendered much loyal service.

O.L.Q.s. Officer-like qualities, the passport to the Quarter-deck, as distinct from *L.D.A.*, lower-deck attitude.

on. Possible. Used most often negatively in the phrase, 'It's simply not on'.

on dags. On leave. (An old Naval term.)

One. Short term for **Number One** or First Lieutenant. (Navy.)

one, get one's. To be promoted to A.C.1. (Air Force.)

one for the gangway. A last drink for the guests before they leave the ship.

one gun salute. A Court Martial; so called because at Colours Ceremony on the day of the Court Martial a salute of one gun is fired.
    Cf. **rogue's salute.**

One O. A First Officer in the Women's Royal Naval Service.

one-pause-two. Short for the also used *one-pause-two course*. An officer's initial training course, held at an O.C.T.U. (colloquially: an *Octu*). . . .

A Dictionary of Slang and Unconventional English, Vol. 1

─────

pross. One who, to an (itinerant) actor, throws money: low theatrical: 1851, Mayhew; very ob. Prob. ex *prosperous*: cf. *pros.* adj.—2. Hence, a cadged drink; theatrical: from ca. 1860.—3. A prostitute: low (mostly London): from ca. 1870.—4. See pross, on the, and of *prosser* and *pross.* v.—5. A variant of *pros.* n.

pross, v. To cadge (a meal, a drink); occ. v.i.: theatrical: from ca. 1860. H., 3rd ed. Either ex *pross*, n., 2, or *pross*, v., 2. Anon., ca. 1876, 'I've pressed my meats from off my pals.'—2. 'To break in or instruct a stage-infatuated youth', H., 1st ed.: theatrical: from ca. 1858; ob. This sense may have been influenced by Romany *pross*, to ridicule.

pross, on the, adj. and adv. Looking for free drinks, etc.; on the cadge: theatrical >, ca. 1890, low gen. s.: from ca. 1860. P. H. Emerson, 1893.—2. Breaking in (and sponging from) a stage-struck youth: theatrical: from ca. 1865.

prosser. A cadger of refreshment, stomachic or pecuniary: theatrical: from ca. 1880. Cf. *Prossers' Avenue* and 'For he don't haunt the Gaiety Bar, dear boys, | A-standing (or pressing for) drinks,' *The Referee*, Nov. 18, 1883.—2. Hence, a loafer, a hanger-on: 1886, *The Cornhill Magazine*, Nov. Senses 1 and 2, prob. ex:—3. A 'ponce' (q.v.): low: from ca. 1870. H., 5th ed. Ex *pross*, n., 3.

Prosser's, occ. **Prossers' Avenue.** The Gaiety Bar: theatrical: from ca. 1882. Ex *prosser*, 1, q.v.

prostitute. To prostrate: a C. 17 catachresis. O.E.D.

prostituted. (Of a patent) so long on the market that it has become known to all: commercial coll. (— 1909). Ware.

[protagonist. See Fowler.]

protected. Lucky; uncannily or very lucky: Australian and New Zealand: C. 20, but not gen. before G.W. Prob. *protected by the gods* or *by one's superiors.* Cf.:

protected man. 'A merchant seaman unfit for the Royal Service and therefore free of the press-gang', F. & H.: naval coll.: ca. 1800–50.

protervious. An incorrect form of †*protervous*: mid-C. 16–17. O.E.D.—**protest.** See **detest.**—

prothesis, prothetic, are incorrect for the *prosthesis, prosthetic,* of surgery: from ca. 1840. O.E.D.

[proud. Feeling very gratified, delighted: S.E. verging on coll. and dial.: C. 19–20. Whence:]

proud, do one. To flatter (ob.); to honour: to treat very generously: coll.: 1819 (O.E.D.); 1836, Clark, *Ollapodiana Papers*, 1836, 'I really thought, for the moment, that "she did me proud".' Cf. '*the Cull tipt us Rum Prog*, the Gentleman Treated us very High,' B.E. and:

proud, do oneself. To be delighted (ob.); . . .

A Dictionary of Slang and Unconventional English, Vol. 2 (Supplement)

pross, n., 3 (p. 663); e.g. in *Sessions*, Feb. 8, 1905. 3. Proscenium: theatrical: since ca. 1910. (Gavin Holt, *No Curtains for Cora*, 1950.)

*****prospector.** A confidence trickster: Australian c.: since ca. 1925. (B., 1953.) For mugs' gold.

pross about. To 'mooch' or hang about: low: from ca. 1890. Pugh (2), 'Afternoon I prosses about in 'Ampstead.' Ex **pross,** v., 1 (*Dict.*).

prossie. An Australian late C. 19–20 variant of **pross,** n., 3 (p. 663). B., 1942. But also English; it occurs in. e.g., Ada E. Jones (Mrs Cecil Chesterton), *Women of the Underworld*, 1931, at p. 164.

prosso. A prostitute: Australian: since ca. 1925. (Dick.) Cf. **prossie.**

prostitute, the. The twelfth man, or a *substitute*, in a cricket match: cricketers': ca. 1870–1914. Sir Home Gordon, *The Background of Cricket*, 1939.

Prot, n. and adj. (A) Protestant: Catholics': mid C. 19–20.

*****protection, take** (a girl) **under one's.** To take care of a girl and send or accompany her out to the Argentine: (Polish) white-slavers' c.: C. 20. Albert Londres, 1928.

Protestant herring, a. A stale, a bad, herring: hence, any inferior provender, as in 'Oh, that butter is a Protestant herring' (P. W. Joyce, *English . . . in Ireland*, 1910); Anglo-Irish coll.: mid C. 19–20.

Prudential men, or **men of the Prudential.** Officers in the Special

Branch of the R.N.V.R.: Naval: 1939–45. With a pun on the Prudential insurance company. (P.G.R.)

prune is short for *Prune, P/O.* John Moore in *The Observer*, Oct. 4, 1942, ' "Lost anybody?" "Some prune who thought he could beat up the searchlights" '; B., 1942.

prune, v. To adjust or otherwise tinker with (a ship's engines): Naval: since ca. 1930. (P.G.R.)

Prune, P/O; in speech, **Pilot Officer Prune.** 'A pilot who takes unnecessary risks, and generally loses his neck through his *prunery*' and ' "P/O Prune" is the title bestowed upon a pilot who has several "prangs" on his record' (H. & P.); R.A.F.: since ca. 1935. He is a constant emblematic monitory figure in the pages of *The R.A.F. Journal.* Not unconnected with the impracticality of 'prunes and prisms'. Created, Jackson tells us, by S/Ldr Anthony Armstrong and L.A.C.W. Hooper ('Raff').

prune-juice. Hard liquor: since ca. 1935. (Richard Gordon, *Doctor and Son*, 1953).

Prussian Guard. A flea: Army: 1914–18. 'Dignity and Impudence.' —2. In the game of House, a card: rhyming s.: C. 20.

psych. A 'psychological' bet, one made on a bunch: Australian two-up players': since ca. 1930. (Lawson Glassop, *Lucky Palmer*, 1949.)

*****psyche man.** See **front man.**

H

A Dictionary of Catch Phrases

S

S.A.B.U. See **T.A.B.U.**

S.N.A.F.U. and S.N.E.F.U. See **snafu.**

said he. In 1927 Collinson, in his invaluable book, recorded this example.

'Do you like that?'
'No, said he frowning.'

Current since the early 1920s and, although somewhat 'old hat', still far from having become obsolete. It derives, I'd say, from a novelists' trick that is also a journalists' mannerism.

sailors don't care – natural enough, with their girls in every port: latish C19–20. Canonized by inclusion in Benham. But Laurie Atkinson's gloss (18 July 1975) is valuable: 'Among soldiers, airmen and others, apt when what is in hand is not likely to be straightforward if niceties are allowed to get in the way: e.g., trespassers will be prosecuted, but if it's a short cut . . .' And, late in 1974, L.A. had glossed the c.p. thus: 'Quip to reject or mitigate undue caution'.

sailor's farewell – **a**, occasionally with **to you** added. A nautical, including naval, parting curse: late C19–20. Perhaps suggested by the apparently slightly earlier (and much sooner obsolete) nautical colloquialism, *sailor's blessing*. But the best comparison is that to be made with **soldier's farewell.** Cf also **the best of British luck (to you)!**

same diff is the Australian counterpart of the next: since *c.* 1945. (Barry Prentice.)

same difference. See **it's the same difference.**

same here! I agree: US: C20. (Berrey.) For 'It is the same here, i.e. with me': 'I think the same as you do'. The drinking sense. 'I'll have the same [drink] as you' is hardly a c.p.

same in a hundred years. See **it'll all be the same. . . .**

same OB. The usual price (for a ticket of entry): lower classes': *c.* 1880–1914. (Ware.) For *same old bob* (shilling), the usual entrance fee for the most popular entertainments and pastimes during that period.

same old shit – **but** (or **only**) **more of it** – **the.** The Canadian Army's version of **snafu**: 1939–45.

same to you and many of them! – **the,** politely synonymous with the phrases immediately following this and is, so far as I've been able to ascertain, rather earlier, for it seems to have arisen *c.* 1880. In Act III of Stanley Houghton's *The Perfect Cure*, produced in 1913, we find:

CRAY: Confound Mrs Grundy! Confound Madge! Confound – yes, hang it, confound, you, Martha.
MARTHA: The same to you, and many of them.

same to you with knobs on! or the fairly common variant . . . **with**

brass fittings! The same to you – only *more so*!: both belong to C20 and were prompted by – were, originally, perhaps euphemistic for – the low-slang expression, '*balls* to you!' Clearly, however, there is reference to brass knobs on a bed, as Norman Franklin has reminded me.

The *knobs on* form was, at one time, very common in schools; it occurs in, e.g. Frank Richards, *Tom Merry & Co. of St. Jim's*, as Mr Petch tells me. Cf the preceding phrase.

san fairy Ann (seldom **Anna**); occasionally **send for Mary Ann** (and **Aunt Mary Ann**). It doesn't matter, *or* It's all the same, *or* Why worry?: late 1914–18, then nostalgically; not, so far as I know, used during WW2, except among a few 'old soldiers'. B & P say:

> An extremely popular phrase, approximated into English from the French *ça ne fait rien*. . . . As the intelligence of the soldier penetrated year after year the infinite layers of bluff and pretentiousness with which military tradition enwrapped the conduct of the War, so his cynicism increased, became habitual. . . . Naturally he adopted a fatalism comparable to that of the Moslem murmuring his enervating '*Maalish*' – It does not *matter*. . . . Let anything happen, the only appropriate comment was – *San Fairy Ann*.

Naturally, the phrase had its lighter uses, especially in defiance of the warnings of friends. It was so much used that variants were almost as popular – chiefly *San Fairy* and *San Fairy Anna*. Hugh Kimber ends his war novel *San Fairy Ann*, 1927, thus: 'There is a magic charter. It runs, "San Fairy Ann".'

sandman (or **the dustman**) **is coming – the,** has, the latter since *c*. 1810, as in Egan's Grose, 1823 and been either addressed to or directed at children beginning to rub their eyes and yawn. From their rubbing their eyes as if sand were in them: the same applies to dust in the eyes.

saucepan runs (or **boils**) **over.** See **your saucepan.** . . .

save a sailor! is a Royal Naval officers' c.p., employed when, in the mess bar, a glass gives off a ringing sound: late C19–20. This sound is, in sailors' superstition, thought to augur a sailor's death by drowning. To prevent this misfortune, one places a finger on the glass, thus stops the ringing – and thus redeems the sailor. (*Sailors' Slang.*)

save the surface and you save all is a US 'sarcastic or cynical c.p. of general application' – derived from a varnish manufacturer's slogan: since the 1920s and 'still heard, though less than formerly' (John W. Clark, 17 May 1975).

saved by the bell. Saved, or spared, by a lucky accident or intervention: Britain and the Commonwealth: late C19–20. In boxing, the bell indicates the end of each round.

say anything but her prayers. See **she will say.** . . .

say au revoir (also, slangily and facetiously, **au reservoir**) **but not goodbye!** We are not parting for ever – we'll see each other again: since *c*. 1910; the facetious form became obsolescent by 1930 and obsolete by 1950.

30

Name This Child

X

XAVIER. This male name – from Arabic *ga'afar*, 'splendid' (cf. the Giafar of *The Arabian Nights*) – is obsolescent except among Catholics, who, in using it, commemorate St Francis Xavier, a noble Spaniard famed for his missions in the middle of the 16th Century to India, Ceylon, the East Indies, Japan and China. Xavier thus appears to have originally been, in Europe, a Spanish surname.

XENOPHON, *m.* There has never been a fashion in, nor much popularity for, Xenophon; but it isn't obsolete. Its most celebrated C20 tenant has been that South African cricketer who specialized in well-spun guile. The name comes from that of the Athenian general and historian of mid C5–early 4, B.C., and, lit., it seems to mean 'speaking a foreign language', from the Greek *xenophōnein*, 'to speak like a foreigner'.

XINA. An occasional diminutive of *Christina* (-*e*). Cf. *Chris* and *Chrissie*.

Y

YDA is a 'literary' variant of *Ida* and should not be encouraged.

YNYR, *f.* The Welsh form of *Honor*.

YSOBEL. See *Isabel*.

YSOLT, YSEULT; ISOLD, ISOLDA, ISOLDE; Anglicized as *Izod*. From the Fr. *Yseulte*, perhaps from *Adsalutta*, a Celtic goddess; apparently the word means 'spectacle'. Though rapidly growing rarer, *Ysolt* is still bestowed by the cultured on a baby girl for whom even a feckless 'highbrow' would wish a less tragic 'life-story' than that which befell Ysolt of the white hands, she who, in medieval romance and beautiful, haunting Swinburnian embroidery, is linked, in deathless story after despairing death, with *Tristram*.

YVETTE, YVONNE, *f.* Mostly Fr.; whence, occasionally, in English use. 'Of all Breton names Yves is the commonest. It is the Old French nominative of Yvain, identical with Evan and John. . . . From it are derived the female names Yvette and Yvonne' (*Jack and Jill*): *Yvette* from *Yves. Yvonne* from *Yvain*. These two names are occasionally bestowed upon girl twins.

Z

ZACHARIAH. In Heb., 'God has remembered'. *Zacharias*, a variant, is obsolete except among Jews and Puritans. One of its pet-forms is *Zach* or *Zack*.

ZACHARY. This is a typical English simplification of *Zachariah* and *Zacharias*; in C19–20, it has been more common than those two names, but it, too, is becoming rare. The only notable Englishman thus named or, rather, the only one with whom memory claims acquaintance at the moment – is the early C19 philanthropist, Zachary Macaulay, the wealthy merchant who, not content with fathering the eminent historian, opposed the slave-traffic.

ZACKY. A diminutive of *Zachariah* and *Zachary*, via *Zack*.

ZED. The diminutive of:

ZEDEKIAH, *m.* Now very rare except among the Jews and, less, among the rural labouring class, and they are much less fond of it than they were. Lit. (in Heb.), 'God is righteousness', it is the name of that king whom direfully prophetic Jeremiah saw led into captivity.

ZENOBIA. Now rare, and apt to excite derision, this was once a favourite 'literary' and fashionable name after that of 'the brilliant queen of Palmyra', who, after annexing Egypt, was defeated and captured by Aurelian in 272 A.D. Of Arabian birth, she probably bore, originally, 'the true Arabic name of Zeenab (ornament of the father),' Yonge.

ZERAH, *m.* Heb., 'rising of light'. From, or akin to, the name of the Biblical prophet Ezra. At one time used by Puritans, it is now, except among Jews, very, very rare.

ZILLA, ZILLAH. In Heb., 'shade, shadow,' *Zillah* (the correct, more usual form) was the name of one of Biblical Lamech's two wives; in C19–20, it has been almost confined to Gypsy women. (Yonge.)

ZOE, *f.* There are two Saints so named; one a Roman lady cruelly done to death late in C3 (Benedictines). Its radical (*zōë*, 'life') is Greek and at the base of such words as *zoology*. As a proper name, it arose thus: – ' "The mother of all living" [Eve] received from the lips of Adam a name signifying life [or life-giving], sounding in the original like *Chavva*. . . . It was not copied by any of her daughters for a long time, and when first the Alexandrian Jews came on it in their translation, they rendered it by *Zoe* . . . , in order to show that connexion of the name with the prophecy,' Yonge.

ZONA; its pet-form being **ZONE.** An American *f.* name, apparently from the Gr. for 'a girdle'.

Envoi

A Short Story

＝

THE NAME *Scholartis* refers to two qualities on which we insist in every reprint: the scholarly and the artistic, thus:

Schol(arly)*artis*(tic).

In a wider sense, it connotes that in every book we demand quality (whether scholarly or literary) and a production that is, at the least, adequate. There have, of course, always been those who, unable to read straight, call us *The Scholastic Press*!!! Variants in perversity are *The Scholastis*, or *Scholars, Press*. It speaks well for our patience that we have not yet been accused of murdering anyone.

The initial Scholartis publication appeared in September 1927; the first three publications had reached the printers in June. As I took a boyish pleasure in keeping the venture a secret until a few days before the appearance of the initial volume, I was bound to edit these books myself . . . and I had finally decided no earlier than March that I would turn publisher. One book I had ready: *Pirates, Highwaymen and Adventurers*, against which Messrs Elkin Mathews and Marrot had decided only because they thought that another book appearing just at this time would spoil the market: 'it's an ill wind . . .' Yet this was to be the third book on the list, for it was too long to be seen through the press in time for September. I had for some months been interested in Disraeli; to write a prefatory note was simple, hence *Ixion in Heaven*, to which I added the little-known but brilliant *Endymion* by Aytoun. That book is out of print and at a premium, partly because *Endymion*, which had never been reprinted, was a deliberate skit on *Ixion*: and Disraeli was, and is, a favourite with the public. The success of *Ixion and Endymion*, allied with that of Messrs

Cape's *Ixion* illustrated by Mr John Austen, caused Messrs Wm. Jackson (Books) Ltd. to issue Disraeli's *The Infernal Marriage* with illustrations by Mr Austen and preface by myself.

The second book issued by the Scholartis Press was *The Three Wartons*, on which I began detailed work in April; I already had by me a number of preliminary notes. At about the same time I commenced to write, on the basis of a previous intensive study, an essay on Blake as a lyric poet to preface a worthy edition of his *Poetical Sketches*, which I considered to be unduly neglected in comparison with the *Songs of Innocence and Experience*; and later on I persuaded Mr Jack Lindsay, an undoubted authority on Blake and a poet himself, to write a study of that poet's metric, the result being a masterly analysis of Blake's technique and an invaluable essay on metre and rhythm in English poetry.

The first season's books were these four, at the rate of one book a month; I actually was so ignorant of publishing as to issue one about the 12th of December! Of those four, the *Ixion* and the *Wartons* are wholly out of print; the fine edition of *Pirates* and the fine edition of *Blake* are also out of print, while the cheaper limited edition of each should be unavailable before very long. Once a book of ours goes out of print, it is permanently out of print.

With January 1928 began the Press's second stage, which still prevails and shall; one of more active and more general publishing. Every book, however, was still limited to either one or two editions: if one edition, limited; if two editions, one cheaper and limited, the other dearer and limited. All the better editions specially bound, signed and numbered. The introduction of fiction marked a widening; not a basic change. Not till July 1928 did I issue a book unlimited in its editions, yet even that, *Poor Women!*, was limited in its first edition. With one exception, every modern copyright book that we have issued is limited in its first edition, either to 500, or to 1,000 copies. This practice is one of the planks of our platform; it makes considerably more work for us, but it gives those who are interested in our publications the certitude that here are modern firsts that on one score at least – that of a genuine limitation of the number of copies – have a tolerably good chance of appreciating; we can do this with the greater security because we are extremely careful to avoid the mediocre book. Somewhat the same principle underlies our reprints: here, *every* book is limited to the one or the two editions; every book is designed to form part of one or other of our series, or, if outside of a series, to further one of our interests (the *Wartons*, for example, indicating our interest in eighteenth-century literature); and every book must be not a mere reprint, however well produced, but a reprint justified of itself on its own merits and made more valuable by thoroughly competent editing. We don't get famous people to write prefaces for our books: we do get capable scholars to edit, and capable or extremely promising authors to write, our books. This may be quixotic, but there it is.

Production has been mentioned. We do not pretend that in our fiction the typography and craftsmanship are of the very best, but we do assert that they are considerably better than the general run of fiction in these respects. The five 'general' books that we have so far published (*Pirates, Bengal Haggis, An Unfrequented Highway, Three Personal Records of the War*, and *Songs and Slang of the British Soldier*) are all very well printed; two of them are excellently produced, two most creditably produced. And in our reprints (all translations, whether from the Classics or from modern European languages, are included) as in our *belles lettres* (modern poetry and the Benington Books) we aim at a consistently high standard of typography and general production. While we have had numerous books printed by such 'fashionable' presses as the Curwen, the Westminster, the Oxford and the Cambridge University, we have had many others printed by firms that, while not so fashionable as those just mentioned, set a very high standard indeed: The Alcuin Press, The Crypt House Press, Messrs MacLehose; Neill; T. & A. Constable; Henderson & Spalding; Gee (typographer: James Shand); Hazell, Watson and Viney. We claim that the following, our best books from the view-point of production, bear comparison with the work of any private press (we think that 'semi-private' is the best description of our own publishing house): *Ixion, Wartons, Blake, Horace, Man of Feeling, Sextette, I See the Earth, Orion, Vigny, Highway,* the Sand volumes, *The Vicar, Sentimental Journey, Otranto, Rowe, Joseph Andrews, Melancholike Humours, Verjuice, The Very End, Pomegranate, François and Katherine, Alexander, Socrates, Werther, Hymns, White Jade, Villon, Legion, Fanfare.* Our best produced novel is either *Forbidden Marches* or *Honour Lost, All Lost.*

In our first year, we published nineteen books, of which one was issued privately for a friend: it is, perhaps, our rarest book, rarer even than *Sleeveless Errand.* In our second year, twenty-four, of which one was a brochure; in our third, nineteen – or twenty-one if one considers the three self-contained issues of *The Window* as three books (the fourth and last number, to appear in October, belonging to next year's publishing). We intend to keep to the twenty-to-thirty-volumes-a-year mark, for we believe firmly in quality rather than quantity; to be frank, we remember also that while a number of persons can afford say £10 a year to possess a copy of every book we publish, few could afford £30–£50 a year to do so, and we are encouraged in this only-seemingly commercial attitude by our knowledge that those persons who have obtained a copy of every book bearing the imprint *The Scholartis Press* (September 1927–October 1929), *Eric Partridge Ltd.* (November 1929–July 1930), or *Eric Partridge Ltd. at the Scholartis Press* (November 1929–July 1930), have done pretty well, for several of our books issued at 7s. 6d. or thereabouts are now worth between 21s and 30s., one at 7s. 6d. is now fetching between £5 and £9, several at 21s are now priced at £3 – £10, and several more expensive books have appreciated considerably, while not a single book has depreciated; I refer, of course, to collectors and knowledgeable booksellers, for sleepy booksellers often let future 'prizes' go without a suspicion that they possess 'a good thing'. One cannot blame them, however, for neglecting to possess a complete set of our catalogues and leaflets, yet complete sets are now sought after.

From the beginning until October 21, 1929, the sole style of the firm was *The Scholartis Press,* which was a wholly private concern owned by myself; on October 21, last year, it was turned into a private company, with the trade-name of *Eric Partridge Ltd.* but with the full publishing style of *Eric Partridge Ltd. at the Scholartis Press*, the *Ltd.* being often omitted; for our modern fiction we frequently content ourselves with *Eric Partridge*, – for our reprints with *The Scholartis Press*. We are not to be confused with Messrs S. W. Partridge, now incorporated with Messrs A. C. Black and Co.; to assist in the avoidance of confusion, we shall in future imprint on most of our books either simply *The Scholartis Press* or *Eric Partridge at the Scholartis Press*. We take pleasure in mentioning that nearly all reviewers have kindly helped us in this matter by putting our name after a book as 'Scholartis Press' or 'Eric Partridge'.

I began with a capital of £100, afterwards increased to £300; but, in small-scale publishing I advise at least £5,000 as an initial capital, and an infinite patience. For the first year I did absolutely all the work by myself, even to delivering parcels. It may have been good physical training, but it was somewhat exhausting. From September 1928 till March 1929 I used to have a friend help me at each publication for a couple of days. From April 1929 I had the constant services of one man. When the private company was formed, we got a secretary, and a boy to run messages and deliver parcels; there were two directors, Captain Bertram Ratcliffe, M.C., and myself, the latter as working director. In April 1930, our third director joined us: Mr Wilson Benington, who shares the editorial and advertising activities with me; I attend to production; Captain Ratcliffe acts as an adviser. We have made our way almost on our own; without acquaintances among reviewers, without friends among journalists, without taking another publisher's authors with us, and without previous experience.

For the first month, I had a tiny office at 1b New Oxford Street; from mid-October 1927 to mid-March 1928, an infinitesimal office at 5 New Oxford Street; then I moved to 30 Museum Street to rooms on the third floor previously occupied by Mr Jack Lindsay. Our rooms are quiet and homely, but visitors usually arrive panting: we have them at an iniquitously unfair advantage, for they remain exhausted for quite two minutes. It has been suggested that we should install an American Bar halfway up, for some people are so ungracious as to claim that the starward climb is not its own reward. What we do ourselves miss is a window in which to display our books (though book-collectors are always welcome to come to inspect our publications): this defect we hope shortly to remedy.

We issue catalogues in February, May, and October; these are always complete, for we are steadily gaining new friends, who naturally like to have a complete list.

Only two lesser matters remain to be mentioned: in 1929 we had a colophon that we used on our catalogues. Three maidens with the caption 'Liberality, Originality, Distinction', indicating the liberalism (in the widest sense) of our views, the originality of our authors, and the (we hope) distinction of our books. But we were dissatisfied with these young women, and some one unkindly called them 'The Three Disgraces' – although I may add that they were respectably clothed. We now seek for a better colophon. The other matter is fourfold: our books, with the exception of one or two very special *éditions-de-luxe*, are now obtainable in all the British Colonies at the English published price; in North America all our books published up to December 31, 1929 (with the exception of *Rousseau*, *Vigny*, *Rowe*, *Wyatt*, *Daphnaïda*; the modern fiction, though *Glimpses* is a counter-exception; and the books of modern verse) may be obtained from Messrs Walter V. McKee Inc., 56 West 45th Street, New York; our agents in New Zealand are Messrs George J. Hicks & Co., 54 Victoria Street, Wellington, and in Australia the same firm at The Rialto, Collins Street, Melbourne. Finally we are always willing to inform collectors and general readers of our books where they will most likely be able to procure an edition, or a book, that is out of print.

Note. On all our catalogues we print the following words, as our motto, taken from Ambrose Bierce: 'At best, a book is not too beautiful, at worst, it is hideous.'

A Partridge Bibliography

Verse Translations from French Poetry. Privately printed, 1914.

The Bakara Bulletin: A Souvenir Book of the Voyage of the Bakara, Dec. 1918–Feb. 1919, and more especially of the Diggers abroad. (Ed.) Brisbane: Outridge Printing, *c.* 1919.

The French Romantics' Knowledge of English Literature (1820–1848), According to Contemporary French Memoirs, Letters and Periodicals. Paris: E. Champion, 1924.

Eighteenth-Century English Romantic Poetry, up till the Publication of the 'Lyrical Ballads', 1798. Paris: E. Champion, 1924.

The Poems of Cuthbert Shaw and Thomas Russell, with a biographical and critical introduction. (Ed.) London: Dulau, 1925.

A Book of English Prose, 1700–1914, with an introduction. (Ed.) London: Edward Arnold, 1926.

A Critical Medley; Essays, Studies and Notes in English, French and Comparative Literature. Paris: H. Champion, 1926.

Pirates, Highwaymen and Adventurers. (Ed.) London: Scholartis, 1927.

A Christmas and a New Year Dinner, Garnished with the Compliments of the Season, 1927–8. London: Scholartis, 1927.

Robert Eyres Landor: A Biographical and Critical Sketch. London: the Fanfrolico Press, 1927. (Also issued as a one-volume edition with the next item.)

Selections from Robert Landor. (Ed.) London: the Fanfrolico Press, 1927.

The Scholartis Press: Prospectus and First List. London: Scholartis, 1927.

The Three Wartons: A Choice of their Verse, with a note and a select bibliography. (Ed.) London: Scholartis, 1927.

Poetical Sketches, by William Blake (with an essay on Blake's metric by Jack Lindsay). (Ed.) London: Scholartis, 1927.

Ixion in Heaven, and Endymion (B. Disraeli), with an introductory note. (Ed.) London: Scholartis, 1927.

IX poems by V (C. Clive), with an introduction on Mrs Archer Clive. (Ed.) London: Scholartis, 1928.

A Journal of Summer Time in the Country (R. A. Willmott), with a critical and biographical introduction. (Ed.) London: Scholartis, 1928.

Horace on the Art of Poetry (ed. E. H. Blakeney), with an edited and annotated transcript of Ben Jonson's translation by E. P. London: Scholartis, 1928.

Orion (R. H. Horne), with a biographical and critical introduction. (Ed.) London: Scholartis, 1928. Revised for *Literary Sessions*; repr. in *A Covey of Partridge*, pp. 153–67.

Lettres à Malesherbes (Rousseau), annotated by E.P. London; Scholartis, 1928.

Glimpses (Corrie Denison/Eric Partridge). London: Scholartis, 1928.

Paul Ferroll (C. Clive), with an introductory note. (Ed.) London: Scholartis, 1929.

The Autobiography of Pel. Verjuice (C. R. Pemberton), with a biographical and critical introduction. (Ed.) London: Scholartis, 1929.

Three Personal Records of the War, by R. H. Mottram, John Easton and Eric Partridge. London: Scholartis, 1929; reprinted as *Three Men's War: The Personal Records of Active Service*, New York and London: Harper, 1930. E.P. extract part reprinted in *A Covey of Partridge*, pp. 73–149.

The Window. A quarterly magazine, ed. by Eric Partridge and Bertram Ratcliffe. Vol. 1, Nos. 1–4, Jan.–Oct. 1930.

The First Three Years: An Account with a Discursive Bibliography of The Scholartis Press. London: Scholartis, 1930.

Songs and Slang of the British Soldier (1914–1918), ed. with John Brophy. London: Scholartis, 1930; 2nd edn, rev. and enl. 1930; 3rd edn, rev., enl. and corr. 1931. Repr. as *The Long Trail*, André Deutsch, 1965.

American Tramp and Underworld Slang (ed. Godfrey Irwin, asst. ed. Eric Partridge, with an essay by E. P. on 'The American underworld and English cant'). London: Scholartis, 1931.

A Martial Medley, by Various Hands. (Ed.) London: Scholartis, 1931. Includes a chapter 'From Two Angles', by Corrie Denison.

Francis Grose's A Classical Dictionary of the Vulgar Tongue (3rd edn, 1796), with biographical notice and linguistic commentary. (Ed.) London: Scholartis, 1931; repr. with minor corr. 1962, London: Routledge & Kegan Paul.

The Scene is Changed (Corrie Denison). London: Scholartis, 1932. A chapter, 'Utopian', repr. in *A Covey of Partridge*, pp. 193–201.

Why not? (Corrie Denison). London, n.d.

Literary Sessions. London: Eric Partridge Ltd. at the Scholartis Press, 1932.

Words, Words, Words! London: Methuen, 1933.

Slang Today and Yesterday: A History and a Study. London: Routledge, 1933; New York: Macmillan, 1934; 2nd edn, carefully rev. and somewhat augm., 1935; 3rd edn rev. and brought up to date, 1950, Routledge & Kegan Paul/Macmillan (: *With a Short Historical Sketch; and Vocabularies of English, American and Australian Slang*); 4th edn, rev. and brought up to date, 1970; Bonanza Books edn, 1963.

Name This Child: A Dictionary of English (and American) Christian Names. London: Methuen, 1936; 2nd edn, rev. and enl. 1938; New York: O.U.P., 1942; 3rd edn rev. and much enl. 1951, London: Hamilton (: *A Dictionary of Modern British and American Given or Christian Names*); abridged edn, 1959; rev. and enl. paperback edn, 1968, London: Evans (*Name Your Child*).

A Covey of Partridge: An Anthology from the Writings of Eric Partridge. London: Routledge, 1937.

A Dictionary of Slang and Unconventional English. London: Routledge, 1937; Supplement, 1938; 2nd edn, rev. and enl., 1938; 3rd edn, rev. and much enl. 1949 (Routledge & Kegan Paul); 4th edn, rev. 1951; 5th edn, rev. and enl., 2 Vols. 1961; 6th edn, rev. and enl. 1967; 7th edn, rev. and enl. 1970. New York: Macmillan. Mid-Century Book Society selection, 1961. Abridged as *A Dictionary of Historical Slang*, ed. Jacqueline Simpson, 1972, Penguin Reference Book, *The Routledge Dictionary of Historical Slang* (Routledge & Kegan Paul, 1973).

The World of Words: An Introduction to Language in General and to English and American in Particular. London: Routledge, 1938; New York, Scribner's, 1939; 2nd edn, rev. 1939; 3rd edn rev. 1948 (Hamilton/Scribner's).

For These Few Minutes: Almost an Anthology. (Ed.) London: A. Barker, 1938.

An Original Issue of The Spectator, together with the Story of the Famous English Periodical and of its Founders, Joseph Addison and Richard Steele. San Francisco: the Book Club of California, 1939.

Précis Writing: Passages Judiciously Selected with an Introduction on the Art of Précis. London: Routledge, 1940.

A Dictionary of Clichés, with an introductory essay. London: Routledge; New York: Macmillan, 1940; 2nd edn, rev. 1941; 3rd edn, rev. and minor addns 1947; 4th edn 1950, with further addns 1962, 1966; 5th edn 1978, and paperback edn, Dutton, 1963.

Slang. Society for Pure English. Tract No. LV. Oxford: Clarendon Press, 1940.

A New Testament Word-Book: A Glossary. London: Routledge, 1940.

The Teaching of English in His Majesty's Forces: A Representative Library. For private circulation, 1941.

A Dictionary of Abbreviations, with Especial Attention to War-time Abbreviations. London: Allen & Unwin, 1942; 2nd edn, rev. and enl. 1943; 3rd edn, rev. and enl. 1949.

Usage and Abusage: A Guide to Good English. New York: Harper, 1942; 1st British edn 1947, rev. and enl., London: Hamilton; 4th edn, rev. 1948; 5th end, rev. and enl. 1957; 6th edn, rev. and slightly enl., 1965; postscript and addenda add. 1969. Penguin Reference Book, 1963.

A Dictionary of RAF Slang, with an introductory essay. London: Michael Joseph, 1945.

Journey to the Edge of Morning: Thoughts upon Books, Love, Life. London: Frederick Muller, 1946.

Shakespeare's Bawdy: A Literary and Psychological Essay and a Comprehensive Glossary. London: Routledge, 1947; New York: Dutton, 1948; new pop. edn 1955 (Routledge & Kegan Paul); 3rd edn, rev. 1958; 4th edn, rev. and enl. 1968. Everyman paperback, 1960.

Words at War: Words at Peace. Essays on language in general and particular words. London: Frederick Muller, 1948.

A Dictionary of Forces' Slang, 1939–45, with Wilfred Granville and Frank Roberts. (Ed., with the section on Air Force slang by Eric Partridge.) London: Secker & Warburg, 1948.

Dictionary of Effective Speech. New York: Grosset & Dunlap, 1949.

English: A Course for Human Beings. London: Winchester Pubs, 1949; London and New York: Macdonald (3-vol. edn.).

Sea Slang of the 20th Century (W. Granville), with an introduction and etymologies. (Ed.) London: Winchester Pubs, 1949.

A Dictionary of the Underworld, British and American: Being the Vocabulary of Crooks, Criminals, Racketeers, Beggars and Tramps, Convicts, the Commercial Underworld, the Drug Traffic, the White Slave Traffic, Spivs. New York: Bonanza Books, 1949; London: Routledge & Kegan Paul/New York: Macmillan, 1950; 2nd edn rev. and enl. 1961; 3rd edn much enl. 1968.

Name into Word: Proper Names that have become Common Property – a
Discursive Dictionary. London: Secker & Warburg, 1949; 2nd edn,
rev. and enl. 1950; New York: Macmillan, 1950.

Here, There and Everywhere: Essays upon Language. London: Hamilton,
1950.

British and American English since 1900, with contributions on English
in Canada, South Africa, Australia, New Zealand and India. (With
John W. Clark.) London; Andrew Dakers, 1951; New York:
Philosophical Library.

From Sanskrit to Brazil: Vignettes and Essays upon Languages. London:
Hamilton, 1952.

*Chamber of Horrors: A Glossary of Official Jargon, both English and
American, by 'Vigilans'* (E.P.), with an introduction by Eric Partridge.
London: André Deutsch, 1952; New York: O.U.P.

Appendix to H. C. Wyld, *The Universal Dictionary of the English
Language.* London: Routledge & Kegan Paul, 1952.

*The 'Shaggy Dog' Story: Its Origin, Development and Nature (with a few
seemly examples).* Illustrated by V. H. Drummond. London: Faber &
Faber, 1953; New York: Philosophical Library, 1954.

You Have a Point There: A Guide to Punctuation and its Allies. (With a
chapter on American practice by John W. Clark.) London: Hamilton, 1953; New York: 4th edn rev., 1978, London: Routledge &
Kegan Paul *(: A New and Complete Guide to Punctuation).*

The Concise Usage and Abusage: A Modern Guide to Good English.
London: Hamilton, 1954; New York: Philosophical Library.

Notes on Punctuation. Oxford: Blackwell, 1955; 2nd edn, rev. 1956;
3rd edn 1963.

*What's the Meaning? The Young People's Book of Answers to Baffling
Questions in the English Language.* London: Hamilton, 1956.

English Gone Wrong. London: Phoenix House (Background Books),
1957.

A First Book of Quotations. London: Hamilton, 1958; 2nd edn, rev.
1960.

Origins: A Short Etymological Dictionary of Modern English. London:
Routledge & Kegan Paul, 1958; New York: Macmillan; 2nd edn,
corr. and addns 1959; 3rd edn rev. and enl. 1961; 4th edn, rev. and
addns 1966. Mid-Century Book Society Selection, 1960.

A Charm of Words: Essays and Papers on Language. London: Hamilton,
1960; 2nd edn, minor corr., 1961.

Comic Alphabets: Their Origins, Development, Nature. Illustrated by
   Michael Foreman. London: Routledge & Kegan Paul, 1961.
Swift's Polite Conversation, with introduction, notes and extensive
   commentary. (Ed.) London: André Deutsch, 1963 (Language
   Library); New York: O.U.P.
Adventuring Among Words. London: André Deutsch, 1961 (Language
   Library); New York: O.U.P.
Smaller Slang Dictionary. London: Routledge & Kegan Paul, 1961;
   New York: Philosophical Library; 2nd edn, corr. and addns, 1964.
*The Gentle Art of Lexicography, as Pursued and Experienced by an Addict:
   A Memoir,* London; André Deutsch, 1963; New York: Macmillan.
By the Brisbane River: The University of Queensland 1914–15, 1919–21.
   London: 1972.
*A Dictionary of Catch Phrases: British and American, from the Sixteenth
   Century to the Present Day.* London: Routledge & Kegan Paul, 1977;
   New York: Stein & Day.

Indexes

Name and Subject Index

Addison, Joseph, 182
Alan, A. J., 164
alphabetization, 60, 64–80
Austen, John, 234
Authorized Version, 138

Bache, Richard, 146
Bartlett, John Russell, 146
Bauche, Henri, 142
B.E.'s Dictionary, 193
Benington, Wilson, 237
Bentham, Gurney, 152
Bentley, Edward Clerihew, 163
Berrey, Lester V., 123
Bierce, Ambrose, 196, 238
Binder, Frank, 133
Black, Alexander, 122
Blake, William, 234
Boileau, Nicholas, 182
Bone, James, 132
Borrow, George, 192
Bosson, Olof E., 106
Bradley, Henry, 57, 104, 106, 191
Brander Matthews, J., 112
Brophy, John, 57
Browning, Robert, 185
Burdett, Osbert, 51
business English, 154–61

Calder, Robert, 187
cant, 104, 114, 115, 120–30, 214–15
Carlyle, A. J., 50, 56
Carnoy, A. J., 142, 145
Castle, Don, 125–6
catch phrases, 150–3, 228–9
Celtic languages, 93–5
Chaucer, Geoffrey, 198
Clark, John W., 58, 82, 83, 84, 86,
    89, 154

clerihews, 163
clichés, 131–40, 216–17
colloquialisms, 114–15
comic alphabets, 151
commercialese, 155, 157–61
Corry, John, 182, 185
Cotgrave, Randle, 183
Craigie, William, 103
Creech, Thomas, 193
culture, 90

dead languages, 82
Defoe, Daniel, 52
Dennison, Corrie, 52–3
dialect, 115
Dickens, Charles, 116, 124
Disraeli, Benjamin, 233
Donne, John, 37
Drummond, V. H., 162
Duméril, A., 189–90
dysphemism, 143

Easton, John, 57
economese, 155
Egan, Pierce, 129
Ernout & Meillet, 96, 128
etymology, 38, 63, 81–100
euphemisms, 141–9

familiar English, 114–17
Farmer & Henley, 80, 123, 148
Farrar, Dean, 52
Fishman, Joseph, 123
Fowler, H. W., 104, 111, 112–13,
    141, 154
Franklin, Benjamin, 139
Fraser & Gibbons, 194
Funk, Charles Earle, 170
Furphy, Joseph, 173

Goldsmith, Oliver, 163
Gordon, George, 50, 56
Gosse, Edmund, 132
Gowers, Ernest, 154
Greene, Robert, 129, 151
Greenough & Kittredge, 103, 107, 110, 111–12, 141, 192
Grimm, Jacob, 85
Grose, Francis, 57, 184, 192–3

hackneyed phrases, 136–7
Haldane, Robert, 171–2
Haliburton, Thomas Chandler, 152
Henry, O., 131–2
Herbert, Alan, 154
Holt, Alfred H., 169
homonyms, 88–9
Hood, Tom, 149, 163
Horsley, J. W., 124–5
Hotten, John Camden, 105, 106, 107, 110, 112, 128, 148–9, 191–2
Hughes, Thomas, 52

idioms, 135
Indo-European, 39, 83–4
Irwin, Godfrey, 123, 169, 170–1, 195

Jamieson, John, 187
Johnson, Samuel, 41, 51, 155, 193
Jones, William, 85
Jonson, Ben, 129
journalese, 154–6

Karr, Alphonse, 138
Keats, John, 138
Kingsley, Henry, 195
Kluge, Friedrich, 46

language, change in, 82–3
    nature of, 46, 108
Lee, Nathaniel, 139
lexicography, 41, 51, 62–3
Lindsay, Jack, 234, 237
literary English, 115–17
Longfellow, Henry, 139
Lowry, Malcolm, 203

Marryat, Frederick, 147, 192
Mathews, M. M., 176
Maurer, David, 123
McKnight, G. H., 104, 111, 141–2, 143
Mencken, H. L., 107, 110, 141, 146–148
Milton, John, 138
Moisant de Brieux, Jacques, 189
Molière, 138
Morley, Christopher, 165
Morris, E. E., 194
Moss, Henry St L. B., 200
Mottram, R. H., 57
Murray, James, 193–4

naming, 196–9, 212–13, 226–7
Niceforo, Alfredo, 107–8, 110, 112, 142
Nichol Smith, David, 50
Nock, Alfred Jay, 41–2

officialese, 154, 157

Paracelsus, 185
passives, 160–1
philology, 38–9, 85–6, 90
phonetics, 39
Piddington, Henry, 203
Poe, Edgar Allen, 128
Pope, Alexander, 162
proverbs, 151

Quiller-Couch, Arthur, 154

Rask, Rasmus, 85
Ratcliffe, Bertram, 237
Reade, Charles, 124
regional English, 47–9, 54–5
repetition, 135–6
Romance languages, 92–3
roots, 81
Rudler, Gustav, 50

Sandberg, Carl, 103
Scholartis Press, 233–8
semantics, 87–8

Sewel, William, 183
'shaggy dog', 162–6
Shakespeare, William, 138, 220–1
Sheridan, Richard, 184
similes, 136
Skeat, W. W., 60, 99, 189–90
slang, 103–19, 222–5
    reasons for, 109–10
Smith, A. H., 198
Smith, L. P., 57
sound laws, 39, 86–7
Souter, Alexander, 91
Spinke, J., 184
Standard English, 49, 114–19
Stable, J. J., 57
stems, 81
Stevenson, R. L., 173
Sullivan, Frank, 132
Swift, Jonathan, 152
Synge, J. M., 141
synonyms, 145

taboos, 144–5
Tennyson, Alfred, 132
Thomas, J. P., 110
transliteration, 90–2

underworld, 60–2, 120–30

van den Bark, Melvin, 123
van de Water, Frederick, 170
van Helmont, Jan, 180
Vaux, James Hardy, 129
Verner, Karl, 85
vogue-phrases, 134
Voltaire, 85
vulgarisms, 114, 116

Webster, Noah, 46, 85
Weekley, Ernest, 57, 87, 104, 105,
    127, 141, 145, 147, 183, 186, 192–
    195, 197, 199
Welby, Earle, 107
Whitaker, Frank, 133
Whitney, W. D., 107–8
Whyte, Robert, 173
Wilson, Edmund, 42
Wilson, F. P., 151
Wright, Joseph, 186, 188, 194
Wyld, H. C. K., 50, 56, 57, 104, 148

Yonge, Charlotte, 198

Word Index

anaesthetic, 180

blitz, 118–19
bo, 195
bogus, 184
booze, 128–9
boy, 96
buddy, 195
bum, 201
bumble bee, 44
burnous, 200–1

cant, 120
charlatan, 183
chloroform, 180
chum, 193
cliché, 133
cobber, 194–5
cow, 81
colleen, 98
crime, 81–2
cure, 178
cyclone, 203

digger, 194
doctor, 177
dream, 86
drug, 180

ether, 180
etymology, 81

fez, 200

gale, 203
gas, 180
girl, 97–8

heroin, 180

hobo, 195, 201–2
hogmanay, 186–90
hospital, 179
hurricane, 203

lad, 95
lass, 95
lucent, 87–8

mate, 191–2
mayonnaise, 38
medicine, 177
morphine, 180
mountebank, 183

nurse, 178–9

opium, 180

pal, 192–3
palmer, 201
pedlar, 201
penicillin, 181
policy, 88
pugilist, 202
punctuation, 202

quack, 183–4
queer, 88, 118, 127

racket, 129
real McCoy/Mackay, the, 169–76
rum, 88, 118, 127–8

set, 67–77
slang, 104–5
sorry, 193–4
storm, 203
surgeon, 178

tanner, 58–9
tarot, 59–60
tempest, 203
tramp, 201
treatment, 178

turban, 200

west, to go, 130–1
wine, 92